ArtScroll Series

Rabbi Nosson Scherman / Rabbi Meir Zlotowitz

General Editors

RAV ASHER

Translated by **Daniel Worenklein**

Published by

Mesorah Publications, ltd

מנחת אשר
על התורה

WEISS
ON THE
PARASHAH

DEPTH AND INSPIRATION ON
BEREISHIS AND SHEMOS
FROM THE RENOWNED
RAV AND ROSH YESHIVAH

FIRST EDITION
First Impression ... September 2012

Published and Distributed by
MESORAH PUBLICATIONS, Ltd.
4401 Second Avenue
Brooklyn, New York 11232

Distributed in Europe by
LEHMANNS
Unit E, Viking Business Park
Rolling Mill Road
Jarrow, Tyne & Wear NE32 3DP
England

Distributed in Australia & New Zealand by
GOLDS WORLD OF JUDAICA
3-13 William Street
Balaclava, Melbourne 3183
Victoria Australia

Distributed in Israel by
SIFRIATI / A. GITLER — BOOKS
6 Hayarkon Street
Bnei Brak 51127, Israel

Distributed in South Africa by
KOLLEL BOOKSHOP
Northfield Centre, 17 Northfield Avenue
Glenhazel 2192, Johannesburg, South Africa

THE ARTSCROLL SERIES
RAV ASHER WEISS ON THE PARASHAH: BEREISHIS / SHEMOS
© Copyright 2012, by MESORAH PUBLICATIONS, Ltd.
4401 Second Avenue / Brooklyn, N.Y. 11232 / (718) 921-9000 / www.artscroll.com

---

ISBN 10: 1-4226-1314-3
ISBN 13: 978-1-4226-1314-6

Printed in the United States of America by Noble Book Press Corp.
Bound by Sefercraft Quality Bookbinders, Ltd., Brooklyn, N.Y.

לזכרון עולם
ולעילוי נשמת

הורינו היקרים

ר׳ משה בן ר׳ שלמה אהרן ז״ל
נלב״ע י״א מרחשון תשס״ח לפ״ק

מרת גאלדע ליבא בת ר׳ יצחק ע״ה
נלב״ע י״ג שבט תש״ס

ר׳ יעקב יצחק בן ר׳ יום טוב ליפא ז״ל
נלב״ע כ״ט מרחשון תשס״ב

תנצב״ה

הונצח ע״י
יוסף יצחק ואסתר מלכה קזרנובסקי

לזכרון עולם
ולעילוי נשמת

מרת חיה בת ר׳ אהרן ז״ל

נלב״ע יום ב׳ דחג השבועות תשע״א

In loving memory of our
adored mother and grandmother

Eleanor ע״ה

and with deep appreciation for
her unconditional love.

תנצב״ה

Dedicated by

Milton, Lara, Mikhali, Sara,
Daniella, and Joshua Weinberg

Table of Contents

ספר שמות / *Sefer Shemos*

ספר בראשית

SEFER
BEREISHIS

Introduction to
Sefer Bereishis

T HE RAMBAN REFERS TO *SEFER BEREISHIS* AS "THE BOOK of Creation," since it discusses the creation of the world and the deeds of our forefathers, which were also acts of creation:

Sefer Bereishis is the Book of Creation, since it is discusses how the world came into being, the creation of everything that exists, and the lives of our forefathers, which were also a kind of "creation" for their descendants after them, since the events of their lives sketched a pattern for the destiny of their descendants. [1]

The lives of our forefathers were not just signposts, to mark the path for their descendants to follow, as is often said.[2] They actually created the destiny of their descendants. They invested their descendants with the moral strength and fortitude to stand strong against all the torrents of spiritual and material hardship that we would ever have to face. Their deeds were not for their own sake alone, or even for the sake of their generation, but for the sake of the entire world until the end of time.

Since their every deed had such great significance for all time to come, they were judged for even the smallest misdeed with the utmost severity, not as a punishment for the misdeed itself, but for its effects upon later generations. For instance, the Midrash states:

"Avraham took sheep and cattle and gave them to Avimelech,

---

1. *Ramban* on the Torah, introduction to *Sefer Shemos.*
2. *Ramban, Shemos* 12:6.

[and the two of them entered into a covenant. Avraham set seven ewes of the flock by themselves.] And Avimelech said to Avraham, 'What are these seven ewes that you have set by themselves?' [And he replied, 'Because you are to take these seven ewes from me, that it may serve me as testimony that I dug this well.'"[3]]

HaKadosh Baruch Hu said to Avraham, "You gave him seven ewes against My will. I swear by your life, that I will delay the joy of your descendants [*Kabbalas HaTorah*] for seven generations. You gave him seven ewes against My will. I swear by your life, that [the Philistines] will slay seven of your righteous descendants: Chafni, Pinchas, Shimshon, Shaul, and his three sons. You gave him seven ewes against My will. So his descendants will destroy seven of your descendant's sanctuaries: Ohel Moed, Gilgal, Nov, Givon, Shiloh, and the Batei HaMikdash.[4]

The severity of this punishment is astonishing. *Kabbalas HaTorah* could have occurred in the time of Avraham Avinu, thus fulfilling the very purpose for the world's creation. Yet it was delayed for seven generations, as a punishment for Avraham's seemingly innocent mistake of having forged a covenant with Avimelech. So too, the Beis HaMikdash is not just for our benefit, but a benefit for Hashem Himself, Who longed for a place to dwell in this world alongside His beloved children,[5] yet it was destroyed as a result of Avraham's indiscretion.

The Tanna D'Vei Eliyahu also states: There is no nation in the world that subjugates and oppresses Yisrael more than several hundred years, only because Avraham made a covenant with a gentile.[6]

Similarly, the Ramban writes that Avraham should not have subjugated Hagar to Sarah. As a punishment for having done so, the descendants of Yishmael were given the power to harm Bnei Yisrael for generations to come.[7]

Avraham was judged, not for a blatant sin, but for having failed to live up to the high standard of perfection that was expected

---

3. *Bereishis* 21:27-30.
4. *Bereishis Rabbah* 54:4.
5. See *Ramban, Shemos* 29:46.
6. *Tanna D'Vei Eliyahu,* 7:22.
7. *Ramban, Bereishis* 16:19.

of him. Whereas for ordinary people the system of Heavenly Judgment gives a certain amount of leeway for imperfection, Hashem is exacting with the righteous to within a hairsbreadth of perfection.[8] Bnei Yisrael have suffered through thousands of years of grief in *Galus*, as a result of Avraham's mistake.

As a general rule, Hashem rewards on a scale five hundred times greater than that with which He punishes.[9] Furthermore, the mitzvos of the *Avos* far outweighed their misdeeds, both in number and in magnitude, reaching up to the very Heavens in their profundity.

If such suffering resulted from the misdeeds of our forefathers, how much greater is the reward we reap for their good deeds. Their merit stands on our behalf, since we inherited their noble traits and carry on their legacy.

Chananyah, Mishael, and Azaryah were thrown into a fiery furnace, rather than bow to an idol. The Midrash states that Hashem then told the angels, "Descend and kiss the lips of their forefathers. Just as their forefathers went through fire in My service, so do they."[10]

Avraham Avinu was thrown into the fiery furnace of Ur Kasdim, braving death to deny idolatry. Yitzchak Avinu willingly stretched out his neck to be slaughtered, as he was bound as an offering on the *Mizbei'ach*. Thereby, they instilled the trait of martyrdom in their descendants: the willingness to endure any and every sacrifice in Hashem's service.

Perhaps with this we can shed light on the story of Chanah and her seven sons. The Gemara states that Chanah's seven sons were all killed by the Romans, for having refused to worship idols. When her youngest son was taken to the slaughter, she told him, "Go tell Avraham Avinu that he built only one *Mizbei'ach* on which to sacrifice his son, while I built seven."[11] This seems a strange thing for a mother to say as she watches the last of her children taken to be killed. It would seem neither the time nor the place for competition.

Rather, perhaps she meant to say that her ability to sacrifice

---

8. *Bava Kamma* 50a.
9. *Sotah* 11a; *Sanhedrin* 100b.
10. *Shir HaShirim Rabbah* 7:1,10.
11. *Gittin* 57b.

her seven sons was drawn from the precedent of Avraham's having sacrificed his one son. The achievements and spiritual heights of Bnei Yisrael throughout the generations are realizations of the potential planted by our forefathers. Their example gives us the strength to endure the hardships of *Galus*, as we follow them on the path they blazed to perfection.

In Darkness and in Light

ACH OF THE *AVOS* MADE HIS OWN UNIQUE CONTRIBUtion to the destiny of our nation. In Avraham's merit, we received Eretz Yisrael. Our Sages interpret the verse, קוּם הִתְהַלֵּךְ בָּאָרֶץ לְאָרְכָּהּ וּלְרָחְבָּהּ כִּי לְךָ אֶתְּנֶנָּה — *"Rise and walk the length and breadth of the land, for I shall give it to you,"*[12] as an instruction to Avraham to acquire the land on behalf of his descendants, so that it would be easier for them to conquer when the time would come.[13]

In Yitzchak's merit, we received the Beis HaMikdash. When he was bound as a offering on Har HaMoriah, he sanctified it throughout time as the place where our offering would be brought and our prayers would ascend. The verse thus states: וַיִּקְרָא אַבְרָהָם שֵׁם הַמָּקוֹם הַהוּא ה' יִרְאֶה אֲשֶׁר יֵאָמֵר הַיּוֹם בְּהַר ה' יֵרָאֶה — *"Avraham called the name of the place, 'Hashem-Shall-See,' as it is said this day, on the mountain Hashem will be seen."*

Targum Onkelos explains: וּפְלַח וְצַלִּי אַבְרָהָם תַּמָּן בְּאַתְרָא הַהוּא וַאֲמַר קֳדָם ה' הָכָא יְהוֹן פָּלְחִין דָּרַיָּא.

Avraham worshipped and prayed there, and in that place he said before Hashem, "Here, future generations shall worship."

However, Yaakov's contribution was of a totally different nature. Whereas Avraham and Yitzchak laid the foundation for our peaceful years in our homeland, Yaakov prepared us for the long, hard years of *Galus*. By standing strong in his own harsh exile to

---

12. *Bereishis* 13:17.
13. *Bava Basra* 100a.

Aram, remaining steadfast in his devotion to Hashem despite his many troubles, he created a precedent enabling us to do the same. He gave us the strength to endure the *Galus* and the merit to be redeemed.

The Gemara states that Avraham instituted Shacharis, Yitzchak instituted Minchah and Yaakov instituted Maariv.[14] The Chassidic texts explain that since Maariv is the nighttime prayer, it represents our prayers for survival in the dark night of *Galus*. When Yaakov descended to Egypt, Hashem told him: וַיֹּאמֶר אָנֹכִי הָאֵל אֱלֹקֵי אָבִיךָ אַל תִּירָא מֵרְדָה מִצְרַיְמָה כִּי לְגוֹי גָּדוֹל אֲשִׂימְךָ שָׁם. אָנֹכִי אֵרֵד עִמְּךָ מִצְרַיְמָה וְאָנֹכִי אַעַלְךָ גַם עָלֹה — "I am God, the God of your father. Have no fear of descending to Egypt, for I shall establish you as a great nation there. I shall descend with you to Egypt, and I shall also surely bring you up."[15]

The Meshech Chochmah explains that Hashem promised Yaakov, not only that He would remain by Yaakov's side in Egypt, but that He would remain with Yaakov's descendants throughout the many phases of our exile, to protect, preserve, and ultimately redeem us.[16] Before Yaakov's passing he wanted to reveal the "קֵץ," which most simply means the time of the Ultimate Redemption.[17] However, this can also be interpreted to mean that he wanted to reveal Hashem's holiness in the world, which is the element of "redemption" that exists even amid our exile, and to hasten the ultimate redemption. As the heirs of Yaakov, this is our mission in *Galus*, to spread holiness wherever we go, through Torah study and mitzvos, and thereby hasten the redemption.

Yaakov received four *berachos* throughout his life: the first he received from Yitzchak by posing as Eisav; the second he received from Yitzchak before setting forth to Lavan's house; the third he wrested from Eisav's guardian angel, after defeating it in battle; and the fourth he received from Hashem, when he returned from Lavan's house.[18]

The Zohar states that Yaakov weighed the value of each of these *berachos*, and decided to keep the smallest for himself, leaving the

14. *Berachos* 27b.
15. *Bereishis* 46:3.
16. See *Parashas Vayeira*, "*Prayers of the Forefathers.*"
17. *Rashi, Bereishis* 49:1.
18. *Bereishis* 27; 28:3-4; 35:11; 32:28-29.

rest as a merit for his descendants, to protect them in *Galus*.[19] In the merit of these three *berachos*, Bnei Yisrael were destined to be redeemed from three different phases of our exile. This was the intent of Yaakov Avinu, and the contribution he made to the destiny of our nation, to give us strength to endure the *Galus* and the merit to be redeemed.

Throughout the Generations

WHEN YAAKOV'S SONS ASKED HIM TO SEND BINYAMIN down to Egypt with them, he answered: אֹתִי שִׁכַּלְתֶּם יוֹסֵף אֵינֶנּוּ וְשִׁמְעוֹן אֵינֶנּוּ וְאֶת בִּנְיָמִן תִּקָּחוּ עָלַי הָיוּ כֻלָּנָה — "*You have bereaved me. Yosef is gone, Shimon is gone, and you would take Binyamin? All this has befallen me!*"[20]

The Vilna Gaon noted the parallel between the word "עָלַי," used here in reference to Yaakov's misfortunes, and the same word used in an earlier verse. When Rivkah suggested that Yaakov pose as Eisav and claim his blessings, Yaakov hesitated, fearing that the deception would bring on him curse instead of blessing. Rivka answered him, עָלַי קִלְלָתְךָ בְּנִי, which is commonly translated as, "Your curse is on me." (Onkelos explains that she told him of a prophecy she received, that he would not be cursed.) However, the Gaon explains עָלַי in both of these contexts as an acronym for Yaakov's three worst challenges, עֵשָׂיו, לָבָן, יוֹסֵף — Eisav, Lavan, and Yosef.

In the context of Rivkah's assurance, this means that regardless of any precautions he might make to prevent them, these sorrows were destined to befall him. In the context of his refusal to send Binyamin, Yaakov protested that he had already endured the three great tests that had been foreseen, and refused to accept a fourth.[21] Binyamin's descent to Egypt was not foretold to him, since it was

---

19. *Zohar* I, p. 146. See *Parashas Toldos*, "*Blessings of our Forefathers*."
20. *Bereishis* 42:36.
21. Quoted in *Teshuvos Zayis Ra'anan*, end of section II.

not a misfortune at all, but the catalyst for his greatest joy, as Yosef at last reunited with him.

We might add Yaakov's three misfortunes were also catalysts for the good things that were to come for him and his descendants. By enduring these hardships with faith, Yaakov gave his descendants the strength to endure their own suffering, and persevere until the problems would ultimately be resolved and days of light and gladness would follow.

Throughout our *Galus*, Bnei Yisrael have suffered persecution from two types of enemies. There were those like Eisav, who sought the physical destruction of our nation, regardless of our beliefs. There were others like Lavan, who sought our spiritual destruction. Lavan claimed Yaakov's children as his own, seeking to make them into his own spiritual heirs: וַיַּעַן לָבָן וַיֹּאמֶר אֶל יַעֲקֹב הַבָּנוֹת בְּנֹתַי וְהַבָּנִים הוּא לִי רֹאֶה אַתָּה אֲשֶׁר וְכֹל צֹאנִי וְהַצֹּאן בָּנַי — *"Lavan answered and said to Yaakov, 'The daughters are my daughters, the sons are my sons, the flock is my flock, and all that you see is mine.'"*[22]

In truth, our spiritual enemies are worse than our physical ones, since they seek to destroy us both in this world and the next, as we say in the *Pesach Haggadah*, "Lavan sought to uproot everything."

Yaakov endured and overcame both of these adversaries, but the worst of all, which broke his heart and caused the *Shechinah* to depart him for twenty-two years, was the disappearance of Yosef, which was the outcome of senseless strife between brothers. This too was a sign of things to come, since the most difficult of all burdens that our nation has ever had to carry, is the senseless hatred that tears us apart.

In ancient times, we have seen all three enemies rise against us. Haman, the scion of Eisav, sought to physically destroy our nation, men, women and children, regardless of our beliefs. In contrast, the Greeks would have let us live peacefully in our homeland, if we would only embrace their religion and ideology. In Hashem's great mercy, we overcame both hardships, and merited to witness the great miracles of Purim and Chanukah. However, the final and

---

22. *Bereishis* 31:43. See *Doveir Tzedek* by Rebbe Tzadok HaKohen of Lublin, *Ki Savo* 1.

hardest test of all was the senseless hatred that led to the destruction of the Beis HaMikdash. For this, there was no remedy. Until this day, we still suffer its consequences.

"Not one alone, but in every generation they rise up against us to destroy us, but HaKadosh Baruch Hu rescues us from their hand."[23] Like Haman, the Nazis sought to destroy the entire Jewish people, regardless of our beliefs. Hashem rescued the scattered remnants of our nation. From amid the inferno of the Holocaust, the Jewish people survived, "Like a smoking piece of wood, snatched from the flames."[24]

We likewise confronted the hardships of the Communist regime, which forbade us to study Torah or perform Hashem's mitzvos. Thanks to Hashem's great mercy, the Soviet Union fell and Russian Jews were once again free to express their Jewish identity, through Torah and mitzvos.

Now, we face the worst of our adversaries, which is the enmity among ourselves, and the senseless hatred between brothers. To the extent that we overcome our differences and join together in unity, we merit Hashem's protection and are redeemed from all our misfortunes.

The Covenant of Yaakov

THE VERSE STATES REGARDING THE REDEMPTION OF Bnei Yisrael from *Galus*: וְזָכַרְתִּי אֶת בְּרִיתִי יַעֲקוֹב וְאַף אֶת בְּרִיתִי יִצְחָק וְאַף אֶת בְּרִיתִי אַבְרָהָם אֶזְכֹּר וְהָאָרֶץ אֶזְכֹּר — "*I shall remember My covenant with Yaakov, and also My covenant with Yitzchak, and also My covenant with Avraham, and I shall remember the Land.*"[25]

Rashi comments that this is among the five places in which Yaakov's name is spelled with an extra latter *vav*, while in five corresponding places, Eliyahu HaNavi's name is spelled "אֵלִיָּה," with

23. From the *Pesach Haggadah*.
24. *Zechariah* 3:2.
25. *Vayikra* 26:42.

the final *vav* missing. Rashi explains that Yaakov took the letter *vav* from Eliyahu's name as a security to ensure that Eliyahu would come to herald the Redemption of Bnei Yisrael.

Rav Eliyahu Mizrachi explained that these five times correspond to the five books of the Torah, to symbolize that Yaakov made Eliyahu swear over the holy Torah. The Maharal, in Gur Aryeh, explains that they correspond to five fingers, symbolizing that Yaakov made Eliyahu shake hands over his assurance.

During the Melavah Malkah meal on Motza'ei Shabbos, it is customary to sing songs in honor of Eliyahu HaNavi, in hopeful prayer that he may soon come to herald our Redemption. It is also customary to sing the song, אַל תִּירָא עַבְדִּי יַעֲקֹב — "*Do not fear, My servant Yaakov.*"

On Motza'ei Shabbos, we sing of Hashem's assurance that Yaakov has nothing to fear, since Eliyahu will surely come at long last, to usher in the final stage of history, the thousand years of peace, which correspond to Shabbos: "A day that will be entirely Shabbos and contentment for the eternal life."[26]

Forming a Connection
With the Avos

TO DRAW FROM THE WELLSPRINGS OF MERIT THAT THE Avos dug, we must form a connection with them, by emulating their ways and continuing their legacy. Tanna D'Vei Eliyahu states that each person must ask himself, *When will my deeds reach the deeds of my forefathers?*[27] Rebbe Yisrael of Ruzhin explained that we are not expected to match the deeds of our forefathers, which are beyond our ability to equal. We need only

---

26. *Tamid* 7:4. See *Ramban, Bereishis* 2:3; *Vayikra* 25:2, who explains that the seven thousand years of the world's existence correspond to the seven days of creation, with the seventh thousand corresponding to Shabbos.
27. *Tanna D'Vei Eliyahu Rabbah*, 25.

emulate them to the best of our ability, following the path that they blazed before us, and carrying on the ideals they espoused.

However, perhaps we might explain otherwise, that we are indeed able to match the deeds of our forefathers; not in our own merit, but in theirs. Through their great sacrifices in Hashem's service, they created a precedent for us to follow. They planted the seeds of greatness in the hearts of their descendants until the end of time. Like a loving father, they descend to the level of their children, to take our hands in theirs, and lead us on the path to greatness, and to pray together with us that we may be redeemed from all our misfortune.

One important trait of the *Avos* that we must strive to emulate is their dedication to Torah study. The Gemara states that Avraham, Yitzchak, and Yaakov all headed yeshivos, where they disseminated Hashem's holy Torah. Since the very inception of our nation, there has been an unbroken chain of yeshivos, where Jews gather to study Torah and strengthen our commitment to Hashem's service. Never once has Klal Yisrael been without a yeshivah.[28]

The Chida writes that the *Avos* would study Torah for fifteen hours each day.[29] Although this might seem like a lot to us, my Rebbe, the Klausenberger Rav *zt"l*, asked quite to the contrary: How could it possibly be that they learned for only fifteen hours? What did they do during the other nine hours of the day?

He explained based on the Gemara, which states that the righteous of ancient times would prepare themselves for prayer for one hour, pray for one hour, and pause afterward in contemplation for one hour.[30] Thus, they dedicated nine hours to the three daily prayers. The *Avos* also davened each day, since they fulfilled the entire Torah, even before it was given.[31] They too dedicated nine hours each day to prayer, leaving them only fifteen hours to learn Torah.

Kidmos HaAyin[32] notes an apparent discrepancy in the Chida's writings. In the source noted above, he writes that they studied

---

28. *Yoma* 28b.
29. *Midbar Kedeimos* 1.
30. *Berachos* 32b.
31. See *Tosefos Yeshonim* on *Yoma* 28, s.v. *Tzelosei D'Avraham*.
32. A commentary written on the *Chida's Midbar Kedeimos*.

.Torah for only fifteen hours a day, but in his commentary on Sefer Chassidim he writes that they studied Torah even in their dreams as they slept.

According to the Klausenberger Rav's explanation, we see that there is no discrepancy at all. They did indeed devote all twenty-four hours of the day to Hashem's service in Torah study and prayer. If they did not study Torah even as they slept, they could not possibly have had nine hours left for prayer.

The Pillars of Creation

THE ZOHAR STATES THAT THE THREE *AVOS* REPRESENT-ed the three pillars that support creation.[33] Avraham was the pillar of kindness, as is written תִּתֵּן . . . חֶסֶד לְאַבְרָהָם — "*Grant ... kindness to Avraham.*"[34] Yitzchak was the pillar of worship. He himself was bound as an offering on the *Mizbei'ach*, creating a portal through which all our prayers ascend to Heaven. Yaakov was the pillar of Torah study. He was the אִישׁ תָּם יֹשֵׁב אֹהָלִים — "*simple man who dwelt in the tents [of Torah].*"[35] (Yaakov represents the *sefirah* of *Tiferes*, of which the Gemara states, "*Tiferes* refers to *Kabbalas HaTorah.*"[36])

The Ultimate Redemption, which we have so long awaited, depends on the merit of Torah, which was the attribute of Yaakov Avinu. The Ohr HaChaim writes that Moshe Rabbeinu is destined to accompany Mashiach when he arrives, but "Moshe does not want to redeem a nation that is lax in its Torah study."

This cannot be taken at face value. Moshe stood in our defense and prayed on our behalf, after all the sins that we committed in the desert. He never said that we were unworthy of Hashem's kindness. To the contrary, he always advocated on our behalf. Why

---

33. *Zohar* I, p. 146.
34. *Michah* 7:20.
35. *Bereishis* 25:27.
36. *Berachos* 58a.

then would he forsake us in our long, harsh *Galus*, due to our laxity in Torah study?

Rather, it is not that Moshe does not want to redeem us, but that he cannot. He needs the merit of our Torah study to be the catalyst for our redemption. Each of the *Avos* had a special merit that he wielded on behalf of his descendants. Avraham's merit was kindness. Yitzchak's merit was prayer. The merit that Moshe will bring on our behalf is the trait of Yaakov: dedication to Torah. Moshe brought the Torah down from Heaven on our behalf, and only through the Torah's merit can he hasten our redemption.

Had we only the eyes to see or the ears to hear, we would see Moshe Rabbeinu standing before us, pleading with us for our own benefit, "My dear children, just a little more Torah *l'shmah*. Just a little more joy of Torah and depth of understanding. Give me the tools that I need in order to pray for your redemption."

By toiling in Torah, with joy, dedication, and true commitment, we hasten the Redemption of Klal Yisrael from *Galus* and the coming of Mashiach, may it be soon and in our days.

פרשת בראשית
Parashas Bereishis

The Letters of Creation

WHEN A MORTAL KING BUILDS A PALACE, HE DOES NOT follow his whim. He consults an architect, who prepares architectural designs to plan how each room and each passageway will be constructed. So too, when Hashem created the world, He gazed into the Torah, and from it He designed His Creation.[37] Therefore, it is written, "*Bereishis* (*With the 'beginning'*), God created." The Torah is the "*beginning,*" of which it is said, "Hashem created me at the beginning of His path."[38]

Hashem created the world using the Torah's wisdom as His tool and guide, and the Torah letters as the very building blocks of creation. All dimensions of existence, from the most spiritual plane of *atzilus* (although this literally means "aristocracy," Kabbalistically it refers to the most exalted realms) to the most material plane of *asiyah* ("action," i.e. our universe), are formed from the letters of the Torah.

For this reason, our Sages tell us that Betzalel built the Mishkan by "arranging the letters with which the world was made."[39] In other

37. *Bereishis Rabbah* 1:1.
38. *Mishlei* 8:22.
39. *Berachos* 55b.

words, he made the Mishkan into a microcosmic model of the world, by employing the same letters utilized in the world's creation.

Since the world is based on the letters of the Torah, each letter is integral to the world's continued existence. Only a tiny dot distinguishes between the letters ה and ח, yet the Midrash tells us that if we were to replace the word תְּהַלֵּל (praise) with תְּחַלֵּל (defile) in the verse, "Let every soul praise Hashem," the most heinous blasphemy would result. The Midrash cites many similar examples, and concludes that the entire world would be destroyed if even one letter of the Torah would be misplaced.[40]

Creation was not just an ancient event, long ago concluded. "In His kindness, He renews each day the work of creation," as we recite in davening. The world around us continues to unfold, as Hashem constantly re-creates it, based on the novel Torah concepts that are brought to light throughout the generations.

The Midrash tells us that Avraham Avinu was moved by a spirit of Divine inspiration (ruach hakodesh), which enabled him to discover the novel Torah insights that Hashem develops each day.[41] Avraham gazed deeply into the world around him, and perceived Hashem's novel Torah concepts as the vivifying force through which the world is renewed.

Until Kabbalas HaTorah, Hashem renewed the world using His own novel Torah concepts. After Kabbalas HaTorah, this responsibility was entrusted to Bnei Yisrael. As Torah scholars toil in their studies, plumbing the endless depths of the Torah, they provide the building blocks whereby which Hashem renews the world. The verse, "All your sons (בָּנָיִךְ) shall be students of Hashem," is interpreted to mean, "All your builders (בּוֹנַיִךְ) shall be students of Hashem,"[42] to highlight the crucial role of Torah scholars in maintaining creation.

Whereas the world was first created by Hashem's speech, it is now sustained and renewed by our own speech, as we study His holy Torah.[43] For this reason, Rav Chaim of Volozhin zt"l warned that if there would ever be a single moment in which no Jew anywhere would be studying Torah, the basis for the world's continued

---

40. Midrash Tanchuma, Bereishis.
41. See Bereishis Rabbah, Vayeira 49.
42. Yeshayahu 54:13.
43. Degel Machaneh Ephraim, Parashas Bo.

existence would totter, and all creation would crumble into nothing-ness.[44]

II

The initial cornerstone of the world's creation was the letter *beis* from the word "*Bereishis,*" the first letter in the Torah. The *Yalkut Shimoni* explains that this letter stands for "*berachah* — blessing," and was therefore uniquely auspicious: R' Akiva said: The twenty-two letters of the Torah were engraved with a fiery stylus on the awesome crown of HaKadosh Baruch Hu. When Hashem sought to create the world, the letters descended before Him, each one beseeching that the world might be created through it.

First, the letter *tav* approached and said, "Master of the Universe, create the world with me, since through me You will give the Torah to Bnei Yisrael, as the verse says: 'Torah was com-manded to us by Moshe.' "

Hashem refused *tav's* request, since the letter *tav* was des-tined to be engraved on the brows of the sinners at the time of the Churban Beis HaMikdash, marking them for destruction. Dejected by the refusal, *tav* exited, and the letter *shin* entered in its place, only to meet with similar refusal. Each letter entered and was dismissed, until finally the letter *beis* entered and said, "Master of the Universe, create the world with me, since with me You will be praised each day, '*Baruch Hashem* forever, amen and amen.' "

Hashem accepted *beis's* proposal, and used it to create the world, as the Torah begins with the word בְּרֵאשִׁית, *Bereishis,* in the beginning.[45]

The world was created for the glorification of Hashem's holy Name, as the verse states, "Everyone who is called by My Name, and whom I have created for My glory, when I have fashioned, even perfected."[46] The Jewish people, who are the pinnacle of creation, were also formed for this purpose: "This nation which

---

44. *Nefesh HaChaim* 4:25.
45. *Yalkut Shimoni, Bereishis* 1:1.
46. *Yeshayahu* 43:7.

I fashioned for Myself that they might declare My praise."[47] It is therefore only fitting that the world be created with the letter *beis*, by which Hashem is praised in the verse, "*Baruch Hashem* forever, amen and amen."

The Talmud *Yerushalmi*[48] offers a slightly variant explanation, that the letter *beis* was chosen over *aleph*, since *beis* stands for *berachah* (blessing), while *aleph* stands for *arurah* (cursed). Just as *aleph* precedes *beis* alphabetically, Hashem's original intention was to create the world based on a system of strict justice, in which weighty punishment would immediately befall those who sin. However, Hashem saw that a world run with such strictness could not possibly endure. Therefore, He dismissed the *aleph* of *arurah*, and rather chose to use *beis* to create a world sustained by His blessed mercy.

———•———

Another reason why the letter *beis* was chosen to inaugurate the world's creation is its numerical equivalent of two, signifying the two worlds of *Olam HaZeh* (the current world into which man is born) and *Olam HaBa* (the World to Come).[49]

Belief in the World to Come is a core tenet of our faith, yet the Torah makes no explicit mention of it anywhere, as the commentaries note and endeavor to explain. In any case, although no explicit mention is made, an allusion to the existence of the World to Come is found in the very first letter of the Torah.

In a similar vein, another Midrash explains that *beis* signifies the two times that the world was destined to be destroyed and renewed: once by the Flood in the time of Noach, and again in the future, in the year 6093. (The significance of this date is discussed in our commentary to *Parashas V'eschanan*: "*The Heights of the Universe.*") Additionally, *beis* attests to the two times that the Beis HaMikdash would be destroyed and rebuilt.

———•———

The Talmud *Yerushalmi* offers another reason why the world

---

47. *Yeshayahu* 43:21.
48. *Chagigah* 10a.
49. *Bereishis Rabbah* 1:10.

was created with the letter *beis*, based on the shape of the letter as it appears in a *Sefer Torah*: ב.

The *Yerushalmi* states as follows: R' Yonah said in the name of R' Levi: The world was created with the letter *beis* ... *Beis* is asked "Who created you?" It answers by pointing up toward Hashem.

"What is your Maker's Name?" it is asked. It answers by pointing back toward the letter *aleph*, and says, "Hashem is His Name Adon (Master is His Name)."[50]

Here we see that even the shape of the Hebrew letters have great significance, from which we can learn important lessons regarding the nature of existence. The Rosh writes in his commentary to *Nedarim,* "All forms of wisdom and knowledge are hidden in the shapes of the Hebrew letters." From them we learn not only philosophical or kabbalistic concepts, but halachah and *mussar* as well.

There is no end to the depth of the Torah. "Turn it over and over again, for everything is contained within it."[51] May Hashem open our eyes, that we may merit to see the wonders of His holy Torah, and may its study help us to improve ourselves in every way.

The Purpose of Creation

"סוֹף דָּבָר הַכֹּל נִשְׁמָע אֶת הָאֱלֹקִים יְרָא וְאֶת מִצְוֹתָיו שְׁמוֹר כִּי זֶה כָּל הָאָדָם": מַאי כִּי זֶה כָּל הָאָדָם? אָמַר רַבִּי אֱלִיעֶזֶר כָּל הָעוֹלָם כּוּלוֹ לֹא נִבְרָא אֶלָּא בִּשְׁבִיל זֶה.

"In the end, when all is heard, fear God and heed His commandments, for that is the entirety of man."[52] What is meant by "the entirety of man"? R' Eliezer explained that the entire world was created for such a man.[53]

B Y DEDICATING OUR LIVES TO HASHEM'S SERVICE through Torah and mitzvos, we fulfill the purpose of Man and the purpose of all creation. The Gemara states in the

---

50. *Yerushalmi Chagigah* 2:1.
51. *Pirkei Avos* 5:26.
52. *Koheles* 12:13.
53. *Shabbos* 30b.

context of the laws of ritual impurity associated with mankind: *"And you are My sheep, the flock of My pasture. You are men"*[54]: You are called men, while the foreign nations are not.[55]

This does not mean to say that gentiles are any less than human beings, which is obviously not the case. Rather it means that the verse, *"Let Us make Man in Our image,"* refers specifically to those who fulfill the purpose of mankind, as stated in the continuation of the verse *"They shall rule over the fish of the sea, the birds of the sky, and over the animals, the whole earth, and every creeping thing that creeps upon the earth"*[56] — which means to say that through his Torah and mitzvos, Man elevates and sanctifies all creation.

The Midrash[57] interprets the word *Bereishis* to mean "for the sake of the first and foremost thing"; namely, Bnei Yisrael, who are called Hashem's "first produce," as we find in the verse, קֹדֶשׁ יִשְׂרָאֵל לַה' רֵאשִׁית תְּבוּאָתֹה — *"Israel is holy to Hashem. They are the first (reishis) of His crop."*[58]

Alternately, the Midrash interprets *Bereishis* as a reference to the Torah, which is also called "the first," as we find in the verse ה' קָנָנִי רֵאשִׁית דַּרְכּוֹ — *"Hashem acquired me at the beginning (reishis) of His path."*[59]

The Ohr HaChaim notes the apparent contradiction between these two Midrashim. On the one hand, the Midrash implies that the world was created for the sake of Hashem's beloved nation, whether or not we observe His Torah. On the other hand, the Midrash implies that the world was created only for the sake of the Torah and those who study it. Accordingly, those who do not study or support Torah do not contribute to the purpose of the world, and therefore have no right to benefit from the world's plenty.

To resolve this issue, the Ohr HaChaim explains that the unique advantage of Klal Yisrael, for which we were honored with the title of "Hashem's first crops," is only in the merit of our Torah study and mitzvah observance. As such, both Midrashim point toward the

---

54. *Yechezkel* 34:31.
55. *Bava Metzia* 114b; *Yevamos* 61a.
56. *Bereishis* 1:26.
57. *Vayikra Rabbah* 36.
58. *Yirmiyahu* 2:3.
59. *Mishlei* 8:22.

same conclusion: that the entire world was created for the sake of the Torah and for Klal Yisrael who study and promulgate it.

Not only is Torah the reason for the world's existence, it was the very tool by which the world was created, as the Zohar states, "Hashem gazed into the Torah and thereby created the world."[60] Furthermore, the Zohar states that the Ten Commandments mirror the Ten Utterances by which the world was created.[61] Therefore, those who observe and study the Ten Commandments, and indeed the entire Torah, support the world that was created by Ten Utterances.[62]

Torah scholars are called "builders."[63] By means of their Torah study the world is constantly being renewed. Accordingly, both the Baal Shem Tov and Rav Chaim of Volozhin cautioned that if there would ever be a single moment in which no Jew anywhere in the world would be studying Torah, all existence would instantly revert into utter nothingness,[64] as the verse states, אִם לֹא בְרִיתִי יוֹמָם וָלָיְלָה חֻקּוֹת שָׁמַיִם וָאָרֶץ לֹא שָׂמְתִּי — "If not for My covenant studied day and night, I would not have established the statutes of heaven and earth."[65]

— • —

Not only was the present world created for the sake of the Torah and its students, but the light of the World to Come as well was placed in safekeeping until it is time for Torah scholars and their supporters to finally enjoy its radiance. The Midrash[66] states: "The nation that walked in darkness saw great light."[67] This is the great light that was created on the first day. HaKadosh Baruch Hu placed it in safekeeping for those who toil in Torah She'Be'al Peh (the Oral Tradition of Torah study) by day and by night. Their merit supports the entire world, as it is written, "So says Hashem: If not

---

60. *Zohar* II, 161a.
61. *Zohar* III, 11b.
62. *Pirkei Avos* 5:1.
63. *Berachos* 64a; *Ohr HaChaim, Bereishis* 1:1 (6).
64. *Degel Machaneh Ephraim: Bo; Nefesh HaChaim* 4:25.
65. *Yirmiyahu* 33:25.
66. *Midrash Tanchuma, Noach* 3.
67. *Yeshayahu* 9:1.

for My covenant studied day and night, I would not have established the statutes of heaven and earth."[68]

Regarding this primordial light, the Midrash states elsewhere: R' Yehudah Bar Simone taught: By the light from which the world was created Adam could see from one end of the world to the other. When HaKadosh Baruch Hu foresaw the wicked deeds of the Generations of Enosh, the Flood and the Dispersion, He hid the light, as it is written, *"He withholds from the wicked their light."*[69] For what end did He hide it? For the sake of the righteous in the Ultimate Future, as it is written, *"God saw that the light was good."* "Good" refers only to the righteous, as it is written, *"Praise the righteous for the good they have done"*[70] ...

R' Levi taught in the name of R' Nazira that this light shone for thirty-six hours: twelve on erev Shabbos, twelve on Shabbos night (i.e. Friday), and twelve on Shabbos day [before it was hidden].[71]

These thirty-six hours correspond to the thirty-six volumes of the Talmud *Bavli*.[72] According to the depth and diligence with which the Talmud is studied, so will this most beautiful and holy of all lights shine upon the Torah scholars and their supporters in the End of Days. May we soon merit to see the new — actually the original light of creation — light that will shine on Tzion, by which the entire world will be illuminated with the glory of Hashem.

The Fruits of Gratitude

IN OUR PREVIOUS ESSAY, WE CITED VARIOUS MIDRASHIM that discuss the reason for the world's creation: be it Klal Yisrael in general, or those who study Torah in specific. Yet there is another Midrash that suggests a reason that is somewhat surprising: The world was created in the merit of *bikkurim* (the first-fruit

---

68. *Yirmiyahu* 33:25.
69. *Iyov* 38:15.
70. *Yeshayahu* 3:10. See *Metzudos David*.
71. *Bereishis Rabbah* 12:6.
72. *Bnei Yissaschar: Kislev; Midrash Pinchas* by Rebbe Pinchas of Koretz.

offerings), as it is written, "***Bereishis*** — *for the first and foremost thing* — ***God created Heaven and earth***." The word "first" can refer only to *bikkurim*, as it is written, "*The choicest first fruits of your land [shall you bring to the House of Hashem your God].*"[73,74]

What is the unique significance of *bikkurim*, that more than any other of the 613 mitzvos, the Midrash understood it to be the very reason for creation?

Each mitzvah has its own special *segulah* and its own nurturing influence on human character, which helps us become finer, kinder people.[75] The influence of *bikkurim* in particular is to develop the character trait of gratitude, perhaps the most crucial of all traits, without which we cannot possibly hope to develop a healthy relationship with our Creator or with our fellow man.

When a Jew would offer *bikkurim* in the Beis HaMikdash, he would recall all the kindness Hashem has done for him personally, and for his ancestors before him:

"Then you shall call out and say before Hashem, your God, 'An Aramean tried to destroy my forefather. He descended to Egypt and sojourned there, few in number, and there he became a nation — great, strong, and numerous. The Egyptians mistreated us and afflicted us, and placed hard work upon us. Then we cried out to Hashem, the God of our forefathers, and Hashem heard our voice and saw our affliction, our travail, and our oppression. Hashem took us out of Egypt with a strong hand and with an outstretched arm, with great awesomeness, and with signs and with wonders. He brought us to this place, and He gave us this Land, a Land flowing with milk and honey. And now, behold! I have brought the first fruit of the ground that You have given me, O Hashem!' And you shall lay it before Hashem, your God, and you shall prostrate yourself before Hashem, your God. And you shall rejoice with all the goodness that Hashem your God has given you and your household — you and the Levi and the proselyte who is in your midst."[76]

Although a Jew must work to perfect all the traits of his character, the trait of gratitude is the very purpose of creation. Hence the

---

73. *Shemos* 23:19.
74. *Bereishis Rabbah* 1:4.
75. See *Midrash Tanchuma, Shemini* 12.
76. *Devarim* 26:5-11.

paramount importance of *bikkurim*, which nurtures this trait. The Ramban writes: The purpose of all the mitzvos is to express our faith in our God and thank Him for having created us. This is the very purpose of creation, since there is no other fathomable reason for primordial creation, nor any desire that Hashem may have from His lower worlds, but that man should recognize and thank his God Who created him.[77]

The Targum Yonasan interprets the verse, יְהוּדָה אַתָּה יוֹדוּךָ אַחֶיךָ — "*Yehudah, your brothers will acknowledge you*,"[78] to mean that all Jews will be called "Yehudim" in his honor. The significance of this name was first expressed by Yehudah's mother, Leah, when she chose it: וַתֹּאמֶר הַפַּעַם אוֹדֶה אֶת ה' עַל כֵּן קָרְאָה שְׁמוֹ יְהוּדָה — "*She said, 'This time, I shall thank (odeh) Hashem,' and she named him Yehudah.*"[79]

Our title of "Yehudim" highlights the essence of our collective identity, and our purpose as the Chosen Nation, which is to recognize Hashem's involvement in our lives, and to thank Him for His never-ending kindness, as we say in the *tefillah* of *Modim*: נוֹדֶה לְךָ וּנְסַפֵּר תְּהִלָּתֶיךָ עַל חַיֵּינוּ הַמְּסוּרִים בְּיָדֶךָ ... וְעַל נִסֶּיךָ שֶׁבְּכָל יוֹם עִמָּנוּ וְעַל נִפְלְאוֹתֶיךָ וְטוֹבוֹתֶיךָ שֶׁבְּכָל עֵת, עֶרֶב וָבֹקֶר וְצָהֳרָיִם — "*We shall thank You and speak Your praise for our lives that are entrusted to Your hand ... and for Your miracles that are with us each day, and for Your wonders and constant kindness at every time, evening, morning, and afternoon.*"

Gratitude is the foundation of any healthy relationship between husband and wife, between neighbors, or between friends. It teaches a person to be humble and respectful to those around him, in recognition of how much he owes them. It enables him to be happy with his portion, and content to be surrounded by people who do so much for his benefit. It nurtures in his heart a sense of love for mankind, and a peaceful contentment with all the good things in life that might otherwise have been overlooked.

In contrast, those who are not grateful for the gifts they receive are perpetually bitter about everything they lack, and are at odds

---

77. *Ramban* to *Shemos* 13:16.
78. *Bereishis* 49:8.
79. Ibid. 29:35.

with their relatives and friends, whom they resent for denying them the honor or favors they think they deserve.

Gratitude is also the foundation of our relationship with Hashem. In the admonitions of *Parashas Haazinu*, Moshe Rabbeinu scolded Bnei Yisrael by saying: הֲלַה' תִּגְמְלוּ זֹאת עַם נָבָל וְלֹא חָכָם הֲלוֹא הוּא אָבִיךָ קָּנֶךָ הוּא עָשְׂךָ וַיְכֹנְנֶךָ — "*Is it to Hashem that you do this, O vile (naval) and unwise people?*"[80]

The Ramban comments that the Hebrew word *"naval"* refers to those who ungratefully repay kindness with injury. Accordingly, this admonition is not so much for the sins themselves, but for the failure to recognize Hashem's kindness and to conduct our lives accordingly. Since Hashem rewards on a scale five hundred times greater than that with which He punishes,[81] we can only imagine the great reward that awaits those who appreciate His kindness, and who devote themselves to His service with joy and gratitude. It is thus quite clear why *bikkurim* and the attribute of gratitude that this mitzvah engenders are indeed the very purpose of creation and the reason for Klal Yisrael's existence.

———◆———

Another insight into the importance of *bikkurim* can be gleaned from an episode in the life of David HaMelech. After completing his royal palace, he set his thoughts toward building a Beis HaMikdash. But Hashem forbade him from doing so, reserving this honor for Shlomo. The Midrash explains why David did not merit to build the Beis HaMikdash himself: You placed your own honor before Mine. Only after you saw yourself sitting in a house of cedar wood did you seek to build a Beis HaMikdash. But Shlomo your son placed My honor before his own, as it is written, "*In the eleventh year, in the month of bul* (Cheshvan) ... *the Beis HaMikdash was completed, and then Shlomo built his house.*"[82,83]

From here we learn an important lesson in the service of Hashem. The order by which we arrange our lives reveals our

---

80. *Devarim* 32:6.
81. *Midrash Tanchuma, Beshalach* 21.
82. *I Melachim* 6:38.
83. *Yalkut Shimoni, II Shmuel* 144.

priorities. By beginning the day with prayer and Torah study, we show that our relationship with Hashem is the most important part of our day. For this reason, the Gemara cautions so strongly against tending to our own business before davening in the morning, going so far as to compare it to idolatry.[84]

The other *matnos kehunah* (priestly gifts), such as *terumos* and *maasros* (agricultural tithes), are separated only after the crop has been harvested, processed, and brought into the warehouse. *Bikkurim* is unique in that it is marked as sacred from the moment the fruit first begins to bud, as the Mishnah states:

How are *bikkurim* separated? The farmer descends to his field and notices the first fig, grape, or pomegranate to bud. He ties a cord around it and says, "These are *bikkurim*."[85]

Bikkurim thus represent the importance of dedicating our first moments of every day to the service of Hashem, thereby showing that this is indeed the most important part of our lives. The same may be said of the beginning of each year, which we dedicate to Hashem in prayer and unity during the Yamim Noraim, thus showing that Hashem's service is more precious to us than anything else. May our prayers be answered to draw holiness and blessing upon all our endeavors throughout the year.

Let Us Make Man in Our Image

IN HIS COMMENTARY TO THIS WEEK'S *PARASHAH*, THE Ramban describes the process of Man's creation: "*And God said: Let Us make Man.*" [Whereas all other creatures were formed by Hashem's general decree that there be vegetation, birds, fish, and animals,] Man is unique in that he was created by specific utterance, due to his preeminent greatness, since his nature is unlike that of the animals that were created before him.

The plural of "*Let Us make Man*" is used, since, as we have

---

84. *Berachos* 14a.
85. Mishnah, *Bikkurim* 3:1.

explained above,[86] God alone created [the basic elements of] existence on the first day out of absolute nothingness. Afterward, He formed His creations from those basic elements. When He gave water the power to give forth life, He said, *"Let the waters teem with teeming living creatures,"* and similarly [to create animals] He said, *"Let the earth bring forth living creatures."*

When creating Man, He said, *"Let Us,"* meaning that together with the earth that He had already formed, He would make Man. The earth would give forth Man's body from the elements that had already been used in the creation of animals, as it is written, *"Hashem, God, formed the man of dust from the ground."* He then gave Man a living spirit by His supreme word, as it is written, *"And He blew into his nostrils the soul of life."*

The expression, *"In Our image, after Our likeness,"* means that Man would resemble them both. In the form of his body, he would resemble the earth from which he was taken. In his soul, he would resemble the higher worlds, since the soul has no physical form and can never die.

The verse continues, *"In the image of God He created him,"* to stress the wonder of Man's creation, which exceeds all else [in that he alone is a composite of the spiritual and physical].[87]

Rav Saadiah Gaon describes mankind as the purpose of creation and its crowning splendor.[88] Since Man incorporates within himself all aspects of creation, both physical and spiritual, he has the power to uplift them all through his Torah and mitzvos. The Kabbalists divide creation into three basic categories: עוֹלָם (space), שָׁנָה (time), and נֶפֶשׁ (spirit), the first letters of which spell the word עָשָׁן (smoke).[89] Accordingly, the verse, *"Har Sinai was entirely covered with smoke,"*[90] means that all aspects of creation were brought to perfection by the momentous event of *Kabbalas HaTorah*.

Whereas Adam named each of the animals, revealing the intrinsic nature of each one,[91] there were several aspects of creation that

---

86. 1:1.
87. *Ramban, Bereishis* 1:26.
88. *Emunos V'Dei'os* 6:4.
89. *Sefer Yetzirah* 6:1, see *Ramak's* commentary.
90. *Shemos* 19:18.
91. *Ramban, Bereishis* 2:19.

Hashem named Himself, since these were the essential building blocks by which everything else was formed: וַיִּקְרָא אֱלֹקִים לָאוֹר יוֹם וְלַחֹשֶׁךְ קָרָא לָיְלָה . . . וַיִּקְרָא אֱלֹקִים לָרָקִיעַ שָׁמָיִם . . . וַיִּקְרָא אֱלֹקִים לַיַּבָּשָׁה אֶרֶץ וּלְמִקְוֵה הַמַּיִם קָרָא יַמִּים . . . וַיֹּאמֶר אֱלֹקִים נַעֲשֶׂה אָדָם — *"God called the light 'Day' and the darkness He called 'Night' ... God called the firmament 'Heaven' ... God called the dry land 'Earth' and the gathering of the waters He called 'Seas' ... And God said, 'Let Us make Man.'"*[92]

Day and night represent the creation of time. (Until Hashem had so decreed, there was no concept of before or after.)[93] Heavens, Earth, and Seas represent the creation of space. Man represents the creation of spirit.

After completing each stage of creation, Hashem declared that His work was good. The sole exception is Man. After creating Man, Hashem did not say that this creation was good. Since Man is the pinnacle of creation, its purpose, and its crowning splendor, we would think that his creation would be especially worthy of Hashem's praise, yet it was not until Hashem finished all His work on the sixth day, that Man was included in the general approval of *"God saw everything that He made, and it was very good."* [94]

The Akeidas Yitzchak explains that the praise "it was good" was extended to each stage of creation in turn, since by its very existence Hashem achieved His objective. Hashem desired there to be light, and so there was. He desired there to be seas, and so there were. As soon as they came in to being, Hashem was pleased to see their existence. However, Hashem's objective in creating Man was not achieved by Man's very existence. Rather, Man must justify his existence by the sweat of his brow and the fruits of his own labor, as he toils in Torah, mitzvos, and character improvement, thus ascending beyond the level of beasts to express the Divine aspect of his nature.

The Sefer HaChinuch writes regarding the mitzvah of Bris Milah, "Just as Man has the power to perfect the appearance of his body [through the mitzvah of Bris Milah], he has the power to perfect his soul by the worthiness of his deeds." Only after he perfects his soul does he earn the accolade, אִמְרוּ צַדִּיק כִּי טוֹב כִּי פְרִי מַעַלְלֵיהֶם

---

92. *Bereishis* 1:5,8,10,26 .
93. *Rambam: Moreh Nevuchim II,* Chapter 30; *Vilna Gaon: Aderes Eliyahu, Bereishis* 1:1.
94. *Bereishis* 1:31.

יֹאכֵלוּ — *"Praise the righteous for the good they have done, for they shall eat the fruits of their labors."*[95,96]

With this we can understand why the name "Adam" was chosen for mankind. The Midrash states: R' Acha said: Before HaKadosh Baruch Hu created Man, He first consulted the ministering angels. "Let Us make Man," he told them.

"What will be the nature of this Man?" they asked.

"His wisdom will be greater than yours," Hashem said. Hashem then brought them all the different animals, beasts, and birds, and asked the angels their names, but the angels were unable to name them. Hashem then presented the animals to Adam and asked him to name them, to which Adam answered, "Ox, donkey, horse, camel," each one in turn.

"And what is your name?" Hashem asked him.

"It is fitting that I be called 'Adam,' since I was created from the earth (*adamah*)."[97]

In this context, the name "Adam" represents Man's coarse, earthy elements. However, the name "Adam" can also be understood to mean "*adameh l'Elyon* — I shall resemble God,"[98] thus representing the lofty, spiritual aspects of his being, of which Hashem said, *"Let Us make Man in Our image."* How can one name, which reveals the essence of one single being, allow for two such extreme opposites?

A similar paradox is found in the verse: וַיֹּאמֶר אֱלֹקִים נַעֲשֶׂה אָדָם בְּצַלְמֵנוּ כִּדְמוּתֵנוּ וְיִרְדּוּ בִדְגַת הַיָּם וּבְעוֹף הַשָּׁמַיִם וּבַבְּהֵמָה וּבְכָל הָאָרֶץ וּבְכָל הָרֶמֶשׂ הָרֹמֵשׂ עַל הָאָרֶץ — *"And God said, 'Let us make Man in Our image, after Our likeness. They shall rule over the fish of the sea, the birds of the sky, and over the animals, the whole earth, and every creeping thing that creeps upon the earth.'"*[99]

"וְיִרְדּוּ" can mean either "rule" or "descend," thus hinting that if Man is true to his Divine image, he rules all creation, but if he is unfaithful to his intended purpose, then he descends to the level of the beasts to become their prey.[100]

---

95. *Yeshayahu* 3:10. See *Metzudas David.*
96. On *Chinuch*, Mitzvah 2.
97. *Bereishis Rabbah* 17:4.
98. See *Shnei Luchos HaBris I, Toldos Adam* p. 3 s.v. *Achar kach.*
99. *Bereishis* 1:26.
100. *Rashi.*

Yet this paradox is in fact the essence of Man, who finds himself in a constant state of battle between the two warring forces of his consciousness. Man's duty in the service of Hashem is to rouse his *yetzer tov* against his *yetzer hara*,[101] thus letting his aspect of "*adameh l'Elyon*" overpower his aspect of "*adamah*." If a person devotes his life to his spiritual ideals, then his soul ascends above after his passing. But if he squanders his life in pursuit of earthly pleasures, then after his passing he will return to the earth, as Rabbeinu Yonah cautions: The wicked spend their lives in pursuit of bodily desires that draw them away from the service of the Creator and thus uproot them from their spiritual source in Heaven. Therefore, after their passing they will descend into the earth, toward which their desires had been focused throughout their lives.[102]

We can thus understand the verse, "*Let Us make Man*," as Hashem's invitation to mankind to join Him in their own creation, by deciding which element of their being would be superior. Hashem did not declare that Man's creation was good, since it is up to Man himself to decide whether his creation was in fact good, by choosing to be good by shunning evil.

הַחַיִּים וְהַמָּוֶת נָתַתִּי לְפָנֶיךָ הַבְּרָכָה וְהַקְּלָלָה וּבָחַרְתָּ בַּחַיִּים — "*I have placed before you life and death, blessing and curse. Choose life!*"[103] If Man chooses spiritual life over death, blessing over curse, then he proves that his creation was in fact good, and becomes Hashem's partner in the creation of the most noble and splendid species in all existence — mankind.

The Sefer Mitzvos Katan (*Smak*) writes regarding the mitzvah of teshuvah:

When HaKadosh Baruch Hu created His world, He made angels on the second day, giving them a *yetzer tov* but no *yetzer hara*. He then made animals, giving them a *yetzer hara* but no *yetzer tov*.

"What benefit do I have from these creations?" Hashem asked. "If the angels serve Me, it is only because they have no *yetzer hara*. If the animals do not serve Me, it is only because they have no

---

101. *Berachos* 5a.
102. *Shaarei Teshuvah* 2:18.
103. *Devarim* 30:19.

yetzer tov. I shall create a being with both inclinations."

Therefore, when the *yetzer hara* tempts Man to pursue his physical desires, his *yetzer tov* should tell him, "Not for this were you created. There were already animals (in existence, who devote themselves to physical pleasures)."

If the *yetzer tov* subdues the *yetzer hara*, then how great is Man, since he excels beyond the angels. If, however, the *yetzer tov* is defeated by the *yetzer hara*, then Man is inferior to animals.[104]

Many suggestions have been offered to explain the "image of God," with which Man was created. Surely this cannot be interpreted literally, since God has no physical image. Rav Chaim of Volozhin writes as follows in Nefesh HaChaim: Why was Man was created in the image of "Elokim," rather than any other Name of God? The Name Elokim represents Hashem's role as the Master of All Powers.[105] ... When Hashem first created all the worlds, He originated them from absolute nothingness. Since then, at every moment of every day, their continued existence and order depends entirely on Hashem's power, and the new light that He constantly pours into them. If Hashem would withhold His power from them for even one moment, they would instantly revert to a state of total nothingness . . .

As far as it may be said, Hashem appointed Man as master of all the myriad powers of creation and worlds without number. Hashem placed them all in Man's hand, that he would be their lord, to guide them by every nuance of his action, speech, and thought, and the general manner of his behavior, for good or for its opposite, *chas v'shalom.*

Through Man's good actions, speech, and thought, he sustains and grants strength to the supernal forces of holiness, increasing their sanctity and light, as it is written, *"And I shall place My words in your mouth ... to stretch out the heavens and establish the earth."*[106] Our Sages thus say of the verse, *"And all your children shall be students of Hashem"*[107]: do not read 'your children' (*banayich*) but 'your builders' (*bonayich*).[108] Torah scholars are called builders since they

---

104. *Smak*, Positive Commandment 53.
105. *Tur, Orach Chaim,* 5.
106. *Yeshayahu* 51:16.
107. Ibid. 54:13.
108. *Berachos* 64a.

design the uppermost worlds, as an architect designs a building. They are the ones who give the upper worlds their power.

The opposite is also true, *chas v'shalom*. Through a person's unworthy deeds, speech, and action, he destroys many vivifying forces and supernal holy worlds beyond number, as it is written, "*Your destroyers and demolishers have gone forth from among you*,"[109] while meanwhile strengthening the power of the Chambers of Impurity.

The Zohar explains the ladder in Yaakov's dream as an allusion to the soul of Man. The angels ascending and descending the ladder indicated how all the forces of creation rise and fall according to Man's deeds.[110]

We can thus well understand the Midrash that states that after Hashem created Adam, He led him through Gan Eden and showed him all its beautiful trees. "See how beautiful and praiseworthy are My works," Hashem told him. "I made them all for you. Take care not to destroy My world."[111]

May we merit to fulfill the true purpose of mankind, by serving Hashem with Torah study and good deeds, and may our Creator testify that the creation of Man was indeed good, with the arrival of the eternal day that will be perfectly good, when the righteous will sit with crowns upon their heads and delight in the radiance of the *Shechinah*, and may our portion be among them.

---

109. *Yeshayahu* 49:17.
110. *Zohar, Parashas Vayeitzei,* p. 53.
111. *Koheles Rabbah* 7.

פרשת נח
Parashas Noach

The Four Elements of Chein

THE TORAH TELLS US THAT "NOACH FOUND FAVOR (*chein*) in Hashem's eyes."[112] In this merit he was spared from the floodwaters that devastated the earth. Rabbi Shimshon Raphael Hirsch writes in his commentary to the Torah, that finding favor in Hashem's eyes constitutes the highest level of perfection that we can hope to achieve.

How does one find *chein* in Hashem's eyes? What traits are necessary to earn His favor? Our Sages point to four different traits, each of which is conducive to finding *chein* before Hashem: humility, *temimus* (perfect innocence), *yiras Shamayim* (fear of God), and Torah study.

Regarding humility, the *pasuk* states, "To the humble, He will give *chein*."[113] The Malbim explains that this refers to those who would not deign to contradict the Torah. In their humility, they realize that their understanding is often too limited to understand the depth of wisdom inherent in the Torah. To such people, Hashem grants *chein*, such that they earn the favor and goodwill of those around them.

Regarding *temimus*, we find in *Tehillim*, "Favor and glory does

---

112. *Bereishis* 6:8.
113. *Mishlei* 3:34.

Hashem bestow; He withholds no goodness from those who walk in perfect innocence."[114] The Radak explains that Hashem grants *chein* and honor to those who walk with integrity, and who return to Him with all their hearts.

Regarding *yiras Shamayim* (fear of Heaven), our Sages tell us, "Anyone who has *chein* is certain to have *yiras Shamayim*, as the *pasuk* states, 'The lovingkindness of Hashem is forever upon those who fear Him.'"[115,116]

Regarding Torah study, we find an interesting Gemara,[117] which discusses a contagious disease called *ra'asan*, which the Sages of the Talmud feared, taking every precaution to distance themselves from those infected with this terrible disease. R' Zeira would not sit downwind from them. R' Elazar would not enter their homes. R' Ami and R' Assi would not eat eggs laid in their neighborhood. The sole exception was R' Yehoshua ben Levi, who would wrap himself in a cloak together with *ra'asan* patients, and study Torah with them. He relied on the *pasuk*, "It (the Torah) is a beloved doe, which imparts *chein*."[118] He reasoned that if Torah imparts *chein* on those who learn it, it will certainly protect them as well.

This Gemara can be understood in greater depth, by comparing it to another Gemara,[119] in which the Sages taught the same R' Yehoshua ben Levi, that the letters of the *aleph-beis* can be interpreted as an acrostic, which teaches us the path of life. א,ב stands for *aluf binah*: learn wisdom. ג,ד stands for *gomeil dalim*: help the poor. ה,ו stands for the Name of Hashem. ז,ח,ט,י,כ,ל stands for the reward that will be granted to those who study Torah and help the poor. Hashem will provide, זָן (*zahn*) for them, grant them favor, חֵן (*chein*), be good to them, טוב (*tov*), grant them an inheritance, יְרוּשָׁה (*yerushah*), and crown, כֶּתֶר (*keser*), them in the World to Come, לְעוֹלָם הַבָּא (*L'Olam HaBa*).

In this context, the entire *aleph-beis* is interpreted as a guide book, which leads a person from the first step, which is Torah study,

---

114. *Tehillim* 84:12.
115. Ibid. 103:17.
116. *Sotah* 49b.
117. *Kesubos* 77b.
118. *Mishlei* 5:19.
119. *Shabbos* 104a.

to the ultimate reward of *Olam HaBa*. The lessons of the letters are not individual instructions, but a comprehensive system of self-improvement, which proceeds from one step to the next. We are not taught to study Torah, as one virtue, and also be kind to the poor, as another. But that we should study Torah, and the Torah study itself will lead us to be kind to the poor, and from there to the next stage.

If we follow the path of the letters, we will merit the special *chein* reserved for those who pursue the charitable aspect of Torah, by teaching it to the unfortunate. With this we can understand how R' Yehoshua ben Levi, after having learned the lesson of the *aleph-beis*, implemented it to its fullest extent. By teaching Torah to the *ra'asan* patients, he was simultaneously pursuing wisdom and helping the unfortunate. Therefore, he was confident that he would merit the *chein* and protection of the Torah.

In *Mishlei*, we find the *pasuk*, "Good discernment provides *chein*, but the way of the faithless is harsh."[120] From here it seems that discernment is a fifth path to *chein*. However, it seems that the discernment referred to here is the same type of discernment espoused elsewhere, in the *pasuk*, "The beginning of wisdom is *yiras Hashem*, it is good discernment to all who perform it."[121] Therefore, in this context, discernment falls under the category of *yiras Shamayim*, which we already noted above as one of the four paths to *chein*: Torah, humility, *yiras Shamayim,* and straightforwardness.

It is interesting to note that these same traits are stipulated as conditions to achieve *hashra'as haShechinah* — the indwelling of the Divine Presence. Regarding Torah, we find in *Pirkei Avos*,[122] that if even one individual studies Torah alone, the *Shechinah* rests upon him, as the *pasuk* states, "In any place that I permit My Name to be mentioned, I shall come to you and bless you."[123]

Regarding humility and *yiras Shamayim*, the *pasuk* states, "What house could you build for Me? What place could be My restful dwelling? . . . Toward this I will look, to the impoverished and broken spirited, who fears My word."[124]

---

120. *Mishlei* 13:15.
121. *Tehillim* 111:10.
122. 3:7.
123. *Shemos* 20:21.
124. *Yeshayahu* 66:1-2.

Regarding straightforwardness, the *pasuk* states, "You shall be *tamim* (wholehearted) with Hashem your God."[125] Rashi explains, "Walk with Him in simple sincerity, and then you will be with Him as His portion."

Noach merited Hashem's favor, since he excelled in all four of these traits. He was humble. Rashi explains the Gemara that states that "Noach was simple in his ways,"[126] to mean that he was humble and of contrite spirit. He was *tamim,* as the *pasuk* tells us that he was "*tamim* in his generation."[127] He was Godfearing, as the *pasuk* states, "Noach walked with the Lord." Onkelos translates this to mean, "Noach walked with the fear of Hashem." Finally, Noach studied Torah, as Rashi observes from the fact that Noach knew which animals were kosher, and allowed seven pairs of each kosher animal to enter the Ark.

In the merit of these four fundamental virtues, Noach survived the Flood, and survived to continue the propagation of the human race.

The New World

AFTER THE FLOOD, NOACH EMERGED FROM THE ARK and brought offerings to Hashem, Who then made a covenant with him, never again to destroy the world: וַיָּרַח ה' אֶת רֵיחַ הַנִּיחֹחַ וַיֹּאמֶר ה' אֶל לִבּוֹ לֹא אֹסִף לְקַלֵּל עוֹד אֶת הָאֲדָמָה בַּעֲבוּר הָאָדָם כִּי יֵצֶר לֵב הָאָדָם רַע מִנְּעֻרָיו וְלֹא אֹסִף עוֹד לְהַכּוֹת אֶת כָּל חַי כַּאֲשֶׁר עָשִׂיתִי —

"*Hashem smelled the pleasing aroma, and Hashem said in His heart, I will not continue to curse again the ground because of man, since the heart of man is wicked from his youth. Nor will I again continue to smite every living being as I have done.*[128]

Here it seems that Hashem's recognition that "the heart of

---

125. *Devarim* 18:13.
126. *Avodah Zarah* 6a.
127. *Bereishis* 6:9.
128. Ibid. 8:21.

man is wicked" is a plea in our defense, as if to say that we are not entirely responsible for our misdeeds, since we are prey to our evil inclinations. However, an apparent contradiction is found in the *pesukim* that precede the Flood, in which the very same argument is used against us: וַיַּרְא ה' כִּי רַבָּה רָעַת הָאָדָם בָּאָרֶץ וְכָל יֵצֶר מַחְשְׁבֹת לִבּוֹ רַק רַע כָּל הַיּוֹם. וַיִּנָּחֶם ה' כִּי עָשָׂה אֶת הָאָדָם בָּאָרֶץ וַיִּתְעַצֵּב אֶל לִבּוֹ. וַיֹּאמֶר ה' אֶמְחֶה אֶת הָאָדָם אֲשֶׁר בָּרָאתִי מֵעַל פְּנֵי הָאֲדָמָה מֵאָדָם עַד בְּהֵמָה עַד רֶמֶשׂ וְעַד עוֹף הַשָּׁמָיִם כִּי נִחַמְתִּי כִּי עֲשִׂיתִם — "*Hashem saw that the wickedness of Man was great upon the earth, and the entire inclination of his heart was only for evil the entire day. Hashem reconsidered having made man upon the earth, and He had heartfelt sadness. Hashem said, 'I will blot out Man whom I created from the face of the ground — from Man to animal, to creeping things, to the birds of the sky; for I have reconsidered My having created them.'*"[129]

Here it seems that for this same reason, that the heart of man is inclined toward wickedness, Hashem decided to destroy the world. How could this very same reason be His basis for vowing to never again destroy it?

It seems that a subtle distinction must be drawn between the two *pesukim*. Before the Flood, Hashem said that Man's *entire* inclination was *only* for evil for the *entire* day. Man had no thoughts other than how to indulge his desires at the expense of others. After the Flood, the *pasuk* states only that Man's heart is wicked from his youth. It does not state that he is *always* or *entirely* wicked. Man continued to have wicked thoughts, but he was no longer entirely wicked. Therefore, Hashem swore to spare mankind from annihilation.

The difference between the condition of the human race before the Flood, and its condition after the Flood, was that before the Flood there was no Torah. The Midrash Tanchuma[130] states that had Adam observed the Torah, he would have lived forever. From that time until the Flood, the world continued to exist in a dark abyss, devoid of the light of Torah.

After the Flood, however, Noach built a new world based on the foundation of Torah study. He himself studied Torah, and was

---

129. *Bereishis* 6:5-7.
130. Beginning of *Parashas Bechukosai*.

therefore able to discern which animals were kosher, and to allow seven pairs (one male, one female) into the ark.[131] His son, Shem, established a house of study, where Rivkah Immeinu inquired regarding the fate of her unborn children.[132]

Hashem, Who created the world, and created the *yetzer hara*, informed us of its only remedy: "I created the *yetzer hara*, and I created the Torah as its antidote."[133] In a world where Torah flourishes, there is still a *yetzer hara*, and Man's heart still wanders to thoughts of wickedness from time to time, but it is no longer true that "Man's *entire* inclination is *only* for evil for the *entire* day." Since Torah helps to subjugate Man's evil inclination, it is the merit of Torah that preserves the world.

This thought is expressed in the Zohar,[134] which states that as long as Torah exists in the world, and mankind labors in its study, HaKadosh Baruch Hu rejoices in His creation, and His joy permeates all the worlds. The heavens and earth are supported in this merit.

Although Man continues to have a natural inclination toward evil, the Torah has the power to subdue this inclination, and to redirect it toward good. The Gemara[135] states:

R' Alexanderi said: Anyone who toils in Torah for its own sake brings peace to the Court of Heaven, and to the Court of Earth, as the *pasuk* states, "If [Israel] would grasp hold of My mighty Torah, then he will make peace for Me. Peace, he will make for Me."[136]

Rav said: It is as if he builds the palaces of Heaven and Earth, as the *pasuk* states, "I have placed My words in your mouth, and covered you with the shade of My hand, to implant the Heavens, and to set a foundation for the earth."[137]

R' Yochanan said: He also protects the entire world, as the *pasuk* states, "And I will cover you with the shade of My hand."[138]

---

131. *Rashi, Bereishis* 7:2.
132. Ibid. 25:22.
133. *Kiddushin* 30b.
134. *Parashas Terumah.*
135. *Sanhedrin* 99b.
136. *Yeshayahu* 27:5.
137. Ibid 51:16.
138. Ibid.

Levi said: He even hastens the Redemption, as the *pasuk* continues, "And to say unto Zion, 'You are My nation.'"[139]

From here we learn that in the merit of immersing ourselves in the wisdom of the Torah, we support the entire world, ensure its preservation, rectify it with the Kingdom of Heaven, and hasten the Ultimate Redemption, may it be soon and in our times.

Perfect in His Generations

THE TORAH DESCRIBES NOACH AS AN אִישׁ צַדִּיק תָּמִים הָיָה בְּדֹרֹתָיו, *"A righteous man, perfect in his generations."* Rashi cites two explanations of the emphasis "in his generations":

Some expound [this word] as praise. Had he been in a righteous generation, he would have been even more righteous. And there are those who expound it to his deprecation. According to the [wicked standards] of his generation, he was righteous. But if he had been in the generation of Avraham, he would not have been considered anything [of significance].[140]

Why did the second opinion interpret the expression "in his generations" to Noach's denigration? The Torah itself testifies that "Noach found favor in Hashem's eyes," implying that he was indeed a *tzaddik*, in whose merit life on earth endured. Would it not then be more reasonable to judge him favorably, and presume that in a righteous generation, Noach would have risen to even greater heights?

Furthermore, why does the first opinion compare Noach to a generation of "*tzaddikim*" in a general sense, whereas the second opinion compares him specifically to Avraham? What was unique about Avraham Avinu that made Noach pale in comparison?

Yeshayahu HaNavi called the great Flood "the Waters of Noach,"[141] implying that Noach was in some way responsible for them. The Zohar in fact says so explicitly: Hashem told Noach that

---

139. *Yeshayahu* 51;16.
140. *Rashi, Bereishis* 6:9.
141. *Yeshayahu* 54:9, read as the *haftarah* to this week's *parashah*.

He would protect him in the ark, as it is written, "Behold, I am about to bring the Floodwaters ..." and "I will blot out all existence I have made from upon the face of the ground, but I will establish My covenant ... and you shall enter the ark." When Hashem told Noach that he and his sons would survive, Noach failed to pray on behalf of the world, and everything was destroyed as a result. For this reason, the Floodwaters were called by his name, as it is written, "For they are the Waters of Noach before Me, and I have sworn never again to bring the Waters of Noach."[142]

Although Noach was perfectly righteous in his own affairs, he was called to account for failing to pray on behalf of the sinners of his generation, that they might be forgiven and spared from destruction. Those who explain the expression "righteous in his generation" to demonstrate Noach's sole fault compare him to Avraham, who prayed on behalf of the wicked sinners of Sodom, that they might be saved despite their many iniquities. The Zohar states as follows: R' Yochanan said: Come and see the difference between Noach and the *tzaddikim* that arose in Israel after him. Noach did not defend his generation, nor pray on their behalf as did Avraham. When Hashem informed Avraham that He intended to destroy Sodom, Avraham immediately approached Him in prayer. He continued to beseech Him, until Hashem ensured that if only ten righteous people were to be found in Sodom, He would spare the entire city on their behalf. Avraham assumed that including Lot and his family, Hashem would certainly find ten. Therefore he concluded his prayers. Had he realized that there were not even ten, he would have prayed that Sodom be spared in the merit of even fewer.[143]

Someone who inadvertently kills another person is exiled to a city of refuge (*ir miklat*), where he must remain until the death of the Kohen Gadol. The Kohen Gadol's mother would often send food packages to the exiles, to forestall them from praying for the death of her son. Although the Torah assures us that "As a bird that wanders off, so an unwarranted curse will not arrive,"[144] the

---

142. *Zohar, Bereishis* 67b.
143. *Zohar* I, 254b.
144. *Mishlei* 26:2.

prayers of the exiles were not considered "unwarranted curses," since the Kohen Gadol was held responsible for their predicament. Had he prayed sufficiently for peace, the tragedies would never have occurred, and they would never have been forced into exile.[145]

From all these sources we draw an important conclusion. Torah leaders are responsible for the physical and spiritual welfare of their entire generation, even for the sinners among us. They must pray on our behalf, even when we prove unworthy. Noach's failure to do so left a blemish on his reputation, despite his perfect righteousness in all other matters.

The Liar's Folly

THE GEMARA DISCUSSES CERTAIN SITUATIONS IN WHICH a person is technically able to renege on a business commitment. However, Beis Din extends to him the severe curse that, "He Who punished the Generation of the Flood and the Generation of the Dispersion (who built the Tower of Bavel) will punish those who break their word."[146]

Throughout history, countless nations have met their demise at the hand of Heaven in retribution for their sins. Why were the Generations of the Flood and of the Dispersion chosen as the examples with which to warn dishonest businessmen? Why was any example necessary? Would it not have been enough to simply say, "He Who punishes sinners will punish you"? By focusing on these two generations in particular, it seems that there must be some relation between their sins, and the baleful sin of cheating in business.

The Generation of the Flood were faulted primarily for the rampant theft that plagued their era. The Gemara states: R' Yochanan taught: Come and see the terrible result of thievery. The Generation of the Flood transgressed all Hashem's commands, yet their judgment was not sealed until they stretched their hands out in theft,

---

145. *Makkos* 11a.
146. *Bava Metzia* 44a.

as it is written, "For the land is filled with robbery; therefore, I shall destroy them from the earth."[147, 148]

In contrast, the Generation of the Dispersion was united by a bond of common purpose. There was no theft, dissent, or strife among them, as they combined their efforts toward a common goal of evil, to ascend the Heavens and wage war against the Creator Himself.[149] Their sin was not *bein adam la'chaveiro* (between man and his fellow), but *bein adam la'Makom* (between man and his Creator).

The deceitful businessman sins not only against his victim, but against Hashem, and against himself too. He invites his own ruin in this world and the next, by blocking the channels of Hashem's blessing. He shakes the very foundations of society, since truth is the first and foremost pillar of existence, as our Sages teach, "The world endures on three things: justice, truth, and peace."[150] A person who cheats in business cannot hope to have any relationship with Hashem, Who signs His Name with a seal of Truth.[151]

For this reason, our Sages warn the deceitful businessman that "He Who punished the Generation of the Flood and the Generation of the Dispersion will punish all those who do not keep their word." His sin is doubly heinous, since it offends both his God and his fellow man. Therefore, he is destined to receive a twofold punishment, equivalent to the punishments of the Flood and the Dispersion.

Shunning Evil

IN THIS WEEK'S *PARASHAH*, NOACH IS DESCRIBED ONCE AS "A righteous man, perfect in his generations" (6:9), while elsewhere Hashem describes him as "righteous in this generation" (7:1), without mentioning his perfection. For which attribute was he

---

147. *Bereishis* 6:13.
148. *Sanhedrin* 108a.
149. *Bereishis Rabbah* Ch. 38, cited by *Rashi*.
150. *Pirkei Avos* 1:28.
151. *Shabbos* 55a.

lauded as righteous; for which was he lauded as perfect; and why was the second praise subsequently omitted?

Noach lived in two corrupt eras: one before the Flood, and one after. The generation before the Flood surrendered itself to the unbridled pursuit of physical pleasure, such that filth and perversion became a normal way of life.[152] The generation of the Dispersion, which thrived after the Flood, followed instead the path of arrogance and heresy. Blinded by their delusions of grandeur, they had the preposterous audacity to assault the very Heavens and confront God Himself.[153]

We are all influenced by the deeds, words, and ideologies of our peers, as the Rambam warns:

Man's nature is to be drawn after the opinions and deeds of his friends and peers. He acts as the people of his environs act. Therefore, Man must befriend the righteous, and always associate with the wise, so that he may emulate their ways. He must distance himself from the wicked, and from those who walk in darkness, to avoid their influence. As Shlomo said, "He who walks with the wise will become wise, while he who pastures with the foolish will be harmed,"[154] and it says, "Fortunate is the man [who does not walk in the counsel of the wicked]." [155]

If he lives in a country whose ways are evil, and its people walk on crooked paths, he should move to a place of righteous people, who act properly. If all the countries of which he knows, or has heard their reputation, all act improperly (as in our own time), or if he cannot travel to a country with proper customs because of war or disease, he should isolate himself, as is written, "Let him sit alone and be silent."[156] If people are so wicked that they will not allow him to remain in their country unless he mingles with them and follows their evil ways, he should go to live among the caves, brushland, and deserts, rather than learn to emulate the wicked, as is written, "Who would make the wilderness into my guest-hostel."[157,158]

---

152. *Rashi, Bereishis* 6:11,12.
153. Ibid. 11:1.
154. *Mishlei* 13:20.
155. *Tehillim* 1:1.
156. *Eichah* 3:28.
157. *Yirmyahu* 9:1.
158. *Rambam, Hilchos Dei'os* Ch. 6.

When perversion and arrogance covered the face of the earth, Noach alone remained true to his values. The corruption of the world could not penetrate the stalwart barriers of faith he had built around his heart. In the perverse Generation of the Flood, Noach's purity of heart and strength of character put him on par with Yosef HaTzaddik, who withstood the lascivious advances of Potiphar's wife. He too earned the title of "*Tzaddik* — righteous." Therefore, in reference to the particular sins of the Generation of the Flood, Hashem described him as "righteous in his generations." He was righteous in his self-control, in stark contrast to the wild abandon that destroyed his generation.

"Enter the ark together with your family, for it is you [alone] I have seen to be righteous before Me," Hashem told him. Noach was the "*Tzaddik yesod olam* — the righteous man who is the foundation of the world."[159] In kabbalistic texts, the attribute of "*Yesod* — foundation" refers to the ability to contain one's desires. From Noach's righteousness in this particular area, a new world was founded after the Flood. (In contrast, our Sages warn that anyone who allows himself to be drawn after selfish pleasure brings a deluge of destruction to the world, as cited in *Shulchan Aruch*.[160])

In the Generation of the Dispersion, Noach was exposed to a different, but equally destructive influence: that of heresy and arrogance. When his neighbors gathered in unison to throw off the yoke of Hashem's Kingdom, Noach alone remained perfectly faithful.

The Torah therefore introduces Noach as "a righteous man, perfect in his generations." He was righteous in standing against the hedonism of the Generation of the Flood, and perfect in standing against the arrogance and heresy of the Generation of the Dispersion. However, when Hashem told Noach that He would save him from the Flood, He refers to Noach as "righteous," making no mention of his perfection.

Throughout our lives, we face many challenges to our ideals. We find ourselves in situations where we must cling to our religious and moral values, despite an overwhelming tide of social influence

---

159. *Mishlei* 10:25.
160. *Shabbos* 41a. See *Shulchan Aruch: Orach Chaim* 3:14, *Even HaEzer* 23:4.

to the contrary. The main test of our character is not when things go easy, but when we must sacrifice for our beliefs. When we block out the tumultuous, confusing din of social pressure, and focus on the still, small voice of Hashem that calls to us from our innermost hearts, we rise to the level of Noach, the "righteous man, perfect in his generations," who built an ark of stalwart idealism that preserved the human race.

פרשת לך לך
Parashas Lech Lecha

A Sacrifice of Love

I N THIS WEEK'S *PARASHAH,* HASHEM COMMANDS AVRAHAM Avinu to circumcise himself and his household, and to pass the covenant of the Bris Milah on to his descendants, for all generations to come: וַיֹּאמֶר אֱלֹקִים אֶל אַבְרָהָם וְאַתָּה אֶת בְּרִיתִי תִשְׁמֹר אַתָּה וְזַרְעֲךָ אַחֲרֶיךָ לְדֹרֹתָם. זֹאת בְּרִיתִי אֲשֶׁר תִּשְׁמְרוּ בֵּינִי וּבֵינֵיכֶם וּבֵין זַרְעֲךָ אַחֲרֶיךָ הִמּוֹל לָכֶם כָּל זָכָר ... וְאַבְרָהָם בֶּן תִּשְׁעִים וָתֵשַׁע שָׁנָה בְּהִמֹּלוֹ בְּשַׂר עָרְלָתוֹ — *"And the Lord said to Avraham, And for you, you shall keep My covenant — you and your offspring after you, throughout their generations. This is My covenant that you shall keep, between Myself and you, and between your offspring after you; every male shall be circumcised' ... and Avraham was ninety-nine years old when he was circumcised on the flesh of his foreskin."*[161]

The Bris Milah is a sign that our entire lives are dedicated to Hashem's service. Not only does the Jewish soul reach up to the highest Heavens, but even his physical body, formed from coarse earth, is a sanctified vessel, dedicated to the service of Hashem. When a child is brought into the covenant of the Bris Milah, he becomes like an offering, which is accepted with good favor before Hashem. The Zohar states, "Fortunate is Israel, who present a

---

161. *Bereishis* 17:9-10,24.

favorable offering before HaKadosh Baruch Hu, when they bring their eight-day-old sons as offerings."[162]

There is a most perplexing Midrash concerning Avraham Avinu's Bris Milah:

"On this very day, Avraham was circumcised." ... R' Abba bar Kahana explained that he felt [pain] and suffered from it, in order that Hashem would multiply his reward. R' Levi explained that the *pasuk* does not say that Avraham circumcised himself, but rather that he was circumcised, meaning that Avraham examined himself and discovered that he was already circumcised. R' Berachya said that at that time (when R' Levi said this), R' Abba bar Kahana cursed R' Levi, and said, "Liar! Deceiver! He felt and suffered from it, in order that HaKadosh Baruch Hu would multiply his reward."[163]

Why did R' Abba so fiercely oppose R' Levi's explanation, such that he was moved to insult his peer, and hurl such harsh words at him? Certainly we should not interpret this to mean that there was any kind of personal feud between them. The Talmud *Yerushalmi* tells us that R' Abba once heard R' Levi speak, and was so touched by his words, that he kissed him on his head, and blessed him, saying, "Just as you have lectured while standing up and young of age, so may you merit to lecture while sitting down, in old age, serving as Rosh Yeshivah, and speaking before the multitudes."[164]

In Koheles Rabbah we find another incident, in which R' Abba kissed R' Levi on his head. If so, why did their disagreement over Avraham Avinu's Bris Milah move R' Abba to disparage R' Levi to such an extent?

It seems that R' Abba did not argue against R' Levi simply based on logic. Rather, he had a clear and obvious proof for his explanation, and therefore maintained that R' Levi's explanation must certainly be false. It cannot possibly be true that Avraham Avinu discovered himself circumcised, and suffered no pain in the process. The covenant he forged with Hashem, by means of the Bris Milah, was one of personal sacrifice and suffering. It was this suffering that created an eternal bond between Hashem and the

---

162. *Zohar* I, 93.
163. *Bereishis Rabbah*, 47:9.
164. *Yerushalmi, Horayos* 3:5, see *Pnei Moshe* commentary.

Jewish people. From where else could his descendants have drawn the strength of character to serve Hashem, and be loyal to the covenant of Avraham Avinu, in the most harsh and bitter circumstances of the *Galus*? We draw our strength from the precedent that Avraham Avinu set for us. Therefore, R' Abba could find no other way to express himself, but to say that R' Levi was lying.

There is a general principle that all mitzvos are best performed personally, and not through an intermediary. This is especially true regarding the Bris Milah. When a father circumcises his son, he must control his natural compassion, and cut the flesh of his own beloved infant. This is a greater display of dedication to the mitzvah than having it done by a *mohel*.

With this, the Ksav Sofer explains the *pasuk*, "Avraham circumcised his son Yitzchak ... as the Lord commanded him."[165] Just as Hashem personally commanded Avraham to perform the Bris Milah, and did not convey this instruction through any intermediary, so too Avraham personally circumcised his son, and did not appoint any intermediary to do so for him.[166]

Amazing stories are told about the dedication of Klal Yisrael to the mitzvah of Bris Milah, even in the most difficult conditions. One story is told of a *mohel* who would travel from city to city throughout Russia, performing clandestine Bris Milahs, risking the threat of horrific punishment. One time he performed a Bris Milah on a baby who was already three months old, but had been unable to have a Bris any earlier. As soon as the Bris was completed, the mother snatched the infant out of the *sandek's* arms, and smothered him with hugs and kisses. When asked for an explanation for this sudden outburst of emotion, the mother explained that she had been afraid that she would be unable to give her son a Bris. In order to strengthen her resolve, she had sworn never to hug or kiss her baby, until after he had entered into the covenant.

Another story is told of a Bris Milah that took place in a hidden cellar, in the Kovna Ghetto, in the midst of the Holocaust. Ten men had secretly met in this hiding place, in order to be present for a Bris Milah. Suddenly, a messenger burst into the room to warn

---

165. *Bereishis* 21:4.
166. *Teshuvos Ksav Sofer, Y.D.* 121.

them that the Germans were conducting a raid. The men hastened to hide any trace of the Bris Milah, but the mother was adamant in her demand that the baby be circumcised immediately. If her son were to die, she wanted him to die as a Jew, after having entered into the Bris Milah.

———•———

Our Sages tell us that any mitzvah for which our forefathers sacrificed their lives is still faithfully observed by their descendants. Our Sages then tell us that any mitzvah which our forefathers performed joyously is still joyously performed by their descendants. As an example of both these principles, the Gemara cites the mitzvah of Bris Milah.[167] One might think that the two sentiments of self-sacrifice and joy are mutually exclusive. Yet in the merit of Avraham Avinu's joyous sacrifice to fulfill Hashem's command, we too are able to harbor both sentiments simultaneously in our hearts.

The Gemara elsewhere states that the Bris Milah should be performed "until one's soul expires."[168] This is because the Bris Milah is an expression of our burning desire to deliver our very lives to Hashem *Yisbarach*, and become a living sacrifice to His holy Name, such that our "soul expires" in longing for Hashem.

The Maharal said in his *derashah* for Shabbos Shuvah that the number seven represents the realm of nature, while the number eight represents that which is beyond nature. Bris Milah is performed on the eighth day. When a father subjugates his innate, paternal love to cut the flesh of his infant son, Hashem correspondingly rewards him in a manner that transcends nature.

An allusion to this can be found in the Baal HaTurim's commentary on the *pasuk*, "Who shall ascend to the Heavens for us?", מִי יַעֲלֶה לָּנוּ הַשָּׁמַיְמָה[169]; the first letters of each word spell the word מִילָה, and the last letters spell Hashem's Name. This teaches us that in the merit of the Bris Milah, Hashem raises us above the Heavens, and guides us by His Holy Name, which transcends nature.

---

167. *Shabbos* 130a.
168. *Avodah Zarah* 27a.
169. *Devarim* 30:12.

The Midrash states: Even if Bnei Yisrael have no other good deeds, HaKadosh Baruch Hu will redeem them in the merit of the Bris Milah... When Bnei Yisrael were in Egypt, they worshiped idols ... and were redeemed only in the merit of the Bris Milah... When they left Egypt and came to the Reed Sea, they rebelled, and the Sea wished to drown them ... When the water reached the hem of their clothes, and lifted up the clothing, it saw the Bris Milah and fled... It split for them only in the merit of the Bris Milah.

When they came to the Desert, they did not observe the Bris Milah for forty years, except for the Tribe of Levi, which circumcised its sons... When Bnei Yisrael came to the Jordan River, they were all uncircumcised, except for the Tribe of Levi, which carried the *Aron*. The Jordan wanted to drown Bnei Yisrael, since they were uncircumcised, but HaKadosh Baruch Hu performed for them a miracle. He took all 600,000 Jews and placed them between the poles of the *Aron*, among the Leviim, in order that the waters of the Jordan would see the Bris Milah of the Leviim and flee.[170]

We pray that just as our forefathers were redeemed in the merit of the Bris Milah, so may we also speedily be redeemed.

Dawn of a New Era

וַיִּקַּח אַבְרָם אֶת שָׂרַי אִשְׁתּוֹ וְאֶת לוֹט בֶּן אָחִיו וְאֶת כָּל רְכוּשָׁם אֲשֶׁר רָכָשׁוּ וְאֶת הַנֶּפֶשׁ אֲשֶׁר עָשׂוּ בְחָרָן וַיֵּצְאוּ לָלֶכֶת אַרְצָה כְּנַעַן וַיָּבֹאוּ אַרְצָה כְּנָעַן.

Avram took his wife Sarai, and Lot his brother's son, and all their wealth they had amassed, and the souls they made in Charan; and they left to go toward the Land of Canaan, and they came to the Land of Canaan.[171]

---

170. *Aggadas Bereishis*, Ch. 17.
171. *Bereishis* 12:5.

THE HISTORY OF THE WORLD IS DIVIDED INTO THREE eras: two thousand years of confusion, two thousand years of Torah, and two thousand years of the era of Mashiach.[172] The two thousand years of Torah began not with *Kabbalas HaTorah* at Har Sinai, but with "the souls Avraham made in Charan," a reference to the converts he drew beneath the wings of the *Shechinah*.

Avraham was credited with being the first to spread God's wisdom in the world, thereby drawing the era of confusion to an end. However, he was not the first to study or teach Torah. Noach also studied Torah. (Otherwise, he could not have distinguished between the pure and impure animals, to know how many of each to take into the ark.[173]) Shem and Eiver also studied Torah, and even established Torah academies where Avraham himself studied. Accordingly, Avraham seems no more than a link in the chain of Torah study that stretches all the way back to Adam HaRishon. Why is he credited with inaugurating a new era of Torah?

Rav Yosef Karo explains in his commentary on the Rambam: "Shem and Eiver revealed to their students the ways of Hashem, but they were never inspired to call out to the world as did Avraham. Therefore, his merit was greater than theirs."[174]

The spiritual leaders who preceded Avraham did no more than allow any who were so inclined to come and learn from them, to drink from the proverbial waters of Torah. However, the wellsprings of Torah never spread outside the Beis Midrash. No one ever took the Torah and carried it out into the streets and marketplaces to disseminate its wisdom, until Avraham arose and proclaimed, "There is a Master of the Palace," and gathered throngs of followers to his banner.

The Rambam writes: Avraham arose and began to call out to the world in a great voice, proclaiming the existence of a single God of the entire world, Whom alone it is fitting to serve. He would travel from city to city, from country to country, gathering crowds as he went, until he reached the Land of Canaan, as it is written, "There he called in the Name of Hashem, God of the world." When

---

172. *Avodah Zarah* 9a.
173. *Eiruvin* 18.
174. *Kesef Mishnah, Hilchos Avodas Kochavim* 1:3.

people would approach to ask about his message, he would explain to each according to his wisdom, guiding him back to the path of truth. Eventually, he gathered a following that numbered tens of thousands. These were the members of Avraham's household. He planted the roots of faith in their hearts, authored books, and passed the tradition on through his son, Yitzchak.[175]

By spreading Hashem's wisdom beyond the walls of the Beis Midrash, Avraham began a new era of Torah, which shone like the dawn, shattering the darkness and confusion of the night that preceded it. In this merit, Avraham earned the title of "Hashem's beloved."[176] He sealed a covenant with Hashem that would last throughout the generations.

II

Another insight into Avraham's revolutionary message can be found in Targum Onkelos's interpretation of "the souls they made": וְיָת נַפְשָׁתָא דְּשַׁעְבִּידוּ לְאוֹרַיְתָא — *the souls they subjugated to the Torah.* For the Torah to revolutionize a person's very being, thereby allowing him to ascend to the greatest heights, it is insufficient for him just to study or even teach Torah. He must subjugate himself to the Torah, dedicating his body to its laws, and his mind to its wisdom, until it transforms him into a new being. This was the message of Torah that Avraham taught, when he "acquired the souls" of his followers in Charan.

The Eternal Covenant

WHEN AVRAHAM PERFORMED THE BRIS MILAH, HE forged a covenant with Hashem that would endure until the end of time. The commentaries offer several insights

---

175. *Rambam, Hilchos Avodas Kochavim* 1.
176. See *Rambam, Hilchos Teshuvah* 10:2.

as to how and why this important mitzvah is the basis of our eternal covenant with Hashem.

In the Guide for the Perplexed, the Rambam explains that the Bris Milah curtails the overwhelming desire for physical pleasure, allowing one's mind to focus on the pursuit of the spiritual.[177] He adds a further explanation, that just as soldiers wear a uniform to show their common purpose, it is only fitting that the legions of Hashem, Bnei Yisrael, show their united allegiance to Hashem with a badge of honor carved into their very flesh.

Rabbeinu Bachaye explains that Shabbos, tefillin, and Bris Milah are all signs of the covenant between Hashem and Bnei Yisrael, as it is written:

בֵּינִי וּבֵין בְּנֵי יִשְׂרָאֵל אוֹת הִוא לְעֹלָם כִּי שֵׁשֶׁת יָמִים עָשָׂה ה' אֶת הַשָּׁמַיִם וְאֶת הָאָרֶץ וּבַיּוֹם הַשְּׁבִיעִי שָׁבַת וַיִּנָּפַשׁ.

Between Me and Bnei Yisrael, it is an eternal sign, that in six days Hashem made Heaven and earth, and on the seventh day He rested and was refreshed.[178]

וְהָיָה לְךָ לְאוֹת עַל יָדְךָ וּלְזִכָּרוֹן בֵּין עֵינֶיךָ לְמַעַן תִּהְיֶה תּוֹרַת ה' בְּפִיךָ כִּי בְּיָד חֲזָקָה הוֹצִאֲךָ ה' מִמִּצְרָיִם.

It shall be for you a sign on your arm, and a reminder between your eyes, in order that Hashem's Torah may be in your mouth — for with a strong hand, Hashem removed you from Egypt.[179]

וּנְמַלְתֶּם אֵת בְּשַׂר עָרְלַתְכֶם וְהָיָה לְאוֹת בְּרִית בֵּינִי וּבֵינֵיכֶם.

You shall circumcise the flesh of your foreskin, and that shall be the sign of the covenant between Me and you.[180]

Just as two witnesses are sufficient to prove a point of law, any two of these three mitzvos are sufficient tesimony to our covenant with Hashem. On Shabbos, we need not wear *tefillin*, since the mitzvah of Shabbos takes its place. Bris Milah is the only witness that testifies to our covenant throughout the week, and throughout the cycle of time.

---

177. *Moreh Nevuchim* III, Chapter 49.
178. *Shemos* 31:17.
179. Ibid. 13:9.
180. *Bereishis* 17:11.

The Chasam Sofer writes that the *orlah* is the remnant of the leather garment with which Hashem clothed Adam after his fall. Since wearing this garment was a result of Adam's sin, the *orlah* serves as a lasting memorial to his disgrace. By removing it, we purge ourselves from the memory and residual influence of Adam's sin.[181]

With this we can better understand the following Midrash: The wicked TurnasRufas once asked R' Akiva, "Whose works are more beautiful: those of God, or those of mortal man?"

"The works of man are more beautiful," R' Akiva answered.

"Can man make anything as beautiful as the Heavens and the earth?" asked TurnasRufas.

"Do not compare our achievements with that which is above the realm of man. Compare our works with those of Hashem that are within our realm," said R' Akiva.

"Why do you practice circumcision?" asked TurnasRufas.

"I realized your intention, therefore I preceded your challenge by saying that the works of man are more beautiful." R' Akiva then produced a bundle of wheat and a loaf of bread, and said, "These are the works of Hashem, and these are the works of man. Are the works of man not greater?"[182]

R' Akiva's argument seems puzzling. Is bread truly greater than stalks of wheat? If not for Adam's curse, "By the sweat of your brow, you shall eat bread," we would have been content to have been able to eat wheat as it grows, without having to toil through ten stages of production until it is made into bread. This seems scarce proof for R' Akiva's claim, that the works of man are greater than those of Hashem. TurnasRufas's argument still hovers before us. What is lacking in man's natural form, as God made it, that it must be so severely altered by the Bris Milah?

According to what we have explained above, this is well understood. Before Adam's fall, trees sprouted loaves of bread, ready to be eaten without any further preparation.[183] Angels roasted meat and chilled wine for his pleasure.[184] Creation offered him its

---

181. *Chasam Sofer on the Torah*, citing *Maaseh Hashem*.
182. *Midrash Tanchuma, Tazria* 5.
183. *Shabbos* 30b. See *Teshuvos Avnei Nezer* 168 (111):4.
184. *Sanhedrin* 59b.

bounty, fully prepared, and within his easy reach. Only after his sin was the world corrupted to the extent that he needed to prepare his food by the sweat of his brow. It then became his responsibility to rectify the spiritual flaws in creation through his Torah and mitzvos, and its physical flaws through his hard work.

By comparing wheat to bread, R' Akiva displayed the harm that was wrought in creation, as a result of Adam's sin. His food would no longer grow perfectly prepared for his enjoyment. He would need to labor by the sweat of his brow, to process wheat into bread. His very body was impaired in the same way, requiring us to perfect it by removing the *orlah*, just as we must perfect wheat by making it into bread.[185]

Another insight into the significance of the Bris Milah is offered by the Zohar, which states that when a father presents his son to be circumcised, he offers him as a *korban* (sacrificial offering) to Hashem.[186] The lap of the *sandek*, on which the Bris Milah is performed, serves in place of the Golden *Mizbei'ach*, where the *ketores* (incense offering) was burned.[187] Accordingly, officiating as a *sandek* at a Bris Milah is a *segulah* for livelihood, as was the *ketores* offering in the Beis HaMikdash. The comparison between Bris Milah and *ketores* can be understood in light of the following Midrash:

R' Aivu taught: When Avraham circumcised the members of his household, he piled the severed *orlahs* into a mound. When the heat of the sun shone upon them, they began to decay, and the odor of the rotting flesh ascended before Hashem like the fragrant smoke of incense, and like the meat of the *korban olah* consumed by the fire of the *Mizbei'ach*.

Hashem then said, "When his descendants sin, I shall remember this smell and show them mercy for its sake."[188]

---

185. *Ohr HaChaim, Vayikra* 12:3.
186. *Zohar, Bereishis* 91a.
187. *Rema, Y.D.* 265:11.
188. *Bereishis Rabbah* 47:7.

פרשת וירא
Parashas Vayeira

Prayers of the Forefathers

וַיַּשְׁכֵּם אַבְרָהָם בַּבֹּקֶר אֶל הַמָּקוֹם אֲשֶׁר עָמַד שָׁם אֶת פְּנֵי ה׳.

Avraham rose early in the morning, to the place
where he had stood before Hashem (in prayer).[189]

ROM HERE WE LEARN THAT AVRAHAM AVINU INSTITUT-
ed the morning prayer of Shacharis. Similarly, Yitzchak
instituted Minchah, and Yaakov instituted Maariv.[190] An
allusion to this can be found in the second letter of each patriarch's
name. The letter ב from אַבְרָהָם stands for בֹּקֶר (*morning*), the צ from
יִצְחָק stands for צָהֳרַיִם (*afternoon*), and the ע from יַעֲקֹב stands for
עֶרֶב (*night*).

The Maharsha explains that in fact, each of the *Avos* prayed all
three prayers, just as they fulfilled all other Biblical and Rabbinical
mitzvos. Nonetheless, since each one applied particular effort to
a specific *tefillah*, he is considered to have instituted it for generations to come. What is the special significance of each *tefillah*, and
how did it correspond to the Forefather who established it?

---

189. *Bereishis* 19:27.
190. *Berachos* 26b.

Avraham sanctified Hashem's Name through his kindness and hospitality. Therefore, he was uniquely attuned to the morning prayers, of which it is said, לְהַגִּיד בַּבֹּקֶר חַסְדֶּךָ וֶאֱמוּנָתְךָ בַּלֵּילוֹת — *"To relate Your kindness in the dawn, and Your faith in the nights."*[191] For serving as the pillar of kindness, Avraham was granted the Shacharis prayer, in which he and his descendants would be able to draw Hashem's mercy and lovingkindness into the world.

Yitzchak's fear of Heaven, and the sense of strict justice that pervaded his very being, is alluded to by the Name used for Hashem: *Pachad Yitzchak* — "The Awe of Yitzchak."[192] Yitzchak offered his life to Hashem as a *korban* upon the *Mizbei'ach*, and became the living embodiment of awe and trepidation. [193]

Before nightfall, a spirit of strict judgment rests upon the world, as the Zohar states.[194] Yitzchak instituted Minchah to advocate on our behalf, and protect us from the very attribute of judgment that he embodied.

Yaakov was the foremost of our forefathers. When he fled his father's home to wander alone in exile, he prepared the path upon which his descendants were destined to journey in their own exiles throughout the ages. The blessings he received from Yitzchak were passed down as an eternal inheritance to every Jew, providing us with the strength and fortitude to persevere and remain loyal to our ideals, until at last the dawn of redemption breaks. He instituted Maariv, the nighttime prayer, to beseech Hashem for mercy in the long, dark night of *Galus*.

The Meshech Chachmah writes as follows: "And God spoke to Yisrael in night visions."[195] This expression is never used anywhere in the Torah in regard to Avraham or Yitzchak. Yaakov alone received "night visions" as he descended from Eretz Yisrael to sojourn abroad. Hashem then revealed Himself to Yaakov at night, signifying that even in the dark night of exile, the *Shechinah* would remain with Bnei Yisrael, as our Sages teach: "When they were

---

191. *Tehillim* 92:3.
192. *Bereishis* 31:42.
193. See *Maharsha*, *Yevamos* 64a.
194. *Zohar*, *Parashas Yisro* 88b.
195. *Bereishis* 46:2.

exiled to Babylon, the *Shechinah* traveled with them."[196] ... David HaMelech prayed, "May Hashem answer you on the day of distress; may the Name of the God of Yaakov make you impregnable."[197] When darkness and suffering would befall Bnei Yisrael, Hashem would remain by their side to protect them, as He remained with Yaakov in the dark night of his own exile.

Each of our forefathers served Hashem in his own unique way, and thereby prepared a channel through which our own prayers ascend to Heaven, as we emulate their traits of kindness, justice, and fortitude in the darkness of exile. May Hashem remember on our behalf the covenant He forged with our forefathers, and redeem their descendants from exile, speedily and in our days.

A Son and a Slave

וַיִּקְרָא אֵלָיו מַלְאַךְ ה' מִן הַשָּׁמַיִם וַיֹּאמֶר אַבְרָהָם אַבְרָהָם וַיֹּאמֶר הִנֵּנִי. וַיֹּאמֶר אַל תִּשְׁלַח יָדְךָ אֶל הַנַּעַר וְאַל תַּעַשׂ לוֹ מְאוּמָה כִּי עַתָּה יָדַעְתִּי כִּי יְרֵא אֱלֹקִים אַתָּה וְלֹא חָשַׂכְתָּ אֶת בִּנְךָ אֶת יְחִידְךָ מִמֶּנִּי.

An angel of Hashem called to him from Heaven and said, "Avraham, Avraham!" And he said, "Here I am." And he said, "Do not stretch out your hand against the lad nor do anything to him for now I know that you are a God-fearing man, since you have not withheld your son, your only one, from Me."[198]

THE MIDRASH DESCRIBES AVRAHAM'S FEELINGS AS HE prepared a knife to slaughter his beloved son as a *korban* to Hashem:

He stretched out his hand to grasp the knife, while tears

---

196. *Megillah* 29a.
197. *Tehillim* 20:2.
198. *Bereishis* 22:11-12.

streamed from his eyes and fell into the eyes of Yitzchak, with the compassion of a father for his son. Nonetheless, his heart was filled with joy to do the will of his Creator.[199]

The angels gathered above him in groups, and cried, "*Roads are desolate, wayfarer has ceased [to travel]. He has annulled the covenant, and despised the cities. He does not consider the man.*"[200] "Does He have no desire for Yerushalayim and the Beis HaMikdash that He had planned to give to Yitzchak's children as their inheritance?" they asked. "*He does not consider the man.*" "If the merit of Avraham did not stand, then no creature can stand before Him."

We find here a poignant juxtaposition of conflicting emotions. On one hand, Avraham wept over the imminent loss of his precious son, whom he had hoped would carry on his legacy. On the other hand, he rejoiced over the opportunity to fulfill Hashem's command. How can one heart carry the burden of these two contrary emotions?

The Rambam describes the importance of serving Hashem with love: He who serves Hashem with love toils in Torah and mitzvos, and walks the pathways of wisdom, not for the sake of any personal benefit; not for fear of punishment, nor for hope of reward. He does what is true because it is true, and his reward consequently follows. This is a very lofty level, which many scholars fail to achieve. It was the path walked by Avraham Avinu, whom Hashem called His beloved, since he served Hashem purely out of love. This is the level toward which we must aspire, as Hashem commanded Moshe, "And you shall love Hashem, your God." If one's love for Hashem is strong, he will fulfill all the mitzvos for the sake of this love.[201]

The Zohar states that we must relate to Hashem both as His servant and His son.[202] A servant stands in awe of his master, and would never dare question his master's will. A son loves his father with all his heart and soul, and rejoices to fulfill his father's will, with no thought of his own benefit. Nevertheless, he may ask a respectful question and expect to receive a loving explanation.

---

199. *Bereishis Rabbah* 56.
200. *Yeshayahu* 33:8.
201. *Rambam, Hilchos Teshuvah* 10:2.
202. *Zohar, Parashas Behar.*

In every aspect of our service of Hashem there must be a delicate balance between love and awe; between the desire to draw close to Hashem, and the fear of overstepping the boundaries of servitude. We must be servants and children of Hashem.

Hashem presented Avraham with a test that would try both aspects of his being at once. *"Take your only son, whom you love."* At a time when Avraham's fatherly love was at its peak, he would be forced to show total, unquestioning obedience to Hashem's command — as unfathomable as it seemed. Thereby, he would prove his loyalty to the extent that Hashem personally testified, *"For now I know that you are a God-fearing man, since you have not withheld your son, your only one, from Me."*

The Midrash relates that after the *Akeidah*, Avraham began to wonder what was the meaning of it all. First, Hashem promised him that Yitzchak would carry on his lineage. Then, Hashem ordered him to offer Yitzchak as a sacrifice. Finally, Hashem ordered him to withhold his hand, and spare Yitzchak's life. Hashem then explained that He had only intended for Yitzchak to be raised upon the *Mizbei'ach*, but He had never intended for him to be brought as an offering.[203]

Why did Avraham wait until after the *Akeidah* to question Hashem's command? Why did he not ask these questions before taking his knife in hand to slaughter his son?

As long as Avraham had a responsibility to fulfill, he served Hashem in the capacity of a dedicated servant. No questions or challenges could be brooked. Hashem commanded him to bring Yitzchak as an offering, and Avraham hastened to comply, paying no heed to any misgivings.

After Avraham was told to spare Yitzchak, he no longer had any obligation to fulfill. He now assumed the role of a loving son, who was welcome to ask and understand the depth of his Father's wisdom.

Remember for our sake, Hashem, our God, the covenant, the kindness, and the oath that You swore to Avraham Avinu on Har HaMoriah. Let the memory of the *Akeidah* appear before You, when Avraham Avinu bound his son Yitzchak on the *Mizbei'ach*, and conquered his compassion to fulfill Your will with all his heart.

---

203. *Bereishis Rabbah* 56:8.

So too, may Your compassion conquer Your anger toward us, and in Your great benevolence, withdraw Your fury from Your nation, Your city, Your land, and Your inheritance.[204]

The Foundations of Kindness

THROUGHOUT THE SAD AND SORDID HISTORY OF MAN-kind, there have been many wicked nations who committed horrific atrocities against man and God. Even in *Tanach* we find incidents such as the story of the Pilegesh in Givah, where a man's home was assaulted by a gathering of the townspeople, just as the men of Sodom had assaulted Lot.[205] Yet we never find such a devastating punishment as occurred to Sodom, when an entire segment of the earth's crust was overturned, totally burying four entire cities beneath it, while fire and brimstone descended from Heaven, leaving no survivors other than Lot and his two daughters who fled for their lives.

Rabbeinu Bachaye explains the singularity of Sodom's wicked-ness: Sodom exhibited every wicked trait imaginable, as our Sages infer from the verse, *"And the men of Sodom were wicked and evil to Hashem, very much so."* **Wicked** — with their money; **evil** — with their bodies; **to Hashem** — by cursing Hashem's Name, **very much so** — by spilling innocent blood... Nevertheless their doom was sealed for despising charity and paying no heed to their poor starving brethren ... The Navi testified against them, *"This was the sin of Sodom your sister. She and her daughters had pride, surfeit of bread, peaceful serenity, but she did not strengthen the hand of the poor and the needy"*[206] ...

Since they were consistently heartless toward the poor, this sin sealed their doom. There is no other nation in the world that com-pletely failed to do any kind of charity ... like the people of Sodom, who despised charity and were absolutely cruel.

---

204. From *Rosh Hashanah Mussaf* prayers.
205. *Shoftim* 19:22-28. See *Ramban, Bereishis* 19:8.
206. *Yechezkel* 16:49.

Although the Torah had not yet been given, human reason is enough to obligate giving charity. It is contemptible for a person to see his kinsman starving, while he is rich and satisfied with everything good, yet pitiless toward his fellow man, refusing to revive his soul.

How much worse is it when the poor man is a member of his own nation and a resident of his own city. Therefore, Hashem destroyed Sodom for refusing to practice any form of charity. He thus exacted the vengeance of the poor.[207]

Even among their own kinsmen, the Sodomites showed no compassion or charity, thus revealing themselves to be a cruel and callous nation, entirely pervaded to the extreme with selfish greed. Since they had not even the slightest degree of compassion toward one another, no mercy was shown to them from Heaven.

Another aspect of Sodom's guilt is noted by the Akeidas Yitzchak, who explains that whereas many nations practice acts of cruelty on occasion, there is usually some system of government to restrain them. The incident of Pilegesh of Givah was an act of mob violence that was severely punished by the Tribes of Israel, who waged war to avenge the woman's unfortunate death. In contrast, the cruelty of Sodom and their negligence toward the needy was an established part of their national ideology that was actually enforced by their courts.

The Gemara discusses the corrupt and deliberately evil system of law practiced there:

The four judges of Sodom were named Liar, Deceiver, Forger, and Corrupter of Justice. If a person would strike a wounded woman and cause her to miscarry, the courts would order that she be given to her assailant to conceive again. If a person would cut off the ear of his fellow's donkey, they would order that the assailant be given the donkey to keep until the ear grew back. If a person would wound his fellow, they would order the victim to pay his assailant a doctor's fee for letting his blood.

Eliezer, the servant of Avraham, was once attacked while passing through Sodom. He went to court, where he was ordered to pay his assailant for letting his blood. He then picked up a stone and

_____

207. *Rabbeinu Bachye, Bereishis* 18:20.

threw it at the judge.

"What is this?" asked the judge.

"The fee you owe me for letting your blood can be paid directly to my own assailant, and I will keep my money for myself," he answered.[208]

The Sifri states: "The appointment of fair judges is enough of a merit to ensure the settlement of Bnei Yisrael on their land." In any country or community there are bound to be a certain percentage of wicked and cruel people who perpetrate acts of violence and sin. However, as long as there is a fair system of courts to punish the wicked and prevent such atrocities from recurring, the country as a whole may be considered fair and just.

In his introduction to Shav Shmaitsa, the Ketzos HaChoshen comments on this passage from the Sifri, stating as follows:

If a city is protected by a wall of fair decrees and just statutes, then even if the walls of justice are occasionally breached by the proverbial foxes who trample the laws, the city can soon be healed and the injustices mended. Some distinguished member of the city will eventually rise to rebuke them and lead the city back to its original course of justice.

But if there are no protective walls [of justice], no edicts, and no proper customs, but instead a towering wall of snakes, scorpions, and thorns in the form of unjust laws and statutes by which they cannot live … then they truly emulate the sins of Sodom, who institutionalized their wicked, lowly ways into national laws enforced by fines for all who violated them.

Our Sages assure us that, "If justice is enforced from below, it need not be enforced from Above."[209] If fair judgment is practiced by the earthly courts, then the Heavenly courts need not inflict harsh punishments for our sins. Prior to shofar blowing on Rosh Hashanah, *Mori V'Rebbe*, the Klausenberger Rav *zt"l*, would study the complicated laws of honest business from the Ketzos HaChoshen's commentary on the *Choshen* section of *Shulchan Aruch*. He explained that the study and enforcement of these laws is a great merit to protect Klal Yisrael from retribution.

---

208. *Sanhedrin* 109b.
209. *Midrash Tanchuma, Mishpatim* 4.

May we all merit to be compassionate and merciful toward the poor and to be honest in all our business dealings, and be judged favorably by the Heavenly Courts, for peace and blessing in all our endeavors.

The Test of a Father's Love

THE *SHULCHAN ARUCH* ADVISES READING THE *PARASHAH* of *Akeidas Yitzchak* every day in order to recall the merit of our forefathers and draw the inspiration we need to make our own sacrifices for Hashem, just as Yitzchak willingly offered himself as a sacrifice on the *Mizbei'ach*.[210] The commentaries note that it is insufficient just to mindlessly mumble the words. One must contemplate the great sacrifice made by our Forefathers and the emotional hurdles they had to overcome in the service of Hashem.[211]

We cannot presume to fully understand the hearts and minds of our illustrious Forefathers, who ascended to such towering heights of spiritual greatness that they became the very pillars of Kindness, Awe, and Truth that support the Divine Throne.[212] Nevertheless, we can and must contemplate their deeds in order to pattern our lives after theirs to the best of our ability, as our Sages teach:

Each and every person must ask himself, *When will my deeds approach those of Avraham, Yitzchak, and Yaakov, who acquired this world and the Next World only in the merit of their good deeds and Torah study?*[213]

As such, each incident in the lives of our forefathers must be viewed as a practical lesson in personal growth. Upon studying the episode of the *Akeidah*, one might presume that Avraham Avinu was so consumed by a burning desire to fulfill Hashem's will, that

---

210. *Shulchan Aruch: Orach Chaim* 1:5; *Taz* 4.
211. See *Magen Avraham* s.k. 7, citing *Rabbeinu Bachye*.
212. *Bereishis Rabbah* 47:6; *Ramban, Emunah U'Bitachon* Ch. 15.
213. *Tanna D'Vei Eliyahu Rabbah*, 23.

he could barely sense any attachment to his son, and thus felt no difficulty at all in bringing him as an offering. The *Shulchan Aruch* states that when the pious of previous generations would pray, they would throw off all attachment to the physical world, until they rose to a near-prophetic state.[214] The Kohen Gadol's experience in the *Kodesh HaKodashim* on Yom Kippur was even greater, such that he was transformed from a human being into an angel, as the Midrash states.[215]

Some suggest that Avraham Avinu's experience during the *Akeidah* was similar, in that he had risen to such a lofty spiritual plane that no sentiment in the world could distract him from fulfilling Hashem's will. The Chassidic Rebbe, Menachem Mendel of Vorka, thus explains the *pasuk, "Avraham raised his eyes and saw — behold a ram ... and offered it up as an offering instead of his son,"*[216] to mean that offering his son was no more difficult than offering a common ram.[217]

However, as we earlier noted the Midrash implies, quite to the contrary, that *Akeidas Yitzchak* was a heartbreaking scene of fatherly love being torn asunder:

He stretched out his hand to grasp the knife, while tears streamed from his eyes and fell into the eyes of Yitzchak, with the compassion of a father for his son. Nonetheless, his heart was filled with joy to do the will of his Creator.[218]

This Midrash clearly states that Avraham was not above human emotions. He stretched his hand out to slaughter his son, struggling with all his might to overcome the pangs of a father's innate mercy for his only son. Had it been so ordained by Heaven, perhaps he could have ascended to the level of angels, who have no consideration in the world other than to do Hashem's bidding. However, this would not have been a *nisayon* and would not be proof of Avraham's unfailing loyalty to Hashem. Instead, Hashem deliberately inspired feelings of fatherly love in Avraham's heart, stressing again and again, *"Your son, your only one, whom you love*

---

214. *Shulchan Aruch: Orach Chaim* 98:1.
215. See *Tosafos, Menachos* 109b; *Vayikra Rabbah* 21.
216. *Bereishis* 22:13.
217. *Yismach Yisrael: Vayeira*, 7.
218. *Bereishis Rabbah* 56.

— *Yitzchak*,"[219] in order that his love for his son should expand in his heart. His sacrifice was so much more profound and noble, since he had to balance his love for his son against his obedience to the Creator, and tilt the scales by an effort of willpower that is beyond our imagination — rejoicing all the while to do Hashem's will.

With this we can understand the depth of what might otherwise seem as a mere formality of dialogue stated in the episode of the *Akeidah*: "*And Yitzchak spoke to Avraham his father, 'Father...'*": Yitzchak asked if Avraham intended to perform the *Akeidah* as a loving, merciful father, heartbroken over the loss of his son; or as a holy angel, transcending the bonds of human emotion.

To this Avraham answered, "*Here I am, my son*"[220]: I am still your loving father, and I must conquer my love for you to fulfill the will of Hashem. Since the *Akeidah* was so difficult for him, its merit was so great, as the Midrash states:

Avraham said to Hashem, "Master of the Universe ... I conquered my mercy in order to fulfill Your command. So may it be Your will, Hashem our God, that when Yitzchak's descendants fall into sin and wicked deeds, remember for their sake the *Akeidah* and show them the fullness of Your mercy.[221]

———•———

The lesson of personal growth that *Akeidas Yitzchak* teaches us is that we must also conquer our natural inclinations. At times it is sufficient for a person to take his natural desires and bend them toward the service of Hashem. For example, the Gemara states that if a person is born under the mazal of Mars, and is naturally inclined toward bloodshed, he can use this inclination in the service of Hashem by becoming a *mohel* or *shochet*.[222]

However, the true perfection of character improvement is reached when a person not only bends his natural inclinations, but breaks them entirely. Only then can he choose freely between

219. *Bereishis* 22:2.
220. Ibid. v. 7.
221. *Bereishis Rabbah* 56.
222. *Shabbos* 156a.

right and wrong, with no preconceived dispositions. He is then free to guide his destiny by the dictates of Hashem. Thus, the Noam Elimelech and the Vilna Gaon both write that man was created only in order to conquer his desires:

Man was created only in order to break his natural inclinations.[223]

The main purpose of man's life in this world is to constantly strive to break his negative character traits. If man does not correct his character, then what good is his life?[224]

These great Sages did not suffice with saying that man must correct his nature, but that he must actually break his nature, implying that he must go entirely contrary to his natural inclinations. Such was the *nisayon* of Avraham Avinu who was naturally inclined toward love and mercy, yet was forced to overcome his love, breaking his nature to fulfill Hashem's command.

Our Sages tell us that Torah can only be mastered by he who "kills himself" in its observance.[225] The Chazon Ish explains that sometimes one must "kill" one's natural inclinations, to allow room for a deeper, holier, and more meaningful personality to sprout in their place:

The more that a person breaks his character flaws, the more he lives, since breaking character flaws is the death of a superficial life and the death of the *yetzer hara* that fills the entire body. He is then left with a new life, by which he may walk on the path of Torah.[226]

With this we can resolve a seeming contradiction regarding Avraham's feelings toward Yishmael. On the one hand, when Avraham banished Hagar and Yishmael from his home, he sent them away with bread and water, but without funds. Rashi explains. "He sent away Yishmael with no silver or gold, since he hated him for the evil path he had chosen."[227] On the other hand, when Hashem told Avraham to sacrifice his beloved son, Avraham at first did not know which son Hashem meant. "I love them both," he said.[228]

---

223. *Rebbe Elimelech of Lizhensk, Tzetel Katan,* 16.
224. *Vilna Gaon, Even Shleimah* 1:2.
225. *Berachos* 63b.
226. *Igros HaChazon Ish,* 1:3.
227. *Bereishis* 21:14.
228. Ibid. 22:2.

In truth, for Avraham Avinu this was no contradiction. He was in control of his heart and was able to invoke or subdue his feelings of love as appropriate to the situation. He could simultaneously hate Yishmael for his evil ways, while loving whatever redeeming qualities Yishmael possessed.

How profound then are the words of the Midrash, that whereas the wicked are ruled by their hearts, the righteous rule their hearts. In this way, they resemble their Creator, Who exhibits emotions such as love and anger, only as dictated by His infinite wisdom.[229]

---

229. *Esther Rabbah* 10:3.

פרשת חיי שרה
Parashas Chayei Sarah

Every Precious Moment

THIS WEEK'S *PARASHAH* BEGINS WITH THE *PASUK,* "AND the lifetime of Sarah was one hundred years, twenty years, and seven years. The years of Sarah's life."[230] Rashi comments that all the days of her life were equally good.

There is an interesting Midrash, that points to the significance of Sarah's life span:

R' Akiva was sitting and expounding, and his audience began to slumber. He said to them, "Why was Esther seen fit to rule over one hundred and twenty-seven countries? 'Let the daughter of Sarah, who lived one hundred and twenty-seven years, rule over one hundred and twenty-seven countries.'"[231]

R' Akiva certainly did not mean to bring this parallel as a light-hearted jest, simply to waken his audience from their slumbers. There must have been some deep significance to his words, intended to waken them from their spiritual slumber, so to speak, by inspiring and encouraging them.

Perhaps the point of his message was as follows. The students dozed while their rebbi was expounding an important Torah lesson,

---

230. *Bereishis* 23:1.
231. *Bereishis Rabbah* 58:3.

"Tying crowns to the letters of the Torah," as our Sages say.[232] Torah can only be mastered by those who "kill themselves" in its pursuit, by applying every iota of their strength. This was the path of our forefathers, which we must follow. They utilized every day to its fullest potential. Sarah Immeinu lived for one hundred and twenty-seven years. "All the days of her life were equally good," as Rashi explains. She sanctified every moment of her life, by applying each and every waking moment to the service of Hashem.

This lesson was the basis for R' Akiva's astonishing ascent from an ignorant shepherd to a giant of Torah wisdom. Our Sages tell us that R' Akiva's wife sent him away from home to study in a distant yeshivah. After having spent twelve years there, he came to visit her. Before he entered his home, he overheard his wife saying to a neighbor, "If he would ask me, I would send him to learn for another twelve years." R' Akiva did not even pause to greet his wife, but immediately returned to the yeshivah for an additional twelve years.[233]

Since he had already made the journey home, why did he not take the time to at least greet his wife before returning? Rav Chaim Shmulevitz, Rosh Yeshivas Mir, explained that had he done so, he would have had two twelve-year periods of study, rather than one period of twenty-four consecutive years. When calculating years spent in Torah study, twelve plus twelve does not equal twenty-four.

R' Akiva and his righteous wife understood that this is the key to greatness in Torah: utilizing time to its fullest. This was the path of our forefathers, as we learn from Sarah Immeinu, whose days were all equally good.

Esther HaMalkah merited to rule over one hundred and twenty-seven countries. Ruling over even one country is difficult enough. How does one succeed in ensuring the peace and prosperity of the many countries under their reign? Obviously, one who wished to rule over 127 countries needs to pay individual attention to each and every village, to ensure that there were no sparks of rebellion anywhere in the kingdom, which might then catch fire and

---

232. See *Menachos* 29b.
233. *Kesubos* 62b.

spread to the surrounding regions. Only by paying careful attention to every province is it possible to consolidate one's rule. Esther learned this approach from Sarah Immeinu, who consolidated the years of her life into harmonious perfection, by paying careful attention to every moment of precious life.

David HaMelech had one request that epitomized the sole desire of his entire being, "One thing I asked of Hashem; that shall I seek: Would that I dwell in the House of Hashem all the days of my life, to behold the sweetness of Hashem, and visit His Sanctuary."[234]

The commentaries note that this prayer begins in the past tense ("I asked of Hashem"), and continues in the future tense ("that shall I seek"). Most people's lives are divided into different periods. Their dreams and aspirations may vary from one period to another. The dreams of a young child are not the same as those of an old man, and the aspirations of a pauper are not the same as those of a millionaire. However, this was not true of David HaMelech. "Hashem raises the needy from the dust, from the trash heaps He lifts the destitute."[235] David began his career as a lowly shepherd, ostracized by his own family, and rose to become king of Israel. Yet through all the stages of his life, he had only one desire: "Let me sit in the House of Hashem all the days of my life, to behold the sweetness of Hashem, and to visit His Sanctuary." He wanted nothing else, but to devote his entire life to the service of Hashem.

Another interesting point in this prayer is the apparent contradiction implied in David's request to "sit in the House of Hashem all the days of my life," and to "visit His Sanctuary." By definition, a visitor is a temporary guest. How could David sit in the House of Hashem all the days of his life, yet still remain a visitor?

Often, people take interest in something that is new, but lose interest in it over time. David HaMelech prayed that he might sit in the House of Hashem, studying His holy Torah, all the days of his life; and still experience the same sense of novelty and interest as if he had just come to visit.

---

234. *Tehillim* 27:4.
235. Ibid. 113:7.

Sarah's Sacrifice

וַתָּמָת שָׂרָה בְּקִרְיַת אַרְבַּע הִוא חֶבְרוֹן בְּאֶרֶץ כְּנָעַן וַיָּבֹא אַבְרָהָם לִסְפֹּד לְשָׂרָה וְלִבְכֹּתָהּ.

Sarah died in Kiriath-arba which is Hebron in the land of Canaan; and Abraham came to eulogize Sarah and to bewail her.[236]

Rashi comments on וַיָּבֹא אַבְרָהָם: לָמָּה נִסְמְכָה מִיתַת שָׂרָה לַעֲקֵדַת יִצְחָק, לְפִי שֶׁעַל יְדֵי בְּשׂוֹרַת הָעֲקֵדָה שֶׁנִּזְדַּמֵּן בְּנָהּ לִשְׁחִיטָה וְכִמְעַט שֶׁלֹּא נִשְׁחַט פָּרְחָה נִשְׁמָתָהּ מִמֶּנָּה וּמֵתָה, Why was the death of Sarah recorded in the Torah alongside *Akeidas Yitzchak*? When she was informed about the *Akeidah*, that her son had been readied for slaughter and was almost *not* slaughtered, her soul fled from her [body] and she died.

It would seem more accurate for Rashi to have written that Yitzchak was almost slaughtered, rather than he was almost *not* slaughtered — which seems to imply that he was indeed slaughtered, but just barely. What does Rashi mean to teach us?

The Sifsei Chachamim explains that a messenger informed Sarah that Yitzchak had been bound to the *Mizbei'ach* and prepared for slaughter, but before he could conclude that Yitzchak's life was spared, Sarah died from shock. Thus, Rashi means to say that the messenger was about to *say* that Yitzchak was *not* slaughtered, but he did not have the chance to conclude his words.

On a deeper level, perhaps we may add that Yitzchak was indeed slaughtered in a certain sense, since Klal Yisrael — as his descendants — are accredited with the merit of the *Akeidah* as if it had been carried through to the end. The Midrash states that when Hashem told Avraham Avinu, "Do not stretch out your hand to harm the lad," Avraham asked permission to draw a drop of blood, so that it might be considered as if he had slaughtered Yitzchak. Hashem then added, "Do not do anything (מְאוּמָה) to him," implying

---

236. *Bereishis* 23:2.

that he should not make the slightest blemish (מום). When Avraham then sacrificed the ram instead, he prayed with every stage of the offering, "May this find favor before You as if I had slaughtered my son ... as if I had thrown his blood against the *Mizbei'ach* ... as if I had burned him upon it."[237]

His prayers were answered, and Klal Yisrael did indeed receive the full merit of the *Akeidah* as if Yitzchak himself had been sacrificed. The Gemara thus states that when Ezra returned to Eretz Yisrael to rebuild the Beis HaMikdash, he identified the site on which to build the *Mizbei'ach* due to the ashes of Yitzchak piled there.[238] If Yitzchak was never actually slaughtered and burned, how could his ashes have been seen there? Rather we must explain that although he was not physically slaughtered, the merit was granted to us as if the ashes of the ram were his own.

We can thus explain that Sarah rejoiced with the knowledge that her son had ascended to such a lofty spiritual height that he was chosen as an offering to be brought on the *Mizbei'ach*. When she then heard that he was almost *not* slaughtered, and that only a ram was slaughtered in his stead, her heart broke with disappointment and she died. She did not realize that the sacrifice of the ram was fully accredited to him and to his descendants as if he had actually been sacrificed himself.

II

Alternatively, we can explain that Sarah's soul fled her body after having experienced such a tremendous spiritual ascent that she was unable to retain her hold on this physical world. Such was the case with the Mishnaic Sage, Ben Azzai, who entered the Pardes: the Orchard of Godly Wisdom, and became so enthralled with the awareness of the Almighty that he was unable to return to this world. Regarding this incident, the Gemara states:

---

237. Midrash *Rabbah*, *Parashas Vayeira*.
238. *Zevachim* 62a. See also *Vayikra Rabbah* 36:4; *Rashi* on *Parashas Bechukosai*, *Bamidbar* 26:42, and *Toras Kohanim* loc. cit.

Four entered the Pardes: Ben Azzai, Ben Zoma, Rebbi Akiva, and Acheir ... Ben Azzai gazed and died. Of him it is written, "Precious in the eyes of Hashem is the death of His pious." Ben Zoma gazed and was struck [in his sanity]. Of him it is written, "If you find honey, eat no more than your fill, lest you gorge yourself and vomit." Acheir uprooted his plantings. R' Akiva alone emerged in peace. [239]

The Maharsha comments: "Ben Azzai gazed and died." His soul embraced with powerful love the upper worlds from which it was formed. As he gazed at the radiant light, his soul took leave of his body and shook itself free of all the body's worldly interests. At that moment he found the peace he desired, and chose not to return to his place in this world. This was a lofty spiritual level, for which reason it was said of him, "Precious in the eyes of Hashem is the death of His pious."

In *Parashas Acharei Mos*, Ohr HaChaim applies the same principles to explain the deaths of Nadav and Avihu, of whom the verse testifies, בְּקָרְבָתָם לִפְנֵי ה' — *"They drew close to Hashem and died."* They entered a plane of spiritual awareness that rendered them unable to retain a connection with this physical world.

Similarly, Rav Tzadok HaKohen of Lublin explains that when R' Akiva was being executed and he recited *Shema*, and he then died not from the iron combs that raked his flesh, but of the love and yearning for the Creator that pervaded his entire being and drew his soul to its celestial home.

The same was true of Sarah Immeinu. When she heard of the great sacrifice her son had made, having been all but offered as a *korban* on the *Mizbei'ach*, she also ascended to such a lofty spiritual level that her soul fled its body.

The Pillars of Avraham's Home

AVRAHAM BOUND HIS SERVANT ELIEZER BY A SACRED oath, not to take a wife for Yitzchak from the daughters of Canaan. What fault did Avraham find in the daughters

---

239. *Chagigah* 14b.

of Canaan, and why did he suppose that the daughters of Aram Naharayim were in any way superior? The Rambam tells us that Avraham had tens of thousands of followers in Canaan: "These were the members of Avraham's household, in whose hearts he planted the roots of faith."[240] Could he not have chosen a bride for his son from among them?

The Kli Yakar writes: Avraham forbade his son to marry the daughters of Canaan lest he learn from their wicked ways. But Besuel was no less of an idolater than the Canaanites. What then did Avraham gain by taking Besuel's daughter as his son's bride?

In fact, Avraham had a different concern. Children tend to exhibit traits similar to those of their parents; for example: greed, lust, and similar character flaws that are inherent to the human body. Since parents form their children's bodies, their physical traits are generally passed to their children... However, false ideologies depend on a person's conscious decision. Hashem grants each person a soul and powers of reason with which to choose his own beliefs. Therefore, there is no reason to fear that false beliefs will be passed on from one generation to the next. Avraham rejected the Canaanites, who were steeped in lustful desire, in favor of Besuel's family, since Besuel's lone fault was idolatry, which he would not necessarily transfer to his daughter.[241]

In preparing the foundation for the Jewish nation, Avraham did not fear the influence of Besuel's idolatry. Hashem's Oneness was so evident in Avraham's home, that any bride brought for Yitzchak would instantly abandon any idolatrous leanings she might have entertained in the past. However, the rectification of faulty character traits is a far more difficult task. Rav Yisrael Salanter would say that it is easier to uproot a mountain than to uproot a character flaw. Therefore, Avraham sent Eliezer to his homeland in search of a bride, rather than take a bride from the daughters of Canaan, who were corrupt in their character.

We learn in *Pirkei Avos*: Whoever exhibits the following three traits is a student of Avraham Avinu. Anyone who exhibits the opposite three traits is a student of the wicked Bilaam. A generous

---

240. *Rambam, Hilchos Avodah Zarah* 1:3.
241. *Kli Yakar, Bereishis* 24:3.

eye, a contrite spirit, and a humble soul — these are [the traits of] Avraham's students. An evil eye, a haughty spirit, and a lustful soul — these are [the traits of] Bilaam's students.

What is the difference between the students of Avraham Avinu and those of the wicked Bilaam? Avraham's students enjoy their reward in this world, and inherit the World to Come, as it is written, "*I have what to bequeath to those who love Me, and I shall fill their storehouses.*"[242] Bilaam's students inherit the punishment of Gehinnom, and descend into the pit of destruction, as it is written, "*And You, O God, You will lower them into the well of destruction, men of bloodshed and deceit shall not live out half their days; but as for me, I will trust in You.*"[243]

Rabbeinu Yonah explains that Avraham's students had many other precious qualities besides the three listed here. However, these three traits were the foundations of Avraham's philosophy, and the central message he imparted to his followers.

We see then that Avraham's message to the world was first and foremost one of character improvement. He instilled humility and generosity in his students to such an extent that thousands of years later the Sages pointed to these traits as exemplifying his household.

Avraham was an accomplished scholar.[244] He led an academy where hundreds of orders of Mishnah were taught,[245] in contrast to the Six Orders of Mishnah we currently possess. His *Maseches Avodah Zarah* contained four hundred chapters, in contrast to the five chapters in our own.[246] He foresaw and observed all the Biblical and Rabbinic laws that would ever be decreed.[247] He even perceived the novel Torah insights that are unearthed each day in Heaven.[248]

It is therefore all the more interesting to note that the students of such a prestigious teacher, who drank deeply from the waters of his teachings, were not praised for their erudition, which was surely exemplary, but for their character traits. In Avraham's school

---

242. *Mishlei* 8:21.
243. *Tehillim* 55:24; *Pirkei Avos* 5:22.
244. *Yoma* 28b.
245. *Chagigah* 14a.
246. *Avodah Zarah* 14b.
247. *Kiddushin* 82a; *Yoma* 28b.
248. *Bereishis Rabbah, Vayeira* 49.

of thought, good character was the very foundation of religious observance.

The three traits Avraham espoused more than all others: generosity, contrition, and humility are the central pillars of the entire Torah. They counter the three destructive traits of jealousy, selfish passion, and arrogance, which drive a person from this world.[249]

With these pillars, Avraham built the dynasty that he bequeathed to Yitzchak. Therefore, it was crucial that the woman who joined Yitzchak in this sacred task would exemplify these traits. Although Avraham realized that Besuel's home was tainted by idolatry, he trusted that this influence could be easily overcome, by means of the fine character and kind heart that he sought in his son's destined match.

---

249. *Pirkei Avos* 4:28.

פרשת תולדות
Parashas Toldos

Rivkah's Aspiration

REGARDING THE TIME WHEN RIVKAH WAS EXPECTING, the Torah tells us, "The children struggled within her, and she said, 'If so, why did I desire and pray for this?'"[250] Rashi explains the reason for their struggle:

This passage begs for an explanation. It does not state the reason for their struggles; but rather continues with Rivkah's complaint, "Why did I pray for this?" Our Sages explain that the word "וַיִּתְרֹצֲצוּ" is based on the root word "רִיצָה" which means "to run." When Rivkah passed the entrance to Shem and Eiver's Torah academy, Yaakov would "run," struggling to escape (to go study Torah). When she passed by the entrance to idolatrous places of worship, Eisav would struggle to escape. Another explanation of their struggle is that they vied for the inheritance of two worlds (this world and the next).

The implication of this passage is astounding. After ten years of infertility, during which Yitzchak and Rivkah poured their hearts out in prayer for children, their prayers were finally answered, and Rivkah conceived. In truth, Rivkah was barren, and it was physically impossible for her to have children. Hashem answered their

---

250. *Bereishis* 25:22, translation based on *Rashi*.

prayers in a manner that transcended nature. One would think that her joy would be so overwhelming that nothing could diminish it. Yet when it seemed that her unborn child was inclined toward idolatry, she expressed regret for all her prayers.

When the *Avos* and *Imahos* prayed for children, they did not seek their own personal pleasure. Like all their deeds, their prayers were solely for the sake of Heaven: to bring a new generation into the world, who would toil in the service of Hashem, through Torah study and mitzvah observance. Their intention was solely to plant an orchard, from which holy saplings would grow, to sanctify Hashem's great Name in the world. When it seemed to Rivkah that she was carrying one child who was attracted both to Torah study and idolatry, she realized that this could not possibly be the scion for which she had hoped, and therefore regretted all her prayers.

The Midrash states as follows:

R' Yehudah and R' Aivu said in the name of R' Yochanan: Two men prayed for the same thing: Avraham and David. Avraham prayed, (when Hashem promised him great reward) "Hashem Elokim, what could You give me, if I am desolate (without children)?"[251] He said, "Master of the Universe! If I will father children who will anger You, better that I remain desolate."

David also prayed, "Search me, Lord, and know my heart" — meaning, look toward those who I will father, "And see if the path of anger is before me, and guide me in the way of the world."[252] He said, "Master of the Universe! If I will father children who will anger You, better that You guide me in the way of the world (toward death)."[253]

Avraham and David, the pillars of our nation, preferred to remain childless, rather than bring children into the world who might anger Hashem. Rivkah's sentiments were the same.

We find in the Mishnah that a father passes to his son the physical properties of beauty (נוֹי), strength (כֹּחַ), and wisdom (חָכְמָה).[254] Some explain that when Yitzchak prayed for children "across

---

251. *Bereishis* 15:2.
252. *Tehillim* 139:24.
253. *Bereishis Rabbah* 44:9.
254. *Eiduyos* 2:9.

from" (לָנֹכַח) his wife,[255] he was really praying for a child who would have all three of these properties, the first letters of which spell the word נֹכַח. However, when Rivkah passed the entrance to idolatrous temples, and felt her unborn child struggling to escape, she asked, אִם כֵּן לָמָּה זֶּה אָנֹכִי — "Why did I pray for this?" The first letters of כֵּן stand for כֹּח (strength) and נוֹי (beauty). She did not want a strong and beautiful baby, if he would not grow to become wise in the wisdom of the Torah.

The Blessings of Our Forefathers

וַיְהִי כִּי זָקֵן יִצְחָק וַתִּכְהֶיןָ עֵינָיו מֵרְאֹת וַיִּקְרָא אֶת עֵשָׂו בְּנוֹ הַגָּדֹל וַיֹּאמֶר אֵלָיו בְּנִי וַיֹּאמֶר אֵלָיו הִנֵּנִי. וַיֹּאמֶר הִנֵּה נָא זָקַנְתִּי לֹא יָדַעְתִּי יוֹם מוֹתִי. וְעַתָּה שָׂא נָא כֵלֶיךָ תֶּלְיְךָ וְקַשְׁתֶּךָ וְצֵא הַשָּׂדֶה וְצוּדָה לִי צֵידָה [צָיִד]. וַעֲשֵׂה לִי מַטְעַמִּים כַּאֲשֶׁר אָהַבְתִּי וְהָבִיאָה לִי וְאֹכֵלָה בַּעֲבוּר תְּבָרֶכְךָ נַפְשִׁי בְּטֶרֶם אָמוּת. וְרִבְקָה שֹׁמַעַת בְּדַבֵּר יִצְחָק אֶל עֵשָׂו בְּנוֹ וַיֵּלֶךְ עֵשָׂו הַשָּׂדֶה לָצוּד צַיִד לְהָבִיא. וְרִבְקָה אָמְרָה אֶל יַעֲקֹב בְּנָהּ לֵאמֹר הִנֵּה שָׁמַעְתִּי אֶת אָבִיךָ מְדַבֵּר אֶל עֵשָׂו אָחִיךָ לֵאמֹר. הָבִיאָה לִי צַיִד וַעֲשֵׂה לִי מַטְעַמִּים וְאֹכֵלָה וַאֲבָרֶכְכָה לִפְנֵי ה׳ לִפְנֵי מוֹתִי. וְעַתָּה בְנִי שְׁמַע בְּקֹלִי לַאֲשֶׁר אֲנִי מְצַוָּה אֹתָךְ. לֶךְ נָא אֶל הַצֹּאן וְקַח לִי מִשָּׁם שְׁנֵי גְּדָיֵי עִזִּים טֹבִים וְאֶעֱשֶׂה אֹתָם מַטְעַמִּים לְאָבִיךָ כַּאֲשֶׁר אָהֵב. וְהֵבֵאתָ לְאָבִיךָ וְאָכָל בַּעֲבֻר אֲשֶׁר יְבָרֶכְךָ לִפְנֵי מוֹתוֹ.

And it came to pass, when Yitzchak had become old, and his eyes dimmed from seeing, that he summoned Eisav, his older son, and said to him, "My son." And he said to him, "Here I am." And he said, "See, now, I have aged; I know not the day of my death. Now, sharpen, if you please, your gear — gather your weapons, your sword and your bow — and go out to the field and hunt game for me. Then make me delicacies such as I love and bring it to me and I will eat, so that my soul may bless you before I die." Now Rivkah

---

255. *Bereishis* 25:21.

was listening as Yitzchak spoke to Eisav his son; and Eisav went to the field to hunt game to bring. But Rivkah had said to Yaakov her son, saying, "Behold, I heard your father speaking to your brother Eisav, saying, 'Bring me some game and make me delicacies to eat, and I will bless you in the presence of Hashem, before my death.' So now, my son, heed my voice to that which I command you. Go now to the flock, and fetch me from there two choice young kids of the goats, and I will make from them delicacies for your father, as he loves. Then bring it to your father, and he shall eat, so that he may bless you before his death."[256]

IT IS AMAZING TO CONSIDER YAAKOV AVINU'S APPARENT treachery in wresting the birthright from his brother Eisav, by exploiting his hunger, and then deceitfully usurping the blessings that their father had intended to give Eisav. Is this the honesty and integrity, for which Yaakov was praised as an *ish tahm* — "a simple and straightforward person"? Is this the man of truth, whom we are meant to emulate?

The Chasam Sofer once wrote a scathing rebuke against people who present themselves as religious Jews, yet give free rein to their passion for money, cheating in business to gain a few coins. He warned his students not to associate with dishonest businessmen, regardless of how learned or pious they may seem in other matters.[257]

However, when we consider the essence of the blessings, and Yaakov's fervent desire to merit them, our question becomes moot.

The Ramban tells us that the deeds of our forefathers carved a path for their descendants to follow. Their every action was done with great deliberation, to serve as a merit for the generations to come. Thereby, they ensured that Hashem's blessing would never cease from the Jewish people, during the period when we dwelled peacefully on our Land, throughout the dark and bitter exile, and until the final day when Hashem will ultimately gather us back to our Land.

---

256. *Bereishis* 27:1-10.
257. *Teshuvos Chasam Sofer* VI, 59.

Throughout our history, a bitter conflict has raged between Yaakov and Eisav, and likewise between their descendants. When Yaakov sought the birthright and the blessing of his father, his intention was not for his own personal benefit, but for the sake of the Jewish people, whom he was destined to beget. He realized that these blessings were crucial for them to succeed in their struggle against Eisav's spiritual heirs. The mission of the Jewish people, to sanctify Hashem's great Name in the world, must succeed at all costs.

The pivotal role of Yitzchak's blessing, in deciding the conflict between Yaakov and Eisav, is highlighted in the following passage of the Zohar:

Come and see. How many blessings did Yaakov receive? One from his father, which he gained through his deceitfulness, and by means of which he received all those blessings. One from the *Shechinah*, when HaKadosh Baruch Hu blessed him, as he returned from Lavan, as the *pasuk* states, "And the Lord blessed Yaakov."[258] One blessing from the angel appointed over Eisav. And one blessing from his father, when he left to Padan Aram, as the *pasuk* states, "May the All-Powerful Lord bless you."[259]

When Yaakov saw that he had all these blessings, he thought to himself, *Which blessing should I use now?* (to protect himself from Eisav). *I shall use the weakest of my blessings.* This was the last blessing that his father gave him. Although this was indeed a powerful blessing, he realized that there was no blessing as powerful to achieve worldly gain, as the first blessing that his father had given him.

I will take this blessing now and use it, and I will leave the other blessings for later, for the time when I or my children will need them, when all the nations gather together to eradicate my children from the world, as the *pasuk* states, "All the nations surround me; in the Name of Hashem I will cut them down. They encircle me and surround me ... They surround me like bees."[260] These three crises will be resolved by the three remaining blessings: First, his father's first

---

258. Cf. *Bereishis* 35:9.
259. *Bereishis* 28:3.
260. *Tehillim* 118:10-11.

blessing. Second, the blessings of HaKadosh Baruch Hu. Third, the blessings of the angel [appointed over Eisav].

Yaakov said to himself, *I will need those blessings then, to defend us against the kings, and against all the nations of the world. I will leave them for then. Now, against Eisav, this one is sufficient.*

This is comparable to the story of a king who had many legions of mighty warriors, and many officers to direct his battles. He held these legions in place, in preparation for a great war against the mighty kings who threatened him. Meanwhile, a band of thieves and murderers entered his kingdom. "The gatekeepers shall deal with them," he said.

"Will you not send any of your soldiers to assist?" he was asked.

"For mere thieves, the gatekeepers will suffice. My many legions, and the officers of my armies, I hold in check to fight against the mighty kings, when war breaks out," he explained.

Yaakov's reasoning was the same. "For Eisav, this one blessing will suffice. I hold my other blessings in check, for the day when my sons will need to fight against all the kings and nations of the world. When that time arrives, these blessings will arise from all sides, and the world will be sustained in its proper way."[261]

The Vilna Gaon writes, in his commentary to Chad Gadya in the Pesach Haggadah, that all the benefits that Bnei Yisrael have ever enjoyed, or ever will enjoy, in this world or the next, were an inheritance from Yitzchak Avinu, when he gave his blessing to Yaakov. If not for this blessing, we would have nothing, and all our benefits would have been seized by Eisav.

When Yaakov was given the birthright in place of Eisav, it was only in order to enable him to then claim his father's blessing. His motive was in no way for his own personal benefit. He himself suffered untold hardship throughout his life, with one episode of grief after another, in the incidents with Lavan, Eisav, Dinah, Yosef, and Binyamin. He held Yitzchak's blessing in store for the sake of his descendants, that they would thereby be sustained in the dark and terrible *Galus*, and ultimately be redeemed in the merit of the forefathers and their prodigious blessings.

---

261. *Zohar* I, p. 146.

The Legacy of Our Forefathers

THE RAMBAN CALLS *SEFER BEREISHIS* "THE BOOK OF Creation," since it begins with a description of the world's creation, and continues with the lives of our forefathers who "created" the models that their descendants were destined to follow.[262] Our forefathers' mitzvos and good deeds were not intended for their own spiritual benefit, or even for the benefit of their generation, but for the benefit of the entire world for all generations to come. By standing strong in the face of their many challenges, they created a precedent that enables us overcome our own hardships.

Just as their mitzvos serve as an eternal merit for their descendants, their seemingly minor flaws also brought cataclysmic consequences. For example, Avraham gave Avimelech seven sheep when they made a pact never to harm each other. The Midrash derides him for doing so without Hashem's consent:

Hashem said to Avraham, "You gave him seven sheep without My consent; by your life I swear to postpone the joy of your descendants (*Kabbalas HaTorah*) for seven generations. You gave him seven sheep without My consent, by your life I swear that his descendants will slay seven *tzaddikim* from yours — Chofni, Pinchas, Shimshon, Shaul, and Shaul's three sons. You gave him seven sheep without My consent; by your life I swear that his descendants will destroy the seven sanctuaries of your descendants: the Ohel Moed, Gilgal, Nov, Givon, Shiloh, and the two Batei HaMikdash."[263]

Kabbalas HaTorah, the very purpose for the world's existence, could have occurred in Avraham's time, yet it was postponed for seven generations; and the seven dwelling places of the *Shechinah* were destroyed; all because of Avraham's seemingly minor indiscretion in making a pact with Avimelech. The Tanna D'Vei Eliyahu adds that the nations of the world were given permission to oppress us for thousands of years, as a result of the pact that Avraham made

---

262. *Ramban, Commentary on the Torah*, introduction to *Sefer Shemos.*
263. *Bereishis Rabbah* 54:4.

with them.[264] Furthermore, the Ramban writes that as punishment for Sarah having oppressed Hagar, Hagar's descendants afflict Sarah's for hundreds of years.[265]

These examples illustrate the perfection that Hashem expects of the righteous, such that even a hairsbreadth of error is brought to judgment. Although Avraham and Sarah were not guilty of any actual sin, they did not meet the exacting standards expected of them. Consequently, their descendants suffered untold suffering over the course of many generations.

Hashem rewards on a scale five hundred times greater than that with which He punishes.[266] Furthermore, for every minor failing of our forefathers, they had countless tremendous mitzvos to their credit. Therefore, we can only imagine the great reward that is apportioned to their descendants in their merit. From their great achievements, we draw the strength necessary to persevere through our own difficulties, for all generations to come.

When Chananyah, Mishael, and Azaryah allowed themselves to be thrown into a fiery furnace rather than bow to an idol, Hashem said to His ministering angels, "Descend and kiss the lips of their forefathers. Just as the fathers served Me in fire, so did the sons."[267]

When Avraham Avinu braved death in the fiery furnace of Ur Kasdim for the sake of Hashem's holy Name, and when Yitzchak stretched out his neck to be slaughtered on Har HaMoriah, they instilled in our nation for all subsequent generations the fortitude to sacrifice our lives for Hashem's sake, time and time again.

Chanah's seven sons were killed for refusing to worship Greek idols. Before her youngest son's execution, she bade him to ascend to Heaven and tell Avraham Avinu that he bound only one son on the altar as a *korban* for Hashem, but she bound seven.[268] Did Chanah really intend to compete with Avraham Avinu? Did she take pride in outdoing our illustrious forefather? Rather, she meant to tell him that his example gave her the strength to endure her difficult trial.

---

264. *Tanna D'Vei Eliyahu Rabbah* Ch. 8.
265. *Ramban, Bereishis* 16:10.
266. *Sotah* 11a, *Sanhedrin* 100b.
267. *Shir HaShirim Rabbah* 7:1.
268. *Gittin* 57b.

So too, throughout the generations, in our long and bitter trek through *Galus*, we draw courage from the righteous deeds of our foregathers. They planted in our hearts the strength to stand firm in the face of adversity, and remain loyal to Hashem.

The Foundations of Holiness

Each of the *Avos* had his own unique role in preparing the foundations of holiness upon which the House of Israel was destined to be built. Avraham sanctified the Land of Israel. Hashem told him: "*Rise and walk the length and breadth of the land, for I shall give it to you.*"[269] The Gemara explains that by walking across the Land of Israel, Avraham established a precedent of ownership, which made it easier for his descendants to conquer the Land many generations later.[270]

Yitzchak sanctified the site of the Beis HaMikdash. By allowing himself to be sacrificed on Har HaMoriah, he instilled it with tremendous holiness, preparing it for the construction of the Beis HaMikdash. Even after the Beis HaMikdash was destroyed, its location remains the portal through which the prayers of Bnei Yisrael from all over the world ascend to Heaven.

Yaakov prepared the path for our nation to travel in exile. By serving Hashem faithfully despite all his hardships and wanderings, he created a pool of merit to ensure our survival in *Galus* and our Ultimate Redemption. Yaakov instituted the nighttime Maariv prayer.[271] The Chassidic texts interpret this to mean that he prayed for the welfare of Bnei Yisrael in the dark night of *Galus*.

As Yaakov and his sons prepared to descend to Egypt, Hashem appeared to him in a vision of the night and said, "*Do not fear your descent to Egypt... I shall descend with you to Egypt, and I shall bring you back and ascend together with you.*"[272] The Meshech Chachmah writes: "God spoke to Yisrael in night visions." This expression is never used anywhere in the Torah in regard to Avraham or Yitzchak. Yaakov alone received a "night vision"

---

269. *Bereishis* 13:17.
270. *Bava Basra* 100a.
271. *Berachos* 26b.
272. *Bereishis* 46:2-4.

as he descended from Eretz Yisrael to sojourn abroad. Hashem then revealed Himself to Yaakov at night, signifying that even in the dark night of exile, the *Shechinah* would remain with Bnei Yisrael, as our Sages teach: "When they were exiled to Babylon, the *Shechinah* journeyed with them."[273] ... David HaMelech prayed, "May Hashem answer you on the day of affliction; may the Name of the God of Yaakov support you."[274] When darkness and suffering would befall Bnei Yisrael, Hashem would remain by their side to protect them, as He remained with Yaakov in the dark night of his own exile.[275]

Yaakov's Threefold Trial

When Yaakov was asked to send his son Binyamin to Egypt, he said: אֹתִי שִׁכַּלְתֶּם יוֹסֵף אֵינֶנּוּ וְשִׁמְעוֹן אֵינֶנּוּ וְאֶת בִּנְיָמָן תִּקָּחוּ עָלַי הָיוּ כֻלָּנָה — "I am the one whom you bereaved! Yosef is gone, Shimon is gone, and now you would take away Binyamin? Upon me has it all fallen!"[276]

The word עָלַי is also found in this week's *parashah*, when Yaakov hesitates to deceive his father, lest he be cursed as a result, but Rivkah assures him עָלַי קִלְלָתְךָ בְּנִי — "Your curse be on me, my son."[277] The Vilna Gaon explains that עָלַי is an acronym for עֵשָׂו לָבָן יוֹסֵף (Eisav, Lavan, Yosef). Rivkah warned him that these three trials had already been decreed by Heaven. He need not fear the curse of his father, since his suffering had already been ordained.[278]

Later, when Yaakov complained, עָלַי הָיוּ כֻלָּנָה — "Upon me has it all fallen," he meant to say that he had already borne the three phases of his suffering, and had not expected this last tragedy to occur. (In truth, Binyamin's descend to Egypt was not a tragedy at all, but the first rays of hope for Yaakov's reunion with Yosef.)

Yaakov's three difficulties parallel the difficulties Bnei Yisrael face in *Galus*. Eisav sought to murder Yaakov. He represents adversaries such as Haman, who wish to destroy the entire Jewish nation,

---

273. *Megillah* 29a.
274. *Tehillim* 20:2
275. *See Minchas Asher, Parashas Vayeira: "The Prayers of Our Forefathers."*
276. *Bereishis* 42:36.
277. Ibid. 27:13.
278. Cited in *Teshuvos Zayis Ra'anan* end of volume 2.

regardless of our religious beliefs. Lavan represents adversaries such as the Greeks, who tried to force their pagan cultures upon us. When he accosted Yaakov and said, *"The daughters are my daughters, the children are my children, and the flock (a reference to the six hundred thousand souls of Israel) is my flock,"*[279] he attempted to claim Yaakov's children as the heirs of his own idolatrous beliefs.[280]

Hashem has rescued us from both kinds of adversaries, but the third and most dangerous challenge is that of internal strife, represented by Yosef's conflict with his brothers. Unwarranted hatred between Jews destroyed the Beis HaMikdash and delays our Redemption.

Our own generation has faced all three challenges. Hitler sought to destroy our entire nation, regardless of our beliefs. The Communists sought to destroy religious observance. However, the most difficult blow has been the strife and dissent that plagues our nation. This plague has been our own doing, and it is within our hands to undo it, by treating one another with patience and understanding, and by spreading love and brotherhood within our communities, and from one community to the next.

The Midrash states:

Rebbi (R' Yehudah HaNasi) taught: Peace is so important, that even if Bnei Yisrael were to worship idols, but there would be peace among them, Hashem could not punish them (so to speak) since the peace among them would protect them, as the verse states: "Ephraim is united in their idolatry. Let them be!"

However, when there is strife among them, the verse states, *"Their hearts are divided, now they shall bear their guilt."*[281] From here we see how important is peace, and how detested is controversy.[282]

May Hashem place love and understanding in our hearts, that we may treat one another with the kindness and sensitivity we all deserve. May we all live to see the coming of the Righteous Redeemer soon and in our days.

---

279. *Bereishis* 31:43.
280. *R' Tzadok HaKohen of Lublin, Dover Tzedek, Ki Savo* 1.
281. *Hoshea* 10:2.
282. *Bereishis Rabbah* 38:6.

פרשת ויצא
Parashas Vayeitzei

Torah and Yiras Shamayim

I N THIS WEEK'S *PARASHAH*, WE LEARN OF YAAKOV'S DREAM, in which he saw a vision of a ladder ascending to Heaven: וַיַּחֲלֹם וְהִנֵּה סֻלָּם מֻצָּב אַרְצָה וְרֹאשׁוֹ מַגִּיעַ הַשָּׁמָיְמָה וְהִנֵּה מַלְאֲכֵי אֱלֹקִים עֹלִים וְיֹרְדִים בּוֹ — *"He dreamt, and behold! A ladder was set earthward, and its top reached heavenward; and behold! angels of Hashem were ascending and descending on it."*[283]

The Baal HaTurim notes that the word סֻלָּם, meaning ladder, has the same *gematria* as the word קוֹל, meaning voice. This teaches us that the voice of the *tzaddikim* in prayer is the ladder by which the angels ascend. In a similar vein, we find that angels also ascend to Heaven through the fire in which the offerings are burned (as did the angel that heralded the birth of Shimshon).[284] Now that we no longer have a Beis HaMikdash, heartfelt prayer takes the place of the offerings, to serve as the means by which angels move between Heaven and earth.

The Baal HaTurim further notes that סֻלָם (spelled without the letter *vav*) has the same *gematria* as סִינַי, implying that Hashem showed Yaakov Avinu a vision of *Kabbalas HaTorah* on Har Sinai.

---

283. *Bereishis* 28:12.
284. See *Shoftim* 13:20.

Taking these two factors together, we realize that prayer in conjunction with Torah study enables us to ascend to the heights of spiritual perfection. The Zohar states that the ladder in Yaakov's dream symbolizes the soul of man. (This point is discussed in greater detail by R' Chaim of Volozhin.[285]) When a person improves his soul through Torah study and prayer, not only does he ascend the ladder himself, he also uplifts the very angels of Heaven.

Weighing Torah study against prayer, which one proves of greater importance? Perhaps a hint toward an answer can be found in this week's *parashah*, in the *pasuk*: וַיִּיקַץ יַעֲקֹב מִשְּׁנָתוֹ וַיֹּאמֶר אָכֵן יֵשׁ ה' בַּמָּקוֹם הַזֶּה וְאָנֹכִי לֹא יָדָעְתִּי. וַיִּירָא וַיֹּאמַר מַה נּוֹרָא הַמָּקוֹם הַזֶּה אֵין זֶה כִּי אִם בֵּית אֱלֹקִים וְזֶה שַׁעַר הַשָּׁמָיִם — "*Yaakov awoke from his sleep, and said, 'Surely, Hashem is present in this place, and I did not know!' And he became frightened and said, 'How awesome is this place! This is none other than the Abode of God, and this is the gate of the heavens.'*"[286]

The Baal Shem Tov explained this *pasuk*, based on the Gemara that states: כָּל אָדָם שֶׁיֵּשׁ בּוֹ תּוֹרָה וְאֵין בּוֹ יִרְאַת שָׁמַיִם ... מַכְרִיז רַבִּי יַנַּאי חֲבָל עַל דְּלֵית לֵיהּ דַּרְתָּא וְתַרְעָא לְדַרְתָּא עָבִיד — *Regarding those who have Torah wisdom, but no yiras Shamayim (fear of Heaven), ... R' Yannai proclaimed, "Woe to those who have no home, but make a door."*[287]

This seems to imply that Torah is only a means of achieving a goal, but the ultimate goal is *yiras Shamayim*. Just as a door is of no use unless it leads into a home, so too Torah is of no use unless it leads to *yiras Shamayim*.

As Yaakov Avinu slept, he experienced a revelation that brought him to new heights of *yiras Shamayim*. Therefore, when he awoke, "he trembled and said, 'How awesome is this place! This is nothing other than the House of Elokim.'" With awe and trembling, he entered the House of *yiras Shamayim*, of which R' Yannai spoke, after having passed through the "door" of Torah, by studying for fourteen years in the yeshivos of Shem and Eiver.

However, there is another passage from the Gemara, which seems to contradict the first:

Rabbah bar Rav Huna said, "Anyone who has Torah but no

---

285. *Nefesh HaChaim* 1:19.
286. *Bereishis* 28:16-17.
287. *Shabbos* 31a-b.

yiras Shamayim, is like a custodian who was given the keys to the inner room, but cannot enter it, since he does not have the keys to the outer room that leads into it."

In the first passage cited above, it seems that Torah is the path to the ultimate goal of *yiras Shamayim*. In this passage, just the opposite is implied, that *yiras Shamayim* is the "outer room," through which one must pass, to reach the ultimate goal of Torah wisdom.

The truth is that Torah and *yiras Shamayim* are intertwined. Our Sages tell us, "If a person claims that he has only Torah, then he does not have even that," meaning to say, that if a person studies Torah, but does not observe mitzvos, he receives no reward for his Torah wisdom.[288] On the other hand, they tell us that, אֵין עַם הָאָרֶץ חָסִיד — "An *am ha'aretz* (one ignorant of Torah) *cannot possibly be pious*."[289] One must study Torah in order to properly observe the mitzvos, but without mitzvah observance his Torah study is meaningless. When Yaakov Avinu awoke from his dream, he said, "This is the Abode of God, and this is the gate of the heavens." He realized that the "Gate" of Torah study, and the "House" of *yiras Shamayim* are interdependent.

The Gemara states that Hashem created the *yetzer hara*, and He created Torah study as its antidote.[290] This implies that Torah is the only way to defeat the *yetzer hara*. However, the Gemara also states: R' Levi bar Chama said in the name of R' Shimon ben Lakish: One must always arouse his *yetzer tov* against his *yetzer hara*, as the *pasuk* states, "Tremble, and do no sin."[291] If he defeats it, good, but if not, let him toil in Torah study, as the *pasuk* continues, "Speak unto your hearts." If he defeats it, good, but if not, let him recite *Shema*, as the *pasuk* continues, "and upon your beds." If he defeats it, good, but if not, let him recall the day of his death, as the *pasuk* concludes, "and be silent, Selah."[292]

Here we see that there are other "antidotes" to the *yetzer hara*, such as reciting *Shema*, and recalling the day of death. To resolve these Gemaras, it seems that Torah is in fact the only thing in the

---

288. *Yevamos* 109b.
289. *Pirkei Avos* 2:6.
290. *Kiddushin* 30b.
291. *Tehillim* 4:5.
292. *Berachos* 5a.

world that has the power to break the iron grasp of the *yetzer hara*. However, if a person studies Torah, and sees that the *yetzer hara* still haunts him, he must realize that there is something lacking in his Torah study. Perhaps he does not have sufficient *yiras Shamayim*. As noted above, "If a person claims that he has only Torah, he does not have even that." Therefore, the Gemara advises him to bolster his *yiras Shamayim* by reciting *Shema*, thus accepting upon himself the yoke of Hashem's kingship. Then, he can return to his studies, with hopes that his Torah, together with *yiras Shamayim*, will be effective in warding off the *yetzer hara*.

If this too is insufficient, the Gemara advises developing one's sense of humility. Torah is compared to water, which flows from high places to low. So too, Torah wisdom abandons the haughty, to rest upon the meek. By contemplating the day of one's death, he is humbled, and thereby enabled to study Torah in the proper way, which will protect him from the *yetzer hara*.

Our Sages tell us, "Since the day the Beis HaMikdash was destroyed, HaKadosh Baruch Hu has no place in the world to rest, but the four cubits in which halachah is studied."[293] They also say, "HaKadosh Baruch Hu has nothing in His treasure-house but a store of *yiras Shamayim*."[294] The treasures of Torah study and *yiras Shamayim* are one and the same, since they ultimately depend upon each other. Together, they form the "Abode of God" and the "Gate of the heavens," through which one can draw close to Hashem. May we all merit to do so.

The Envy of Angels

THIS WEEK'S *PARASHAH* BEGINS WITH THE PASSAGE: וַיֵּצֵא יַעֲקֹב מִבְּאֵר שֶׁבַע וַיֵּלֶךְ חָרָנָה. וַיִּפְגַּע בַּמָּקוֹם וַיָּלֶן שָׁם כִּי בָא הַשֶּׁמֶשׁ וַיִּקַּח מֵאַבְנֵי הַמָּקוֹם וַיָּשֶׂם מְרַאֲשֹׁתָיו וַיִּשְׁכַּב בַּמָּקוֹם הַהוּא. וַיַּחֲלֹם וְהִנֵּה סֻלָּם מֻצָּב אַרְצָה וְרֹאשׁוֹ מַגִּיעַ הַשָּׁמָיְמָה וְהִנֵּה מַלְאֲכֵי אֱלֹהִים עֹלִים וְיֹרְדִים בּוֹ. וְהִנֵּה

---

293. *Berachos* 8a, see *Maharsha*.
294. Ibid. 33b.

ה' נִצָּב עָלָיו וַיֹּאמַר אֲנִי ה' אֱלֹקֵי אַבְרָהָם אָבִיךָ וֵאלֹהֵי יִצְחָק הָאָרֶץ אֲשֶׁר אַתָּה שֹׁכֵב עָלֶיהָ לְךָ אֶתְּנֶנָּה וּלְזַרְעֶךָ — *"Yaakov departed from Be'er Sheva and went toward Charan. He encountered the place and spent the night there because the sun had set; he took from the stones of the place which he arranged around his head, and lay down in that place. And he dreamt, and behold! A ladder was set earthward and its top reached heavenward; and behold! angels of God were ascending and descending on it. And behold! Hashem was standing over him."*[295]

The Gemara comments on this passage: It was taught: "The angels ascended" and gazed upon the countenance Above (Rashi — the face of Man, one of the Four Creatures,[296] has the likeness of Yaakov); "they descended" and gazed upon the countenance of Yaakov below. They wished to harm him (Rashi — in their envy), but "Hashem was standing over him" (Rashi — to protect him). R' Shimon ben Lakish said: If the *pasuk* had not been written, it would be forbidden to say, but this is like a man who fans his son (Rashi — to protect him from the heat).

Similarly, we find in the Midrash: R' Abahu said: This is comparable to a prince who slept in his crib, and flies landed on him. When his nursemaid came to feed him, the flies fled from him. So too, at first the *pasuk* states, "The angels of Hashem ascended and descended on it." When HaKadosh Baruch Hu revealed Himself, the angels fled.[297]

Yaakov Avinu merited to have his likeness carved into the Divine Throne. Although the ministering angels, that pass between Heaven and earth, were awed by him, Yaakov himself, in his simple humility, had no concept of his own greatness. Rebbe Shimshon of Ostropole explained that in Yaakov's dream, the gates of Heaven were opened, and he received a revelation of the Divine Throne. Heretofore, he had realized that the likenesses of a lion (אַרְיֵה), child (כְּרוּב), and eagle (נֶשֶׁר) are carved into the Divine Chariot. However, he had never realized that his own image is also engraved in the Chariot. Therefore, he said: אָכֵן יֵשׁ ה' בַּמָּקוֹם הַזֶּה וְאָנֹכִי לֹא יָדָעְתִּי —

---

295. *Bereishis* 28:10-13.
296. This is a reference to the likeness of Four Creatures engraved in the supports of the Divine Throne (see *Yechezkel*, Ch. 1).
297. *Bereishis Rabbah* 69:3.

"Surely, Hashem is present in this place, and I did not know."[298]

He was aware of "אֶבֶן," an acronym for lion (אַרְיֵה), child (כְּרוּב), and eagle (נֶשֶׁר), but he was unaware that the אֶבֶן was in fact אָנֹכִי, since his own likeness (יַעֲקֹב) was engraved in the fourth "leg" of the Throne.

We see that the angels were jealous of Yaakov's greatness, yet it is difficult for us to understand how the angels of Heaven could be prey to the base emotion of envy. This is especially confusing, since the Gemara seems to tell us explicitly, that there is no envy among them: R' Yehoshua ben Levi said: When Moshe ascended to Heaven, the ministering angels said to HaKadosh Baruch Hu, "Master of the Universe, what does this mortal, born of woman, do among us?"

"He has come to receive the Torah," Hashem said.

"The precious treasure, that has been kept by You since nine hundred and seventy-four generations before the world's creation, You now wish to give to flesh and blood? '*What is man, that You recall him, and son of man, that You are mindful of him,*'[299] '*Hashem, our Master, how mighty is Your Name in all the land. Give Your glory* (a reference to the Torah) *to the Heavens.*'"[300]

"Answer them," HaKadosh Baruch Hu commanded Moshe.

"Master of the Universe, I fear that they might burn me with the breath of their mouths," said Moshe.

"Grasp hold of My Throne of Glory, and give them an answer," Hashem said, as it is written, "*From grasping the side of the Throne, His cloud spread over him.*"[301] R' Nachum interpreted this to mean that Hashem spread the radiance of His *Shechinah*, and His cloud (of protection) over Moshe.

Moshe then said to Him, "Master of the Universe, the Torah that You wish to give me, what is written in it? '*I am Hashem, your God, Who took you out of the land of Egypt.*'"[302]

He then turned to the angels and asked, "Did you descend to Egypt? Were you enslaved by Pharaoh? Why should you have the Torah?"

---

298. *Bereishis* 28:16.
299. *Tehillim* 8:5.
300. Ibid. v. 2.
301. *Iyov* 26:9.
302. *Shemos* 20:2.

"What else does the Torah say?" Moshe continued. "*You shall have no other gods.*' Do you dwell among the nations, who worship idols? What else does the Torah say? *'Remember the Shabbos day, to sanctify it.*' Do you have any labors, from which you must rest? What else does the Torah say? *'Do not take (Hashem's Name in vain).*' Do you have business transactions (that might tempt you to swear falsely)? What else does the Torah say? *'Honor your father and mother.*' Do you have fathers and mothers? What else does the Torah say? *'Do not kill, do not be adulterous, do not steal.*' Do you have envy or *yetzer hara* among you (that might tempt you to do these sins)?"

HaKadosh Baruch Hu immediately agreed to Moshe's arguments, as the *pasuk* repeats, "Hashem, our Master, how mighty is Your Name in all the land." But this time, it does not say, "Give Your glory to the Heavens."[303]

Moshe Rabbeinu based his argument on the fact that there is neither envy nor other negative traits among the angels. R' Akiva Eiger, in his gloss on the Talmud, notes an apparent contradiction from Rashi's commentary on the *Chumash*,[304] in which we find that since man resembles the angels, Hashem asked their consent before creating him, in order not to provoke their jealousy. Here we see that angels are indeed tainted by the trait of envy.

R' Akiva Eiger could perhaps have brought an even more convincing proof from the Gemara cited above, in which the angels wished to kill Yaakov Avinu, in their terrible envy of him.

To answer this question, we must take note of the exact wording of Moshe Rabbeinu's argument: "Do you have envy ... *among you?*" The angels are not envious of one another. "They lovingly give permission to one another to sanctify their Creator," as we say in the *berachah* before *Shema* in the morning. Therefore, they have no need of the Torah to make peace among them. However, their envy of mankind, and specifically of Yaakov who represented the perfection of man, is on a totally different level. They realized that by means of the Torah, man can reach a sublime peak of perfection. Man himself can become the ladder that connects Heaven

---

303. *Shabbos* 88b.
304. *Bereishis* 1:26.

and earth. Rav Chaim of Volozhin explains that the "*tzelem Elokim* — image of God*," in which man was created, means that he has the ability to build and destroy, uplift and cast down, influencing all creation through his deeds, in a manner of which the angels are entirely incapable.[305]

Perhaps for this reason Hashem told Moshe to "Grasp hold of His Throne of Glory" before answering the angels, to protect him from their fiery breath. The angels would see Yaakov's likeness engraved on the Throne, and thereby be reminded of the envy they felt toward him long ago, when they realized that he was the very ladder that connects Heaven and earth, and brings all creation to its fulfillment. It was this same envy that they were experiencing once again, when Yaakov's descendant, Moshe, rose to Heaven to receive the Torah, on behalf of Klal Yisrael.

The Gemara elsewhere states that when Eisav's guardian angel struggled against Yaakov Avinu, the dust from their feet ascended to the Throne of Glory.[306] "When he perceived that it was unable,"[307] when Eisav's angel saw that it was unable to remove Yaakov's likeness from the Throne of Glory, it tried to at least conceal his likeness, by covering the Throne with a cloud of dust. Thereby, it hoped to minimize Yaakov's influence on the world.

"A person must always aspire that his deeds touch the deeds of the *Avos*."[308] Rebbe Yisrael of Ruzhin explained that we cannot hope to actually match the greatness of the *Avos*, since their holiness and righteousness are far beyond our grasp. However, we must aspire to at least "touch their deeds," by emulating them to the best of our ability.

Perhaps another explanation is that we can actually hope to "touch" them, since the *Avos* lower themselves, to maintain contact with us, and thereby draw us up to their level. The merit of the *Avos* will persevere until the end of time. They are eternally attached to their descendants until the end of all generations. "A three-ply cord is not easily severed."[309] This refers to the merit of the three *Avos*:

---

305. *Nefesh HaChaim* 1:1.
306. *Chullin* 91a.
307. *Bereishis* 32:26.
308. *Tanna D'Vei Eliyahu Rabbah*, Ch. 23.
309. *Koheles* 4:12.

Avraham, Yitzchak, and Yaakov. They will always be bound to their descendants, with cords of love. Just as we depend on their merit to protect us, they also depend on us to continue their mission, by spreading Hashem's holiness in the world. By following in their footsteps, we can also hope to ascend to the heights of spiritual greatness.

The Vision of Protection

THE RAMBAN DESCRIBES HOW EVERY DETAIL OF OUR forefather's lives was a signpost, indicating future events in the lives of their descendants. Yaakov's wanderings in exile, as he fled first from the wrath of Eisav, and later from the jealousy of Lavan, foretold the exiles that his children would suffer throughout the ages. Yet throughout the difficult epochs of exile that we have endured, Hashem has stretched His protective wings over us, rescuing us from our enemies time and time again, just as He rescued Yaakov Avinu, in fulfillment of His vow, אָנֹכִי עִמָּךְ וּשְׁמַרְתִּיךְ בְּכֹל אֲשֶׁר תֵּלֵךְ — *"I am with you; I will guard you wherever you go."*[310]

Rav Yaakov Emden writes: When we contemplate our situation in the history of the world, we realize that we are a nation exiled, like scattered sheep. After all the thousands of years of hardship that have befallen us, there is no nation as oppressed as ours. Our enemies are numerous. With hatred and jealousy, they have raised their heads to uproot and destroy us. Even so, they have been unable to fulfill their plans. The most powerful of nations have risen against us and long ago fallen, their memory forgotten like a passing shadow, but we who cling to Hashem survive today. Despite all the torments of our exile, we have not forsaken even one letter of the written Torah, and the words of our Sages still stand strong. They have been impervious to the hand of time. What could the clever philosophers possibly say to explain this? That it is a coincidence?

---

310. *Bereishis* 28:15.

By my life, I swear that this is a greater miracle than those Hashem performed for our forefathers in Egypt, in the desert, and in Eretz Yisrael. The longer the *Galus* lasts, the more the miracle becomes obvious and Hashem's might is revealed. Everything that we undergo today was already foreseen by the prophets, who bemoaned the terrible length of the *Galus* long before it began. From all their words, not one has fallen aside. He who would dispute this, his words are like smoke and the passing clouds.[311]

The fortitude necessary to endure our exile was bequeathed to us by our forefathers, who suffered similar hardships throughout their lives. Avraham Avinu, the founder of our nation, also tasted the hardship of exile, when he fulfilled Hashem's command, לֶךְ לְךָ מֵאַרְצֶךָ — *"Go for yourself from your land."* He was the first to assume the role of the wandering Jew, traveling from one land to another, not even knowing his destination, but trusting that Hashem would ultimately bring him אֶל הָאָרֶץ אֲשֶׁר אַרְאֶךָּ — *"to the land that I will show you."*

However, Avraham's exile was very different from Yaakov's. Avraham experienced the hardship of wandering in foreign lands, but Yaakov experienced a much more difficult exile, as he fled the unsheathed sword of a deadly adversary. To give him the encouragement he so desperately needed, Yaakov was granted a prophetic vision, in which Hashem assured him of his survival in exile: an assurance that would stand for his descendants throughout the generations.

וַיַּחֲלֹם וְהִנֵּה סֻלָּם מֻצָּב אַרְצָה וְרֹאשׁוֹ מַגִּיעַ הַשָּׁמָיְמָה וְהִנֵּה מַלְאֲכֵי אֱלֹקִים עֹלִים וְיֹרְדִים בּוֹ. וְהִנֵּה ה' נִצָּב עָלָיו וַיֹּאמַר אֲנִי ה' אֱלֹקֵי אַבְרָהָם אָבִיךָ וֵאלֹקֵי יִצְחָק הָאָרֶץ אֲשֶׁר אַתָּה שֹׁכֵב עָלֶיהָ לְךָ אֶתְּנֶנָּה וּלְזַרְעֶךָ. וְהָיָה זַרְעֲךָ כַּעֲפַר הָאָרֶץ וּפָרַצְתָּ יָמָּה וָקֵדְמָה וְצָפֹנָה וָנֶגְבָּה וְנִבְרְכוּ בְךָ כָּל מִשְׁפְּחֹת הָאֲדָמָה וּבְזַרְעֶךָ. וְהִנֵּה אָנֹכִי עִמָּךְ וּשְׁמַרְתִּיךָ בְּכֹל אֲשֶׁר תֵּלֵךְ וַהֲשִׁבֹתִיךָ אֶל הָאֲדָמָה הַזֹּאת כִּי לֹא אֶעֱזָבְךָ עַד אֲשֶׁר אִם עָשִׂיתִי אֵת אֲשֶׁר דִּבַּרְתִּי לָךְ.

And he dreamt, and behold! A ladder was set earthward and its top reached heavenward; and behold! angels of God were ascending and descending on it. And behold! Hashem

---

311. *Siddur Beis Yaakov: Sulam Beis Keil.*

was standing over him, and He said, "I am Hashem, God of Avraham your father and God of Yitzchak; the ground upon which you are lying, to you will I give it and to your descendants. Your offspring shall be as the dust of the earth, and you shall spread out powerfully westward, eastward, northward, and southward; and all the families of the earth shall bless themselves by you and by your offspring. Behold, I am with you; I will guard you wherever you go, and I will return you to this soil; for I will not forsake you until I will have done what I have spoken about you."[312]

The Ramban interprets this vision as follows: Hashem revealed to Yaakov through a prophetic dream, that everything that occurs here on earth is orchestrated through the angels by Divine decree. The angels that Hashem sends to walk the earth can perform no act, from the trivial to the momentous, until they have first returned to stand before the Lord of the world, to deliver their report, and state whether the land rests peacefully or is plagued by sword and bloodshed. God then directs the angels to return to earth to fulfill His bidding.

Hashem's appearance over the ladder represented His firm assurance that Yaakov's fate would not be entrusted to the hands of the angels. Yaakov was Hashem's own portion, and Hashem would always protect him personally, as it is written, "I shall be with you; I will guard you wherever you go." In this respect, Yaakov was greater than other *tzaddikim*, of whom it is written, "He will charge His angels for you, to protect you in all your ways."[313]

According to Rabbi Eliezer the Great, this vision paralleled Avraham's *Bris bein HaBesarim* (Covenant of the Parts). Hashem showed Yaakov how the four empires would ascend to power, and ultimately crumble. The angels on the ladder were the guardian angels of the empires: Greece, Babylon, Media, and Rome, as described by Daniel.[314] Hashem assured Yaakov that He would stand by Yaakov's side to protect him as he wandered among the nations, and rescue him from their hands.

---

312. *Bereishis* 28:12-15.
313. *Tehillim* 91:11.
314. *Daniel*, Chapter 11.

Hashem showed him each empire's ascent and its subsequent destruction. He showed him the guardian angel of Babylon ascending seventy rungs on the ladder, and then falling. He showed him the guardian angel of Media ascending fifty-two rungs and then falling. He showed him the guardian angel of Greece ascending one hundred and eighty rungs and then falling. He then showed him the angel of Edom ascending higher and higher, but it did not fall. Hashem then assured him, "But in the end, he shall fall into the abyss."[315] Hashem then said to Eisav, "If you raise [your nest] like an eagle, [or if you place your nest among the stars, I will bring you down from there — the word of Hashem]."[316]

Yaakov's adversaries were the spiritual forebears of the empires that were destined to oppress his descendants. Each enemy threatened Yaakov with a particular form of danger, which paralleled the dangers that Bnei Yisrael were destined to endure in exile. Eisav threatened him with physical destruction, representing nations such as Nazi Germany, which waged an open war to destroy Bnei Yisrael, irrespective of our level of religious observance.

The suffering Yaakov endured under Lavan's hand was more insidious. Yaakov worked for him for twenty years, under conditions of hardship and depravation: הָיִיתִי בַיּוֹם אֲכָלַנִי חֹרֶב וְקֶרַח בַּלַּיְלָה וַתִּדַּד שְׁנָתִי מֵעֵינָי — "This is how I was: By day, scorching heat consumed me, and frost by night; my sleep drifted from my eyes."[317]

Yet throughout it all he remained the very model of honest labor, as the Rambam writes: Just as an employer is forbidden to cheat his employees, or withhold their pay; so too an employee is forbidden to cheat his employer by shirking his duties here and there, until finally the entire day is wasted in deceit. He must be punctual and diligent in his work hours, for which reason our Sages exempted him from the fourth blessing of *Birkas HaMazon*. He must serve his employer with all his strength, as Yaakov the *tzaddik* said, "it was with all my might that I served your father."[318] Hashem rewarded him in this world for his honest labor, as it is written,

---

315. *Yeshayahu* 14:15.
316. *Ovadiah* 1:4.
317. *Bereishis* 31:40.
318. Ibid. v. 6.

"And the man was very, very successful."[319,320]

Lavan prospered by Yaakov's honest labor, but he never showed Yaakov the slightest bit of appreciation. Just the opposite, he constantly sought ways to cheat Yaakov, and deprive him of his basic rights. This foreshadowed the plight of Bnei Yisrael in lands such as Communist Russia, where their lives were spared, but their basic human rights were usurped. Jews played a role in the development of science, education, and trade in all the countries where we were exiled, yet we were often denied the opportunity to earn the most basic livelihood.

By enduring these difficult tests, and remaining faithful to Hashem throughout them all, Yaakov instilled in our nation the strength and fortitude necessary to survive the various stages of our exile. In his merit, Hashem stands beside us at all times, to rescue us from our adversaries, in whatever guise they may appear.

בְּכָל דּוֹר וָדוֹר עוֹמְדִים עָלֵינוּ לְכַלּוֹתֵנוּ וְהַקָּדוֹשׁ בָּרוּךְ הוּא מַצִּילֵנוּ מִיָּדָם.

"In every generation they rise against us to destroy us, but HaKadosh Baruch Hu rescues us from their hands."[321]

---

319. *Bereishis* 30:43.
320. *Rambam, Hilchos Sechirus* 13:6.
321. *Pesach Haggadah.*

The Merit of Charity

וַיִּדַּר יַעֲקֹב נֶדֶר לֵאמֹר אִם יִהְיֶה אֱלֹקִים עִמָּדִי וּשְׁמָרַנִי בַּדֶּרֶךְ הַזֶּה אֲשֶׁר אָנֹכִי הוֹלֵךְ וְנָתַן לִי לֶחֶם לֶאֱכֹל וּבֶגֶד לִלְבֹּשׁ. וְשַׁבְתִּי בְשָׁלוֹם אֶל בֵּית אָבִי וְהָיָה ה' לִי לֵאלֹקִים. וְהָאֶבֶן הַזֹּאת אֲשֶׁר שַׂמְתִּי מַצֵּבָה יִהְיֶה בֵּית אֱלֹקִים וְכֹל אֲשֶׁר תִּתֶּן לִי עַשֵּׂר אֲעַשְּׂרֶנּוּ לָךְ.

Then Yaakov took a vow, saying: "If God will be with me, will guard me on this way that I am going; will give me bread to eat and clothes to wear; and I return in peace to my father's house, and Hashem will be a God for me — then this stone which I have set up as a pillar shall become a house of God, and whatever You will give me, I shall repeatedly tithe it to You."[322]

YAAKOV RECOGNIZED THE GREAT DANGERS THAT FACED him on his way, and thus made this vow to doubly tithe his possessions, giving one fifth of all his earnings as a gift to Hashem. Although we are normally discouraged from making vows, Tosefos explains that in times of danger it is advisable to make a vow to charity, in order that its merit might protect us from harm.[323]

Whereas all mitzvos earn great reward, *tzedakah* is the only mitzvah for which we may actually test the Creator and see with our own eyes that in reward for tithing our earnings for charity, we are certain to receive His blessing. The Gemara thus states:

R' Yochanan once encountered Reish Lakish's son and asked him what *pasuk* he was learning. "*Asser ti'asser* — Tithe, you shall tithe,"[324] he answered.

" What is the meaning of this *pasuk*?" asked R' Yochanan.

"Tithe (*asser*) in order that you may become rich (*tisasher*)," answered the boy.

"How do you know this is true?" asked R' Yochanan.

---

322. *Bereishis* 28:20-22.
323. *Chullin* 2b, *Tosefos* s.v. *Aval* citing *Bereishis Rabbah*.
324. *Devarim* 14:22.

"Try it and see," answered the boy.

"Is it permitted to test Hashem? Does the *pasuk* not state, '*You shall not test Hashem*'[325]?"

The boy answered, "R' Hoshea said that this does not apply to tithing, as the verse states, '*Bring all the tithes into the storage house, and let it be sustenance in My Temple. Test Me, if you will, with this, says Hashem Master of Legions, [see] if I do not open for you the windows of the Heavens and pour out upon you blessing without end.*'"[326,327]

Tzedakah is truly a wondrous *segulah* that brings success, good fortune, and protection upon those who practice it. The Gemara states that whereas salt preserves meat, the proverbial salt that preserves wealth is חֶסֶד (kindness), or according to some versions חֹסֶר (diminish).[328] The two versions of the Gemara represent two aspects of *tzedakah*. On the one hand, *tzedakah*'s virtue is kindness, since it benefits the poor. On the other hand, *tzedakah* has another virtue, in that it trains us to overcome our greed by willingly diminishing from our wealth.

Tzedakah furthermore has the power to prolong a person's life, as Shlomo HaMelech said, צְדָקָה תַּצִּיל מִמָּוֶת — "*Charity rescues from death.*"[329] This is the fair and fitting reward, *middah k'neged middah*, since by giving charity one revitalizes the poor by helping to relieve the deathlike depression and despair that accompany poverty.[330]

The power of *tzedakah* to rescue a person from death is well illustrated by the following Gemara:

Binyamin HaTzaddik was the custodian of the *tzedakah* fund. One time, a woman approached him during a year of famine. "Rebbi, support me," she said.

"I swear by the service of the Beis HaMikdash that there is no money left in the *tzedakah* fund," he said.

"Rebbi, if you do not support me, a woman and her seven sons will die," she said. He then used his own money to support her.

---

325. *Devarim* 6:16.
326. *Malachi* 3:10.
327. *Taanis* 9a.
328. *Kesubos* 66b.
329. *Mishlei* 10:2.
330. *Rosh, Pe'ah* 1:1.

Years later he fell sick and was close to death. The ministering angels said before Hashem, "Maser of the Universe, You said that anyone who saves the life of one Jew is considered to have saved the entire world. Binyamin HaTzaddik saved a woman and her seven sons from death. How could he die so young?"

Immediately, the judgment against him was overruled and twenty-two years were added to his life.[331]

The Vilna Gaon explains this Gemara with a brilliant calculation. The Gemara states that someone who gives charity to the poor is blessed with six blessings, but someone who comforts the poor with kind words is blessed with eleven blessings. Since Binyamin comforted eight souls (the poor woman and her seven sons), his eleven blessings were multiplied by eight, for a total of eighty-eight. In *Maseches Sotah* we learn that even if a person is subject to a decree of death, sufficient merit can preserve his life for another three months.[332] Binyamin had eighty-eight merits, which multiplied by three months earned him a total of 264 months, or twenty-two years. He was thus blessed with another twenty-two years of life.

Tzedakah is always an important mitzvah, but in times of personal or national danger it becomes the crucial key to our survival. For this reason, when danger hung over Yaakov's head, he vowed to tithe his possessions, in order that this great merit would protect him.

In our times as well, spiritual and physical danger threaten the Jewish community in Eretz Yisrael and abroad. Therefore, let us all make extra efforts to be considerate and helpful to one another, with kind words and a generous hand, and may we soon merit the fulfillment of the verse: צִיּוֹן בְּמִשְׁפָּט תִּפָּדֶה וְשָׁבֶיהָ בִּצְדָקָה — "*Tzion will be redeemed through justice, and its captives will return through tzedakah.*"[333]

---

331. *Bava Basra* 11a.
332. *Sotah* 20b.
333. *Yeshayahu* 1:27.

Yaakov's Dual Mission

I N THIS WEEK'S *PARASHAH*, WE LEARN OF THE RUSE THAT
Lavan played on Yaakov, by substituting Leah for Rachel on her
wedding night, and thus tricking Yaakov into marrying Leah.
The verse states: וַיְהִי בַבֹּקֶר וְהִנֵּה הוּא לֵאָה וַיֹּאמֶר אֶל לָבָן מַה זֹּאת עָשִׂיתָ לִּי
הֲלֹא בְרָחֵל עָבַדְתִּי עִמָּךְ וְלָמָּה רִמִּיתָנִי — *"Morning came, and behold it was
Leah. He (Yaakov) then said to Lavan, What have you done to me? I
worked for you to earn Rachel's hand. Why did you trick me?'"*[334]

Rashi explains, "Morning came, and behold it was Leah," to
mean that only in the morning did Yaakov realize he had married
Leah. At night, he had assumed she was Rachel. Yaakov and Rachel
suspected that Lavan might resort to trickery, so they agreed on a
secret code by which Yaakov could verify her identity. At the last
moment, Rachel reconsidered. She revealed the signs to Leah, lest
Leah be found out and humiliated by the exposure.

The Midrash adds that when Yaakov confronted Leah in the
morning, he made harsh accusations against her:

The entire night he called her Rachel and she answered him.
"Trickster daughter of a trickster!" he later said to her.

"Am I not a student of the book you wrote?" she answered.
"When your father called you Eisav, did you not answer? So too, I
answered when you called me Rachel."[335]

Lest we misinterpret this as a domestic quarrel regarding matters of dishonesty, we must pause to consider the reasons for
Yaakov and Leah's deception. Yaakov posed as Eisav, not in order
to claim any worldly benefit for himself, but to ensure that the spiritual blessings of Heaven and earth would fall into the right hands,
in order to ensure the destiny of the Jewish people as the heralds of
Hashem's Torah. Without Yitzchak's blessings, Bnei Yisrael could
not possibly endure the hardships of *Galus*.[336]

In Yitzchak's mistaken presumption of Eisav's righteousness,
he thought that Eisav would be the one to sanctify Hashem's Name

---

334. *Bereishis* 29:25.
335. *Bereishis Rabbah* 70:19.
336. See *Minchas Asher, Sichos: Parashas Toldos.*

in the world. Therefore, he planned to grant his blessings to Eisav. However, since Yaakov and Rivkah well knew that this was not the case, they had no choice but to attain Eisav's blessings in any way possible.

Yaakov had good reason for deceiving his father, but what justification did Leah have? By comparing her deception to Yaakov's, Leah hinted to him that she did so with the very same intent.

The Kozhnitzer Maggid and other Chassidic leaders explain that while Yaakov and Eisav were still in their mother's womb, they had already divided this world and the World to Come between them.[337] Eisav was to inherit this world with all its physical pleasures, while Yaakov was to inherit the World to Come.

Eisav was a "man of the field." Had he realized his potential, he could have focused his mighty physical powers toward Hashem's service. Then, he could have used Yitzchak's blessings to sanctify Hashem's Name in the physical world. Yaakov, on the other hand, "sat in the tents." He was meant to devote himself to the purely spiritual pursuit of Torah study in the tents of Shem and Eiver's Torah academies.

Eisav, however, shirked his responsibilities. He misused his inclination toward physicality to fulfill his own lascivious desires. Yaakov then had no choice but to assume both positions.[338] He took over Eisav's role, and with it the *berachos* of material wealth, "*May Hashem grant you the dew of the Heavens, the fatness of the earth, and abundant grain and wine.*"[339]

Rashi hints that Leah was meant to be Eisav's bride, while Rachel was meant for Yaakov: "(Lavan's) older daughter for (Yitzchak's) older son, and (Lavan's) younger daughter for (Yaakov's) younger son."[340] Had Eisav fulfilled his potential and utilized his physicality in Hashem's service, then Leah would have truly been his partner and his helpmate in this lofty endeavor. However, since this task ultimately fell upon Yaakov's shoulders, Leah became his destined bride alongside Rachel.

The Kozhnitzer Maggid thus writes as follows:

337. See *Rashi, Bereishis* 25:22.
338. *Malbim, Parashas Toldos.*
339. *Bereishis* 27:28.
340. Ibid. 29:17

When Yaakov said, "I am Eisav, your firstborn," he spoke the truth. [The good aspects of Eisav's soul] were given over to Yaakov along with the birthright. At that moment, the Heavens appointed Leah as Yaakov's destined bride.

"When your father called you Eisav, did you not answer?" Leah asked him, implying that at that very moment she had become his destined bride.

With this we reach some understanding of the esoteric teaching of the Zohar on this matter:

Two worlds were given to Yaakov: a world of concealment and a world of revelation. From one world, six tribes were born. From the other world, two tribes were born. From the hidden world came six tribes, while from the revealed world came two tribes, corresponding to the two *Cheruvim* below.

Yaakov was found between both worlds, in the exact image of them both. For this reason, all Leah's words were hidden, while all Rachel's words were revealed.[341]

Due to the very nature of her soul, Leah had no choice but to live in a world of concealment. Only in the hidden recesses of the night could she surreptitiously claim her place as Yaakov's bride, to bear for him the six tribes that were destined to emerge from her.

---

341. *Zohar* I, 152a.

פרשת וישלח
Parashas Vayishlach

The Downfall of Eisav

וַיִּוָּתֵר יַעֲקֹב לְבַדּוֹ וַיֵּאָבֵק אִישׁ עִמּוֹ עַד עֲלוֹת הַשָּׁחַר. וַיַּרְא כִּי לֹא
יָכֹל לוֹ וַיִּגַּע בְּכַף יְרֵכוֹ וַתֵּקַע כַּף יֶרֶךְ יַעֲקֹב בְּהֵאָבְקוֹ עִמּוֹ. וַיֹּאמֶר
שַׁלְּחֵנִי כִּי עָלָה הַשָּׁחַר וַיֹּאמֶר לֹא אֲשַׁלֵּחֲךָ כִּי אִם בֵּרַכְתָּנִי. וַיֹּאמֶר
אֵלָיו מַה שְּׁמֶךָ וַיֹּאמֶר יַעֲקֹב. וַיֹּאמֶר לֹא יַעֲקֹב יֵאָמֵר עוֹד שִׁמְךָ כִּי
אִם יִשְׂרָאֵל כִּי שָׂרִיתָ עִם אֱלֹקִים וְעִם אֲנָשִׁים וַתּוּכָל.

*Yaakov was left alone and a man wrestled with him until
the break of dawn. When he perceived that he could not
overcome him, he struck the socket of his hip; so Yaakov's
hip-socket was dislocated as he wrestled with him. Then he
said, "Let me go, for dawn has broken." And he said, "I will
not let you go unless you bless me." He said to him, "What is
your name?" He replied, "Yaakov." He said, "No longer will it
be said that your name is Yaakov, but Yisrael, since you have
striven with the Divine and with man and have overcome."*[342]

THE MIDRASH EXPLAINS THAT THIS INCIDENT IS A SYM-
bol of the conflict between the descendants of Yaakov
and Eisav for generations to come. Bnei Yisrael's success
in business, war, and Torah study is entirely in the merit of the

---

342. *Bereishis* 32:25-29.

dust that rose from the ground, as Yaakov struggled against Eisav's guardian angel.[343] As such, we see that this was indeed a monumental conflict, with great relevance to the future of the Jewish people.

With a mere touch, the angel wounded Yaakov's thigh, causing him to limp. How then was Yaakov able to defeat this mighty angel in battle? Ramban explains:

"The angels are mighty; they do His bidding."[344] Although the angels are mighty, they must do Hashem's bidding. Therefore, Eisav's guardian angel was unable to do more than wound Yaakov in the thigh. The Midrash states that this wound was in fact a blow against all the *tzaddikim* destined to descend from Yaakov, most particularly in the generations of *shmad* (persecution).[345]

The truth is that this entire incident is a portent for future generations, that the descendants of Eisav would overpower the descendants of Yaakov, and come close to eradicating them completely, as occurred in the times of the Mishnah, during the generation of R' Yehudah ben Bava and his peers.[346]

The Midrash cites R' Chiya bar Abba as saying, that if he would be forced to sacrifice his life in sanctification of Hashem's Name, he would do so, provided that he would be killed quickly. He could not bear the torments of the generations of *shmad*, in which Jews are slowly tortured to death with burning hot metal.[347] We have been subjected to these and many worse tribulations, yet we

---

343. *Shir HaShirim Rabbah* 3:2.
344. *Tehillim* 103:20.
345. *Bereishis Rabbah* 73:3.
346. This refers to the generation of the Ten Martyrs, who were executed by the Romans for promulgating Torah study. The Gemara (*Sanhedrin* 14a) tells us that the Romans passed a decree that anyone who gave or received *semichah* (Rabbinic ordination) would be executed, and the city in which the *semichah* was given would be destroyed. R' Yehudah ben Bava then summoned his students to an uninhabited valley, where he conferred *semichah* upon them. The Romans found out, and descended upon them, whereupon R' Yehudah ben Bava commanded his students to flee. He himself was caught and executed on the spot. The students who received *semichah* then were none other than R' Meir, R' Yehudah, R' Shimon bar Yochai, R' Yose, R' Elazar ben Shamua, and according to some opinions R' Nechemiah. Their teachings are extensively cited throughout the Mishnah.
347. *Shir HaShirim Rabbah* 2:7.

persevere, as did Yaakov Avinu, who ultimately returned to Eretz Yisrael unharmed.[348]

Eisav and his descendants were given permission to struggle against Bnei Yisrael, and even to wound us, but they can never completely defeat us. In remembrance of Yaakov's struggle against the angel, and its great significance throughout the generations, we were commanded not to eat the *gid hanasheh* (sciatic nerve), the hind quarters where Yaakov was wounded. The Sefer HaChinuch writes as follows:

The root of this mitzvah is to serve as a reminder for Bnei Yisrael, that although we will suffer many terrible persecutions from the nations of the world, and particularly from the descendants of Eisav, we can rest assured that we will never be destroyed. The name of Yaakov and their descendants will endure forever. Our salvation from the hands of our enemies will ultimately arrive.

By remembering this assurance, through the mitzvah that serves as a memorial, we will stand firm in our faith and our righteousness forever. The angel that struggled against Yaakov Avinu (which tradition tells us was Eisav's guardian angel) wanted to eradicate Yaakov and his children from the world, but it was unable to do so. Instead, it harmed him by striking his thigh. So too, Eisav's descendants torment the descendants of Yaakov, yet in the end our salvation will arrive. Just as the sun shone upon our patriarch, he was healed from his injury, and saved from his adversary. So too shall the proverbial sun of Mashiach shine upon us, to heal us from our many injuries and rescue us. May this be soon and in our days.[349]

As we refrain from eating the *gid hanasheh*, we are given cause to remember Hashem's assurance. As much as the descendants of Eisav torment us, they will never be able to destroy us.

The Zohar states that there are three hundred and sixty-five organs of the body, which correspond to the three hundred and sixty-five days of the solar year. The day that corresponds to the *gid hanasheh* is Tishah B'Av.[350] The Arizal explains that just as Eisav's angel sought to kill Yaakov, but was able to harm only his

---

348. *Ramban, Bereishis* 32:26.
349. *Sefer HaChinuch,* 3.
350. *Zohar* I, *Parashas Vayishlach,* 170b.

gid hanasheh; so too, Eisav's descendants struggle throughout the year to defeat us, but were successful only on Tishah B'Av, a day of harsh judgment, when the Beis HaMikdash was twice destroyed. According to Kabbalah, if a person eats on Tishah B'Av, it is considered as if he ate from the *gid hanasheh*.[351]

This point can be further understood, in light of the Sefer HaChinuch's explanation of the *gid hanasheh's* significance. On this most bitter day in Jewish history, when the Beis HaMikdash was twice destroyed, and Bnei Yisrael were exiled from our land, we must bolster our faith, and remember that no matter how hard Eisav tries to destroy Yaakov, he must ultimately fail. Eisav's angel was not given free rein to destroy us completely.

Why is it that Eisav's angel, which represents evil, chose to confront Yaakov, whereas Avraham and Yitzchak were never opposed by angelic adversaries? It seems that the central player in the ultimate battle between good and evil is none other than Yaakov Avinu. What was unique about Yaakov, that gave him this crucial role?

Last week, we noted the significance of the ladder in Yaakov's dream. The Baal HaTurim explains that סוּלָם, the Hebrew word for ladder, has the same gematria as the word קוֹל, which means voice. When spelled without the letter *vav*, סֻלָם has the same gematria as סִינַי, a reference to Har Sinai. This teaches us that Torah study, and the voice of the *tzaddikim* in prayer, together form the ladder upon which the angels ascend and descend between Heaven and earth.

As mentioned there, our Sages further tell us that the angel Yaakov saw ascending the ladder was none other than Eisav's guardian angel. Yaakov saw it rising ever higher, and feared that there would be no end to the empire that Eisav was destined to build. Hashem then assured Yaakov, that even if Eisav were to ascend to the very Heavens, Hashem would ultimately cast him down, as the *pasuk* states, "If you arise [you act] like an eagle, or if you place your nest among the stars, I will bring you down from there — the word of Hashem."[352] Perhaps Hashem did not tell Yaakov when Eisav's fall would come, but He did tell him how

---

351. *Pri Eitz Chaim, Shaar Chag HaShavuos*, Ch. 1.
352. *Ovadiah* 1:4; *Vayikra Rabbah* 29:2.

it would come about: in the merit of the ladder, which represents Yaakov's prayer and Torah study.

The Ohr HaChaim writes, based on the Zohar, that Bnei Yisrael passed through four stages of exile. We were redeemed from the first three in the merit of the *Avos*: Avraham, Yitzchak, and Yaakov. We will be redeemed from this final stage of our exile in the merit of Moshe Rabbeinu. "For this reason our redemption has been delayed so long. As long as our dedication to Torah and mitzvos is lax, Moshe does not wish to redeem us."[353]

How could the Ohr HaChaim say that Moshe Rabbeinu does not wish to redeem us? As he led Bnei Yisrael through the desert for forty years, he bore our complaints with loving patience. He prayed for us when we sinned, and confronted Hashem on our behalf, demanding that his name be erased from the Torah, if Hashem were to destroy us. Why then would he refuse to redeem us now, for our laxity in Torah and mitzvos?

Clearly the Ohr HaChaim did not mean that Moshe does not want to redeem us, but that he is simply unable. The Ultimate Redemption must be spurred by our Torah study, mitzvah observance, and prayer.

The Chasam Sofer had an interesting insight into the *pasuk* cited above, in which the angel gave Yaakov a new name, "No longer will it be said that your name is Yaakov, but Yisrael, for you have striven (*sarisa*) with the Divine and with man, and have overcome."[354] Eisav's angel wished to remove Yaakov's original name entirely, and replace it with the new name, Yisrael. Although Hashem acquiesced to add a new name for Yaakov, He did not remove Yaakov's original name. When Yaakov descended to Egypt, Hashem called him again by the name Yaakov: "Elokim spoke to Yisrael in night visions and he said, 'Yaakov, Yaakov.' "[355] From here our Sages learn that Yaakov retained both names.[356]

The Chasam Sofer explains that יַעֲקֹב and יִשְׂרָאֵל added together have the same gematria as the words קְרַע שָׂטָן ("tear apart the Satan"), which are part of Hashem's forty-two-letter Name.

353. *Ohr HaChaim, Shemos* 27:20.
354. *Bereishis* 32:29.
355. Ibid. 46:2.
356. *Berachos* 13a.

Therefore, Eisav's angel did not want him to keep both names, which would ultimately give him the power to defeat Eisav.

However, when we count the numerical value of each letter, we reach a different conclusion. יַעֲקֹב יִשְׂרָאֵל equals 723, whereas קְרַע שָׂטָן equals 729. The Chasam Sofer's calculation is correct, only when using alternate spelling, יַעֲקוֹב, including the letter *vav*. In five places in *Tanach*, יַעֲקוֹב is spelled with the extra *vav*; and in five places the name Eliyahu is spelled אֵלִיָּה, without the *vav*. Rashi explains that Yaakov took the letter *vav* from Eliyahu's name, as collateral to ensure that Eliyahu would come to redeem Yaakov's descendants.[357]

When speaking of Yaakov's role in hastening the redemption, his name is spelled with the extra *vav*. He is the one who tears apart the Satan. He struggled with Eisav's guardian angel and defeated it, thereby setting a precedent for his descendants, by which we would also be able to defeat the forces of darkness in the world. Yaakov's parting words to Eisav were: יַעֲבָר נָא אֲדֹנִי לִפְנֵי עַבְדּוֹ וַאֲנִי אֶתְנַהֲלָה לְאִטִּי לְרֶגֶל הַמְּלָאכָה אֲשֶׁר לְפָנַי וּלְרֶגֶל הַיְלָדִים עַד אֲשֶׁר אָבֹא אֶל אֲדֹנִי שֵׂעִירָה — *"Let my lord go ahead of his servant; I will make my way at my slow pace according to the gait of the drove before me and the gait of the children, until I come to my lord at Se'ir."*[358]

Rashi explains that Yaakov is destined to confront Eisav again on the final day, when the forces of evil will be eradicated from the world. This is the day of which it is written, וְעָלוּ מוֹשִׁעִים בְּהַר צִיּוֹן לִשְׁפֹּט אֶת הַר עֵשָׂו וְהָיְתָה לַה׳ הַמְּלוּכָה — *"The redeemers will ascend Mt. Zion, to judge the Mountain of Eisav, and the kingship will be for Hashem."*[359]

May it be soon and in our days.

---

357. *Rashi, Vayikra* 26:42.
358. *Bereishis* 33:14.
359. *Ovadiah* 1:21.

The Eternal Name of Yisrael

AFTER YAAKOV DEFEATED EISAV'S GUARDIAN ANGEL IN battle, the angel said to him as follows: לֹא יַעֲקֹב יֵאָמֵר עוֹד שִׁמְךָ כִּי אִם יִשְׂרָאֵל כִּי שָׂרִיתָ עִם אֱלֹקִים וְעִם אֲנָשִׁים וַתּוּכָל — "*Your name shall no longer be called Yaakov, but instead Yisrael, for you have struggled (sarisa) with angels and men and have been victorious.*"[360]

Later, Hashem gave him the same change of name: וַיֹּאמֶר לוֹ אֱלֹקִים שִׁמְךָ יַעֲקֹב לֹא יִקָּרֵא עוֹד שִׁמְךָ יַעֲקֹב כִּי אִם יִשְׂרָאֵל יִהְיֶה שְׁמֶךָ וַיִּקְרָא אֶת שְׁמוֹ יִשְׂרָאֵל — "*Hashem said to him, 'Your name is now Yaakov; but it shall not be called Yaakov anymore. Yisrael shall be your name.' And He called his name Yisrael.*"[361]

There are two interesting distinctions between the way the angel proclaimed Yaakov's name change, and the way Hashem Himself proclaimed it. First, the angel suggested a reason for the name change: "*For you have struggled with angels and men and have been victorious,*" whereas Hashem offered no apparent reason for the change. Second, after Hashem proclaimed the name change, the Torah repeats it, "*'Yisrael shall be your name.' And He called his name Yisrael.*"

Although there is profound depth and symbolism behind names in general, the name Yisrael has particular symbolism. The Zohar notes that the first initials of the names of all the *Avos* (Patriarchs) and *Immahos* (Matriarchs) are included in the name Yisrael. Yaakov was the greatest of them all, the pinnacle of everything they have striven so hard for three generations to achieve. He combined Avraham's attribute of *chesed* (kindness) with Yitzchak's attribute of *gevurah* (strength), in perfectly balanced *tiferes* (splendor).

Since he incorporated all the myriad facets of human greatness into a complete, well-balanced composition, he was able to pass them down to his children so that every one of his children found meaning and fulfillment in his religious observance. Therefore, albeit that Avraham lost Yishmael and Yitzchak lost Eisav, Yaakov

---

360. *Bereishis* 32:29.
361. Ibid. 35:10.

kept all of his children on the path that leads directly to Hashem. This is another symbolism of his name, יָשָׁר-קל: "straight toward Hashem." For this reason, the entire Jewish nation until the end of time is known not as Bnei Avraham, Bnei Yitzchak, or Bnei Yaakov, but Bnei Yisrael.

Eisav's guardian angel knew that Yaakov's name was destined to be changed to Yisrael, but it did not know, or perhaps did not care to understand, the deeper significance of the name. It realized only that it was defeated in battle, and therefore saw the significance of "*For you have struggled with angels and men and have been victorious.*" It did not realize, however, that this name would be the essence of the Jewish nation until the end of time.

When Hashem gave him the name, He had both intentions. Referring to Yaakov as an individual, He said, "*Yisrael shall be your name.*" Referring to Klal Yisrael as a nation, the Torah adds, "*And He called his name Yisrael.*"

The Midrash[362] adds that Hashem was so proud of Yaakov's achievements that He chose to permanently associate Himself with Yaakov's descendants, by incorporating His own Name (קל) into theirs (יִשְׂרָאֵל). Of this the verse states, יִשְׂרָאֵל אֲשֶׁר בְּךָ אֶתְפָּאָר — "*Yisrael, in you I take pride.*"[363]

By doing so, Hashem granted every Jew that would ever be born an element of His eternal holiness, which can never be destroyed or lost. Regarding this, the Talmud *Yerushalmi* states:

Rabban Shimon ben Lakish said in the name of R' Yannai: HaKadosh Baruch Hu associated His great Name with Bnei Yisrael. This can be compared to a king who had a small key to his inner chamber. He feared that if he would leave the key on its own, it might get lost. Instead, he decided to attach a chain to it, which could easily be spotted if the key would ever be misplaced.[364]

So too, Hashem feared that if He would leave Bnei Yisrael as they are, they might become lost and assimilated among the nations. Instead, He attached His eternal Name to theirs, so that they could endure forever. With this in mind, Yehoshua prayed,

---

362. *Midrash Tanchuma, Kedoshim.*
363. *Yeshayahu* 49:3.
364. *Taanis* 10b (2:6).

"The Canaanite and all the inhabitants of the land will hear[365] *and will surround us and cut off our name from the earth. What will You do for Your great Name?"*[366] Hashem accepted his complaint and said, *"Raise yourself up!"*[367]

To the extent that we are attached to Hashem's holy Name, we can pray for His intervention to rescue us from our adversaries. Even when we are unworthy, Hashem hastens to our defense for the sake of His own honor, lest the nations say, "Where is their God?" However, to the extent that we deny our Jewish heritage and attempt to assimilate among the nations, we lose the best possible defense, which is the Creator's own patronage.

Decades before the Holocaust, the Meshech Chachmah (Rav Meir Simcha of Dvinsk) warned that from Berlin, the very city where Jews considered themselves more successful and integrated into secular society than anywhere else in the world, there would arise a tornado wind of fury and hatred to utterly destroy any bonds of camaraderie that the Jews believed they had forged with the gentiles.

Therefore, in times of peace and in times of war, we must realize that we have no one in the world upon whom to depend, no faithful or sincere ally or political patron, except for our Father in Heaven. By remaining faithful to His Name which is eternally intertwined with our own, we can rely on Him, and Him alone, to come to our salvation at all times.

Bowing Seven Times

וַיִּשָּׂא יַעֲקֹב עֵינָיו וַיַּרְא וְהִנֵּה עֵשָׂו בָּא וְעִמּוֹ אַרְבַּע מֵאוֹת אִישׁ וַיַּחַץ אֶת הַיְלָדִים עַל לֵאָה וְעַל רָחֵל וְעַל שְׁתֵּי הַשְּׁפָחוֹת. וַיָּשֶׂם אֶת הַשְּׁפָחוֹת וְאֶת יַלְדֵיהֶן רִאשֹׁנָה וְאֶת לֵאָה וִילָדֶיהָ אַחֲרֹנִים וְאֶת רָחֵל וְאֶת יוֹסֵף אַחֲרֹנִים. וְהוּא עָבַר לִפְנֵיהֶם וַיִּשְׁתַּחוּ אַרְצָה שֶׁבַע פְּעָמִים עַד גִּשְׁתּוֹ עַד אָחִיו. וַיָּרָץ עֵשָׂו לִקְרָאתוֹ וַיְחַבְּקֵהוּ וַיִּפֹּל עַל צַוָּארָו וַיִּשָּׁקֵהוּ וַיִּבְכּוּ.

---

365. That they lost their battle against the city of Ai.
366. *Yehoshua* 7:9.
367. Ibid. 7:10.

Yaakov raised his eyes and saw — behold, Eisav was coming, and with him were four hundred men — so he divided his children among Leah, Rachel, and the two handmaids. He put the handmaids and their children first, Leah and her children next, and Rachel and Yosef last. Then he himself went on ahead of them and bowed earthward seven times until he reached his brother. Eisav ran toward him, embraced him, fell on his neck, and kissed him; then they wept.[368]

I N THIS WEEK'S *PARASHAH*, WE LEARN THAT YAAKOV BOWED down seven times before he reached his brother Eisav. What did he hope to achieve by bowing? In the Gemara, we learn: Once there was a demon that haunted Abaye's academy. The demon was so powerful that it would even strike two people who entered together, and even during the day. Abaye instructed the people of the city not to invite Rav Acha to stay in their homes. He would then be forced to sleep in the academy, and in his merit perhaps a miracle would occur, by which the demon would be slain.

Rav Acha then entered the academy, and went to sleep. Suddenly, the demon appeared in the form of a seven-headed snake and attacked him. He prayed to Hashem for help, bowing down seven times. With every bow, one head of the demon fell off, until it was killed.[369]

The Sefer HaMakneh explains, based on the Maharsha, that the seven heads of the snake represented the seven forces of impurity that the primordial Snake brought into the world. Each time R' Yaakov bowed to Hashem in prayer, he subjugated one of those forces. The Sefer HaMakneh adds that this was also the intention of Yaakov Avinu, when he bowed down seven times before confronting Eisav. Rashi explains that although Eisav's hatred for Yaakov is well known, he was overcome with mercy at that moment, and kissed Yaakov with all his heart.

Eisav's guardian angel was the Satan, whose name (שָׂטָן) is equal in gematria to the word snake (נָחָשׁ).[370] Before confronting

---

368. *Bereishis* 33:1-4.
369. *Kiddushin* 29b.
370. The rules of gematria allow for a difference of one between the

Eisav, Yaakov first struggled against his angel and subjugated it. As a result, Eisav was inspired to momentary repentance, and he kissed Yaakov with all his heart.

It seems according to this explanation, that Yaakov did not bow down to Eisav. He bowed down to Hashem seven times, and thereby subjugated the seven forces of impurity associated with Eisav's angel.

With this we can understand the Gemara's teaching, that if *a person fails to bow during the Modim prayer of Shemoneh Esrei*, his spine will turn into a snake seven years after his death.[371] These seven years correspond to the seven heads of the primordial Snake, and the seven prostrations necessary to defeat it. If a person fails to bow in submission to Hashem, he strengthens the power of evil in the world. Therefore, his own spine turns into a snake after his death.

Bowing to Hashem is the ultimate symbol of submission and obedience to His majestic splendor. Nothing is as effective as bowing to Hashem, to eliminate the forces of evil from the world, and to draw Heavenly mercy upon us all.

The Sages decreed that upon approaching the Beis HaMikdash, one must bow thirteen times, corresponding to the thirteen breaches that the Greeks made in the walls of the Beis HaMikdash.[372] The breaches in the wall of the Beis HaMikdash were in fact breaches in the hearts and souls of the Jewish people. The Greeks shook the thirteen pillars of our faith, by influencing us with their heretical philosophies and idolatries. Thereby, they hoped to topple the entire spiritual structure of Klal Yisrael. "Carve on the horns of a bull, that you have no portion in the God of Israel," they ordered us. By bowing thirteen times to Hashem, in recognition of His greatness, we repair the thirteen breaches in the wall of our faith. More than any other kind of Divine service, bowing represents total submission, and simple *emunah*. These traits helped our forefathers resist the influence of the Greeks.

The importance of bowing to Hashem is highlighted by the following Midrash:

---

equated words, since in addition to the value of each letter, each word can also count as the number one.

371. *Bava Kamma* 16a.

372. *Middos* 2:3.

R' Yitzchak said: Everything is in the merit of bowing. Avraham returned from Har HaMoriah, only in the merit of bowing, as it is written, "We will bow and return to you."[373] Bnei Yisrael were redeemed only in the merit of bowing, as it states, "The people believed ... and they bowed their heads and prostrated themselves."[374] The Torah was given only in the merit of bowing, as it says, "And you shall bow from a distance."[375] Chanah's prayers were answered in the merit of bowing, as it is written, "And he prostrated there to Hashem."[376] The exiles will be gathered together in the merit of bowing, as it is written, "And it shall be on that day, that a great shofar will be blown... and they will prostrate themselves to Hashem on the holy mountain in Yerushalayim."[377] The Beis HaMikdash was built in the merit of bowing, as it is written, "Exalt Hashem our God, and bow at His footstool."[378] The dead will be revivified in the merit of bowing, as it is written, "Come, let us prostrate ourselves, and bow, let us kneel before Hashem, our Maker."[379]

Portent of Things to Come

THE RAMBAN WRITES IN HIS INTRODUCTION TO THIS week's *parashah*: This *parashah* was written to reveal how Hashem rescued His servant Yaakov from a force mightier than he, and sent His angel to protect him. The *parashah* further teaches us that Yaakov did not rely on the merit of his righteousness, but pursued every practical means to his salvation. Furthermore, the *parashah* is a symbol for generations to come, since everything that occurred to our forefather in his struggle against Eisav is destined to occur to us in our own struggles against

---

373. *Bereishis* 22:5.
374. *Shemos* 4:31.
375. Ibid. 24:1.
376. *I Shmuel* 1:28.
377. *Yeshayahu* 27:13.
378. *Tehillim* 99:5.
379. Ibid. 95:6.

Eisav's heirs. It is therefore fitting that we follow the example set by the *tzaddik*, by preparing ourselves with prayer (as Yaakov prayed), gifts (as Yaakov sent gifts to Eisav), and military tactics (as Yaakov divided his family into two camps, so that one could escape if Eisav were to strike the other).

The Ramban stresses the practical lessons we must glean from the deeds of our forefathers, which were recorded in the Torah to guide us in all our ways. Specifically in the case of Yaakov's struggle against Eisav, the Torah provides us with a survival guide for our long, bitter sojourn in *Galus*. There are times when we can bribe our enemies to loosen their cruel grasp upon us. There are times when tactical maneuvers can prove efficient. And there are times when our only hope is prayer.

In addition to the practical message contained herein, we also learn of the great reservoir of merit that Yaakov left for his descendants. We draw from his great merit, when our own merit would prove insufficient.

The Ramban further explains that with every preparation Yaakov made for his confrontation with Eisav, he included a prayer that Hashem may rescue his descendants from Eisav's heirs.

"*He (Yaakov) said: If Eisav comes to the one camp and strikes it down, the remaining camp shall survive.*"[380] Yaakov realized that Hashem would never let all his children be destroyed by Eisav. At the very least, one camp would survive. This was an omen that Eisav's descendants would never be able to eradicate the name of Israel. They may harm a segment of us in some of their lands, but when one king passes a harsh decree against our possessions or our lives, another king will have mercy on us, and rescue the fugitives that escape to his land. Thus, the Midrash explains this verse, "If Eisav comes to the one camp" — our brethren in southern Israel, "the remaining camp shall survive" — our brethren in the Diaspora.[381] As such, this *parashah* serves as a portent for generations to come.[382]

Later in the *parashah*, we find another hint for the future: "He put

---

380. *Bereishis* 32:9.
381. *Bereishis Rabbah* 76:3.
382. *Ramban, Bereishis* 32:9.

in his servants' charge each drove separately and said to his servants: 'Pass on ahead of me and leave a space between drove and drove.'" The Midrash finds in this another omen. Yaakov prayed before Hashem saying: "Master of the Universe! If suffering must befall my children, do not bring it upon them all at once. Give them time to recover between one blow and the next."[383] This was an omen that Yaakov's descendants would have time to recuperate between the weighty taxes that Eisav's descendants would level upon them.[384]

A third hint is found in this next verse:

"Let my master pass before me, and I will continue on at the slow pace of my herd and children, until I meet up with my master in Se'ir." The Midrash explains that Yaakov is destined to meet up again with Eisav in the Era of Mashiach.[385] Regarding this, the verse states, "The redeemers will ascend Mount Tzion to judge the Mountain of Eisav."[386,387]

When Yaakov assured Eisav that they would meet again, he lifted his eyes toward Heaven in prayer, that Mashiach would one day arrive to lead his descendants into battle against Eisav and the forces of the *yetzer hara* that he represents, to cleanse the world of evil, and herald a new era in which the conclusion of this verse will be fulfilled: וְהָיְתָה לַה׳ הַמְּלוּכָה — *"And the kingship shall be Hashem's."*[388] May it be soon and in our days.

Emulating Our Forefathers

In order to draw from the reservoir of eternal merit that our forefathers created, we must try to the best of our ability to emulate their ways, and walk on the path that they paved. Accordingly, we learn in Tanna D'Vei Eliyahu that each person is obligated to ask himself: מָתַי יַגִּיעוּ מֶעֲשַׂי לְמַעֲשֵׂי אֲבוֹתַי — *"When will my deeds reach those of my fathers?"*[389]

---

383. *Bereishis Rabbah* 75:13.
384. *Ramban, Bereishis* 32:17.
385. *Bereishis Rabbah* 78:14.
386. *Ovadiah* 1:21.
387. *Ramban, Bereishis* 33:14.
388. *Ovadiah* 1:21.
389. *Tanna D'Vei Eliyahu* Ch. 25.

As mentioned in *Parashas Vayeitzei*, R' Yisrael of Rizhin explained that we cannot actually hope to equal their greatness, but we must at least aspire that our deeds may resemble theirs. However, perhaps we may argue that it is indeed possible for our deeds to match theirs to some extent, not due to our own righteousness, but due to the great reserves of moral and spiritual determination that they instilled in our nation. By clearing the path for us to follow, the *Avos* allowed us to climb after them to their towering heights of holiness. They stretch their hands down from Heaven, and if we only reach up as high as we can, they will grasp hold of us to pull us up to their level.

One trait we must learn from our forefathers is diligence in Torah study. The Gemara states that ever since the days of our forefathers, there have always been yeshivos for the Jewish people. Avraham, Yitzchak, and Yaakov all headed yeshivos, where they disseminated Hashem's holy Torah. [390]

The Chida writes that the *Avos* would study Torah for fifteen hours each day.[391] My revered mentor, the Tzanzer Rebbe , would add that it is impossible to presume that our forefathers spent nine precious hours of each day without studying Torah. Rather, he explained based on the Gemara that states that pious men would prepare for prayer for one hour, pray for an hour, and pause for an hour after prayer. Accordingly, the *Avos* spent nine hours in prayer each day, three hours for each prayer — leaving only fifteen hours for them to study Torah.

Thus, we can well understand why the Chida himself writes elsewhere that they contemplated Torah wisdom even as they dreamed. Otherwise, they would not fill their quota of fifteen hours a day.

In any case, we see from here that Torah study has been the cornerstone of Jewish observance ever since the days of our forefathers. Although we cannot hope to match their fifteen hours a day of study, we can and must learn from their example to utilize our time and resources to the best of our ability, in wholehearted dedication to the holy Torah.

---

390. *Yoma* 28b.
391. *Midbar Kideimos: Aleph.*

The Pillar of Torah

The world is supported by three pillars: Torah, *Avodah* (prayer and sacrifice), and Acts of Kindness.[392] The Zohar adds that each of the *Avos* supported a different pillar.[393] Avraham supported the pillar of Kindness, by graciously welcoming guests into his home. Yitzchak supported the pillar of *Avodah*, by offering himself as a sacrifice. Yaakov supported the pillar of Torah, with his unflagging diligence in Torah study.

As we previously noted, five times throughout the Torah Yaakov's name is spelled יַעֲקוֹב, with an extra *vav*; while five times Eliyahu HaNavi's name is spelled אֵלִיָּה, with the *vav* missing. Our Sages explain that Yaakov took the letter *vav* from Eliyahu's name as collateral, to assure that Eliyahu would come to herald the redemption of Yaakov's children.[394]

The commentaries offer several explanations why this hint was repeated five times. R' Eliyahu Mizrachi explains that the five *vavs* represent the Five Books of the Torah. It was as if Yaakov made Eliyahu swear on a *Sefer Torah* (just as an oath is administered in Beis Din) that he would come to redeem Yaakov's children. The Maharal, on the other hand, explains that the five *vavs* represent five fingers, as if to say that Yaakov and Eliyahu shook hands on this deal.[395]

Perhaps on a deeper level this comes to teach us that while Eliyahu will be the one who comes to herald the redemption, Yaakov will be the one to bring the redemption about, in the merit of his own diligence in Torah study, and the diligence he inspires in his descendants.

The *melavah malkah seudah* on Motza'ei Shabbos is dedicated in memory of David HaMelech. During this meal, it is customary to sing about Eliyahu HaNavi, as well as "Do Not Fear, My Servant Yaakov." We sing for Yaakov, that he need not fear for the fate of his descendants. Eliyahu will one day fulfill his vow, and herald the redemption, when the scion of David will at long last come to redeem us. May it be soon and in our days.

---

392. *Pirkei Avos* 1:2.
393. *Zohar* I, p, 146.
394. *Rashi, Vayikra* 26:42.
395. *Gur Aryeh*, ibid.

פרשת וישב

Parashas Vayeishev

In the Image of the Creator

I N THIS WEEK'S *PARASHAH* WE FIND THE EPISODE OF
Yehudah and Tamar. Rather than openly revealing Yehudah's
involvement in her predicament, Tamar made a discreet hint
that only Yehudah would understand: הוא מוּצֵאת וְהִיא שָׁלְחָה אֶל
חָמִיהָ לֵאמֹר לְאִישׁ אֲשֶׁר אֵלֶּה לּוֹ אָנֹכִי הָרָה — "*As she was taken out [to be
executed], she sent word to her father-in-law saying, 'By the man to
whom these belong, I am with child.' "*[396]

Had Yehudah ignored her hint, Tamar would surely have
been burned to death and no one would have been the wiser. Yet
Yehudah confessed and her life was spared. Our Sages learn from
Tamar's example that it is better to be thrown into a fiery furnace
than to humiliate another person in public.[397]

Concern for the feelings of others is in fact the very bedrock of
our Torah, as R' Akiva said, *"Love your neighbor as yourself —* this
is a major rule of the Torah."[398] For this reason, mitzvos that involve

---

396. *Bereishis* 38:25.
397. *Berachos* 43b; *Bava Metzia* 59a; *Sotah* 10b.
398. *Talmud Yerushalmi, Nedarim* 9:4.

helping other people are far more precious in Heaven than mitzvos between man and God alone.[399]

———•———

The importance of being sensitive to other's feelings, and the sacrifices this often entails, is well illustrated by the story of R' Chanina bar Chama. As Rebbi [R' Yehudah HaNasi] lay on his death-bed, he appointed R' Chanina to lead the yeshivah after his demise. Yet when Rebbi died and the time came for R' Chanina to assume the mantle of leadership, he refused, since he feared this might offend his peer, R' Afeis, who was two-and-a-half years older. R' Chanina stepped aside, allowing R' Afeis to lead the Yeshivah until his demise, after which R' Chanina finally accepted the position.[400]

Rebbi knew that R' Afeis was older, and no doubt was also sensitive to R' Afeis' feelings. Nevertheless, he felt that R' Chanina was better suited for the position. Furthermore, Rebbi had already exhibited his powers of *ru'ach hakodesh*, and could thus be assumed to have appointed R' Chanina in accordance with Hashem's will. Moreover, R' Chanina's singular greatness was his unflinching loyalty to Rebbi, such that he never once passed any halachic ruling unless he had heard it directly from Rebbi.[401] R' Chanina also taught, "Who is destined for the reward of the World to Come? He whose teachers are pleased with him."[402]

In light of all this, we can understand that R' Chanina had every incentive in the world to comply with Rebbi's last wishes, yet he felt himself simply unable to do so at the expense of his colleague's honor. Lest we think that R' Chanina erred in this decision, the Talmud *Yerushalmi* relates that when his disciples asked him by what virtue he merited to live to such a venerable old age, he answered that he was granted long life in reward for stepping aside in honor of R' Afeis.[403]

———•———

---

399. *Rosh, Pe'ah* 1:1.
400. *Kesubos* 103b.
401. *Talmud Yerushalmi: Niddah* 2:7.
402. *Shabbos* 153a.
403. *Talmud Yerushalmi: Taanis* 20b.

A similar example may be brought from the story of Rava, the preeminent Sage of his era, who merited to have all his halachic debates decided in his favor (with only six exceptions, in which the halachah follows Abaye). Furthermore, when all the yeshivos of his time were forced to close, only his yeshivah in Mechuza remained open.[404]

How did Rava rise to such a towering level of prominence? One might think that this was in the merit of his passionate devotion to Torah study, such that the Gemara describes how he was so absorbed by his Torah study that he did not even notice that his hands were crushed beneath his feet and were oozing blood.[405]

Yet in truth Gemara provides a different incident in his life, in which we see that it was not the blood of his Torah study that led to his greatness, but the blood of his respect for others. The Gemara states that when Rava parted from his mentor, Rav Yosef, he would walk backward in respect, rather than disrespectfully turning his back to him (even though Rav Yosef was blind and would not have noticed). As he backed out of the room, he crashed into a pillar and stained it with his blood. When Rav Yosef was told what happened he said, "May you be raised to leadership over the entire city," which Rashi explains to be, "May you be the Rosh Yeshivah of the city," while Rabbeinu Chananel explains it to mean, "May the halachah always be decided in your favor." [406]

What better example do we need than the well-known story of R' Akiva's 24,000 disciples whose Talmudic greatness was surely phenomenal, yet they all died within a short period of time for failing to show one another the proper respect. The world was then desolate for lack of Torah wisdom until R' Akiva gave *semichah* to a new generation of disciples, including R' Meir, R' Yehudah, R' Yose, R' Shimon, and R' Elazar ben Shamua. [407]

---

404. *Iggeres Rav Sherira Gaon.*
405. *Shabbos* 88a.
406. *Yoma* 53a.
407. *Yevamos* 62b.

The severity of their punishment is shocking. Where do we ever find that such terrible death and destruction can descend for no sin other than failing to respect someone's feelings? Yet the truth is that each person is held accountable to the level of decency that can rightfully be expected of him. For a person without a proper role model of value and virtue, we must expect a certain amount of coarse behavior. However, these were the disciples of R' Akiva, who taught them throughout their lives, "Man is precious, since he was created in the image of God."[408] In other words, respect for mankind is a necessary extension of respect for God in Whose image we were created. R' Akiva also taught them, *Love your neighbor as yourself — this is a major rule of the Torah."* Having failed to learn from the teachings and personal example of a Rebbi whose entire message was one of respect and consideration for others, they were held accountable to the highest degree.

Realizing the mistake his first generation of disciples had made, he warned his later disciples: "I had 24,000 disciples, all of whom died for failing to respect one another in their Torah study. Do not repeat their mistake."[409]

These new disciples formed the backbone of the Oral Tradition of Torah study, such that the Gemara states:

The unnamed teachings in the Mishnah are from R' Meir; in Sifra from R' Yehudah; in Sifri from R' Shimon; in Tosefta from R' Nechemyah, and all of them follow the teachings they received from R' Akiva.[410]

The entire body of Oral Law that exists in our hands today is the legacy of R' Akiva, in the merit of his second generation of disciples. They internalized his message of *"Love your neighbor as yourself"* and developed it, each adding his own insights. R' Meir taught: כָּל הַמְבָרֵךְ אֶת יִשְׂרָאֵל כְּאִלּוּ מְבָרֵךְ אֶת הַשְּׁכִינָה — *"Anyone who blesses his fellow Jew is considered as if he has blessed the Shechinah."*[411]

He furthermore exhorted us: וֶהֱוֵי שְׁפַל רוּחַ בִּפְנֵי כָל אָדָם — *"Be of meek and humble spirit before all people."*[412]

---

408. *Pirkei Avos* 3:18.
409. *Koheles Rabbah* 11.
410. *Sanhedrin* 86a.
411. *Midrash Tanchuma, Vayechi* 5.
412. *Pirkei Avos* 4:12.

R' Yehudah taught: כָּל מִי שֶׁמְקַבֵּל פְּנֵי חֲבֵרִים כְּאִלוּ מְקַבֵּל פְּנֵי שְׁכִינָה — "Anyone who greets talmidei chachamim is considered as if he has greeted the Shechinah."[413]

R' Yose ben Chalafta, another of R' Akiva's second generation of disciples, once said of himself: מִיָמַי לֹא עָבַרְתִּי עַל דִּבְרֵי חֲבֵרַי יוֹדֵעַ אֲנִי בְּעַצְמִי שֶׁאֵינִי כֹהֵן אִם אוֹמְרִים לִי חֲבֵרַי עֲלֵה לְדוּכָן אֲנִי עוֹלֶה — "In all my life, I never once disobeyed my peers. I am not a Kohen, yet if my peers would tell me to ascend the platform [to recite the Priestly Blessing] I would do so."[414]

He also taught: אֲפִילוּ לֹא הֵאִיר עֵינָיו אֶלָּא בְּמִשְׁנָה אַחַת זֶה הוּא רַבּוֹ — "Even if one's peer has done no more than explain to him a single Mishnah, he must honor him as his rebbi."[415]

R' Elazar ben Shamua taught: יְהִי כְבוֹד תַּלְמִידְךָ חָבִיב עָלֶיךָ כְּשֶׁלָּךְ וּכְבוֹד חֲבֵרְךָ כְּמוֹרָא רַבָּךְ וּמוֹרָא רַבָּךְ כְּמוֹרָא שָׁמַיִם — "Let the honor of your student be as precious as your own; the honor of your peer as the reverence of your teacher; and the reverence of your teacher as the awe of Heaven."[416]

Yet perhaps the most powerfully worded teaching of all is the message that Rabban Shimon ben Yochai gleaned from this week's parashah: נוֹחַ לוֹ לְאָדָם שֶׁיַּפִּיל עַצְמוֹ לְכִבְשַׁן הָאֵשׁ וְאַל יַלְבִּין פְּנֵי חֲבֵרוֹ בְּרַבִּים — "It is better to be thrown into a fiery furnace than to embarrass another person in public."

By risking her life to protect the dignity of Yehudah, Tamar provided an eternal message of respect and consideration, even for those who are guilty of doing us harm. By showing respect to one another, we show respect to the Creator in Whose image we were formed.

---

413. *Shir HaShirim Rabbah* 2:18.
414. *Shabbos* 118b.
415. *Bava Metzia* 33a.
416. *Pirkei Avos* 4:15.

Yosef's Test

YOSEF SAID, "MY FATHER WAS TESTED. MY GRAND-father was tested. Yet I have never been tested."

HaKadosh Baruch Hu then said to him, "By your life I swear, that I will test you more than I tested them."[417]

Yosef's forefathers passed grave and difficult tests to prove their faithfulness to Hashem. Avraham Avinu opted to be thrown into a fiery furnace in Uhr Kasdim, rather than renounce his belief in the one true God. Yitzchak Avinu stretched out his neck to be slaughtered on the altar on Mt. Moriah, in perfect obedience to Hashem's command. Why was Yosef's test, of withstanding the advances of Potiphar's wife, considered more difficult than the tests of his forefathers, who were asked to forfeit their very lives?

The Zohar[418] states that only after Yosef passed this test, did he receive the title of *tzaddik yesod olam* — "the righteous pillar of the world."[419] What does this title imply, and what was so unique about his test, that earned him this prestigious title?

The temptation for promiscuity can be so powerful, that it can ensnare even the most lofty and righteous individuals, dragging them down to the dark abyss. In discussing the laws of separation between men and women, the Gemara cites the following incident:

Once, a group of female captives were led through the city of Naharda'a. Rav Amram raised money to redeem them from captivity, and then provided them shelter in the second floor of his home. (To prevent the risk of sin) he removed the ladder that led to their dwelling. When one of the women passed by the window, a light shone from her down to the house below (Rashi — due to her great beauty). Rav Amram then took a ladder that even ten people could not normally carry. He carried it to the window, and began to ascend. When he reached half its height, he dug his heels down (Rashi — to stop himself from ascending), and began to yell, "Fire in Amram's house! Fire in Amram's house!" (Rashi — to summon

---

417. *Bereishis Rabbah* 87.
418. *Zohar* I, 194b.
419. *Mishlei* 10:25.

his neighbors, who would then rescue him from his uncontrollable urge to sin).

Thinking that his house was on fire, the Sages quickly came to help. "You have shamed us," they told him.

"Better that you be shamed by me in this world, and not be shamed by [your association with] me in the World to Come," he answered.

He then compelled his *yetzer hara* to leave him by oath. As it left, it appeared like a pillar of fire. "You are made of fire, while I am made of mere flesh, yet I have defeated you," he told it.[420]

From here we learn, that the *yetzer hara* is given leave to twist the laws of nature. It can give one man the strength of many, in order to make him sin. No doubt, it directed all its powers against Yosef, to lure him into the trap of sin. The Midrash describes the many ploys Potiphar's wife used to seduce him. Nonetheless, Yosef did not yield to her wiles. He was truly a *tzaddik yesod olam*, standing strong as a marble pillar, in the face of unbearable temptation.

The Torah tells us that when Potiphar's wife grabbed hold of the garments Yosef was wearing and demanded his attention, he fled from her (וַיָּנָס). This same word is used to describe how the waters of the Yam Suf fled before Bnei Yisrael, "הַיָּם רָאָה וַיָּנֹס," allowing them to pass through on dry land. Our Sages infer from this parallel, that the sea split in the merit of Yosef's remains, which Bnei Yisrael carried with them as they left Egypt.[421] This was a fitting reward for Yosef. Just as he rose beyond the restraints of his nature, withstanding unbearable temptation, so too were the laws of nature suspended for the sake of his descendants, making the sea split before them.

Rav Amram needed only to withstand the *yetzer hara* for a short while, but Yosef had to fight against it day after day, for one full year, as Potiphar's wife incessantly made advances upon him.[422] It is much easier to pass even the most difficult test, if it only lasts for a short and limited period. A constant barrage of temptation is much harder, since it leads to the slow erosion of one's ideals. The true

---

420. *Kiddushin* 81a.
421. *Bereishis Rabbah* 87.
422. *Midrash Tanchuma, Vayeishev* 12.

measure of spiritual achievement cannot be judged by a single feat of greatness, but only by a steady commitment, which holds true in the test of time. The Gemara demonstrates this important point with the following: Our Sages taught: When R' Yose ben Kisma fell ill, R' Chanina ben Teradyon went to visit him. "Chanina, my brother," he said. "Do you not realize that Heaven has granted kingship to this nation (the Romans)? They have destroyed His House, burned His Sanctuary, killed His righteous, destroyed the best of His servants, and they still endure. I have heard that you gather assemblies in public to teach them Torah, with a Torah scroll on your lap."

"Heaven will have mercy," answer R' Chanina.

"I offer you logical arguments, and you respond: 'Heaven will have mercy'?! I would be surprised if they don't burn you in fire together with the Torah scroll," said R' Yose.

"Will I have a place in the World to Come?" asked R' Chanina.

"Have you done any good deeds?" asked R' Yose.

"The money I set aside for my Purim meal became intermingled with *tzedakah* money, so I gave it all to the poor," answered R' Chanina.

"If so, may my place in Heaven be close to yours," said R' Yose.[423]

Why did R' Yose ask R' Chanina if he had done any good deeds? Is it not impressive enough that R' Chanina had risked his life to spread Torah in Klal Yisrael? Based on the premise stated above, we can well understand this. R' Chanina had proven that he was willing to die in sanctification of Hashem's Name. However, R' Yose wanted to see if R' Chanina had lived his life, day after day, in all his mundane daily activities, in a way that likewise sanctifies Hashem's Name. This is a totally different challenge. When R' Chanina proved that he had done so, R' Yossi answered that his standing in Heaven was truly enviable.

The Torah tells us that when Yosef fled from the advances of Potiphar's wife, she took hold of his garment, and he was forced to leave it behind, and run out into the street. This was an amazing display of *yiras Shamayim*. Yosef realized that by putting his clothes on display, Potiphar's wife could offer clear "proof" that he had assaulted her. It would have been much more prudent for him to

---

423. *Avodah Zarah* 18a.

retrieve his clothes, and then make his escape. However, he feared to spend even one more moment in her presence, lest he fall prey to sin. Instead, he left his clothes behind, no doubt presuming that he was bringing the death penalty upon himself by doing so. For his great sacrifice, to avoid even the risk of sin, he became the *tzaddik yesod olam* — the pillar of righteousness that supports the world.

May his merit stand on our behalf, that we may also be protected from sin.

The Light of Mashiach

THIS WEEK'S *PARASHAH* PRESENTS US WITH A SERIES OF events that are exceedingly difficult for us to understand. How did Yosef find his way from the peace and tranquility of his father's home to the dungeons of Egypt, and ultimately to the heights of power, amassing the fortunes of the known world? Furthermore, why was the episode of Yehudah and Tamar inserted in the middle of this narrative? The two episodes seem entirely unrelated.

The Midrash states as follows: R' Shmuel bar Nachman expounded on the *pasuk*, "For I know the thoughts that I am thinking of you, says Hashem, thoughts of peace, and not of evil, in order to give you future and hope."[424]

The brothers were occupied with the sale of Yosef, Yosef was occupied with his sackcloth and fasting (in anguish over his enslavement), Reuven was occupied with his sackcloth and fasting (in penitence for moving his father's bed), Yaakov was occupied with his sackcloth and fasting (in mourning over Yosef), Yehudah was occupied in finding a wife, and HaKadosh Baruch Hu was involved in creating the light of Mashiach.

"At that time, Yehudah descended"[425] (to find a wife. He then fathered the line from which Mashiach would ultimately be born).

---

424. *Yirmiyahu* 29:11.
425. *Bereishis* 38:1.

"Before she feels her birthpangs, she will have given birth."[426] The ultimate redeemer was born before the birth of the first oppressor. For this reason, the *pasuk*, "At that time Yehudah descended," follows the *pasuk*, "The Midianites sold him to Egypt."[427]

At the time that events were being set into place, which would ultimately lead to our servitude in Egypt, Hashem was simultaneously setting in place Yehudah's progeny, from which Mashiach would be born, to redeem us from our final exile.

There were many players in this saga. Each person went about his own business, perhaps with little thought of the true magnitude of his role. Everyone minded his own business, yet Hashem was orchestrating all their activities from above, weaving the threads together into the tapestry that He had planned. Unbeknownst to them, they were being guided in the path they needed to travel, to reach the light of Mashiach.

The same holds true for their descendants, the Jewish people throughout the generations. Each person has the free choice to lead his life as he sees fit. He can choose to lead a life of virtue, or the opposite, *chas v'shalom*. Hashem rewards the righteous for their mitzvos, and punishes the wicked for their sins. Yet despite what we might plan to accomplish through our actions, Hashem has His own plans for us. He stands Above, guiding our every movement, in perfect choreography, in order to fulfill His own plan: "thoughts of peace, and not of evil, to give us future and hope." We do not always envision the destination toward which our actions bring us, but Hashem advances us toward this destination nonetheless.

A perfect example of this can be found in the story of Shaul HaMelech. He was commanded to eradicate each and every member of the nation of Amalek. In his misplaced mercy, he spared the life of the Amalekite king, Agag, who then proceeded to father a line of descendants from which Haman would be born. Shaul's own descendants, Mordechai and Esther, defeated Haman, and Haman's nefarious plot to destroy the Jews was turned against him. Instead of the destruction Haman had planned, the Jews enjoyed days of "light, joy, happiness, and glory." They defeated their

---

426. *Yeshayahu* 66:7.
427. *Bereishis Rabbah* 85.

enemies, and Hashem's holy Name was sanctified in the world. Shaul was punished for failing to kill Agag, regardless of the fact that Agag's survival, and the ultimate birth and death of Haman, was a cause of great rejoicing for the Jews.

The same is true in the life of each and every Jew. We must faithfully obey the commandments we were given, although we have little control over our destiny. The development of our personal lives, the progress of the Jewish people, and the unfolding events of history are all in the hands of the Almighty, Who guides everything toward the light of Mashiach, in a manner that is far beyond our comprehension. As the *pasuk* states: כִּי לֹא מַחְשְׁבוֹתַי מַחְשְׁבוֹתֵיכֶם וְלֹא דַרְכֵיכֶם דְּרָכָי נְאֻם ה׳. כִּי גָבְהוּ שָׁמַיִם מֵאָרֶץ כֵּן גָּבְהוּ דְרָכַי מִדַּרְכֵיכֶם וּמַחְשְׁבֹתַי מִמַּחְשְׁבֹתֵיכֶם — "*For My thoughts are not as your thoughts, and your ways are not as Mine, says Hashem. As the Heavens are high above the earth, so too are My ways above your ways, and My thoughts above your thoughts.*"[428]

We pray that our deeds will find favor before Hashem, and that we may merit to participate in spreading the light of Mashiach, may he come soon and in our days.

---

428. *Yeshayahu* 55:8,9.

פרשת מקץ
Parashas Mikeitz

The Bonds of Brotherhood

THE COMMENTARIES STRUGGLE TO UNDERSTAND THE seemingly cruel hoax to which Yosef subjected his brothers, when he concealed his true identity from them, accused them of espionage, incarcerated Shimon, and finally planted his cup in Binyamin's sack to incriminate him for a theft he did not commit.

Yosef is known throughout the generations as "Yosef HaTzaddik," implying that he was perfectly righteous in all matters, both *bein adam la'Makom* (between man and God) and *bein adam la'chaveiro* (between man and his fellow).[429] How could a *tzaddik* cause his brothers such terrible suffering? And why did he show no mercy to his aged father, overwrought with grief and fear for the fate of his sons, as the Torah so poignantly relates:

וַיֹּאמֶר אֲלֵהֶם יַעֲקֹב אֲבִיהֶם אֹתִי שִׁכַּלְתֶּם יוֹסֵף אֵינֶנּוּ וְשִׁמְעוֹן אֵינֶנּוּ וְאֶת בִּנְיָמִן תִּקָּחוּ עָלַי הָיוּ כֻלָּנָה. וַיֹּאמֶר רְאוּבֵן אֶל אָבִיו לֵאמֹר אֶת שְׁנֵי בָנַי תָּמִית אִם לֹא אֲבִיאֶנּוּ אֵלֶיךָ תְּנָה אֹתוֹ עַל יָדִי וַאֲנִי אֲשִׁיבֶנּוּ אֵלֶיךָ. וַיֹּאמֶר לֹא יֵרֵד בְּנִי עִמָּכֶם כִּי אָחִיו מֵת וְהוּא לְבַדּוֹ נִשְׁאָר וּקְרָאָהוּ אָסוֹן בַּדֶּרֶךְ אֲשֶׁר תֵּלְכוּ בָהּ וְהוֹרַדְתֶּם אֶת שֵׂיבָתִי בְּיָגוֹן שְׁאוֹלָה.

---

429. *Sotah* 13b, *Rashi* s.v. *Kiyeim zeh mah she'kasuv b'zeh.*

Their father Yaakov said to them, "I am the one whom you bereaved! Yosef is gone, Shimon is gone, and now you would take away Binyamin? Upon me has it all fallen!" Then Reuven told his father, saying, "You may slay my two sons if I fail to bring him back to you. Put him in my care and I will return him to you." But he said, "My son shall not go down with you, for his brother is dead and he alone is left. Should disaster befall him on the journey which you shall take, then you will have brought down my hoariness in sorrow to the grave."[430]

For the entire period of twenty-two years that Yosef was separated from his father, he must have realized Yaakov's anguish in imagining him to be dead. Common decency should have required him to inform his father of his wellbeing, as soon as he was freed from prison. Why then did he conceal his identity until the very last moment?

According to the Ramban, Yosef understood that his dreams of his family bowing down to him were a prophetic vision. To bring about the fulfillment of this prophecy, he had no choice but to conceal his identity, despite the regrettable anguish that this would cause Yaakov and his sons. [431]

The Akeidas Yitzchak adds that Yosef had to place his brothers in a situation where they would be forced to take a stand in Binyamin's defense, and thereby thoroughly atone for their sins against Yosef.[432]

Based on these insights, we can follow the development of Yosef's plan step-by-step. The sin of the brothers in kidnapping Yosef and selling him as a slave was not as much the act of violence itself, which perhaps could have been justified by any one of the reasons offered by the commentaries.[433] Rather, even after all the justifications, the accusation of their utter mercilessness hovered over their heads, as they themselves confessed: וַיֹּאמְרוּ אִישׁ אֶל אָחִיו אֲבָל אֲשֵׁמִים אֲנַחְנוּ עַל אָחִינוּ אֲשֶׁר רָאִינוּ צָרַת נַפְשׁוֹ בְּהִתְחַנְנוֹ אֵלֵינוּ וְלֹא שָׁמָעְנוּ עַל כֵּן בָּאָה אֵלֵינוּ הַצָּרָה הַזֹּאת — *"They then said to one another, 'Indeed*

---

430. *Bereishis* 42:36-38.
431. *Ramban's* commentary on *Bereishis* 42:9.
432. *Akeidas Yitzchak: Sha'ar* 30. See also *Abarbanel.*
433. See commentaries on *Bereishis* 37:18, *Seforno, Ohr HaChaim,* et al.

we are guilty concerning our brother inasmuch as we saw his heart-felt anguish when he pleaded with us and we paid no heed; that is why this anguish has come upon us.' "[434]

Where was the compassion that every sensitive person should naturally feel toward his own flesh and blood? Where was the brotherly love that is the foundation of our entire Torah? How could they have ignored his desperate cries for mercy, while they sat down to eat a meal? This was their inexcusable sin, which Yosef felt obligated at all costs to expunge, for the benefit of all future generations of Klal Yisrael.

The early Poskim discuss the concept of "*teshuvas hamishkal* — repentance to counterbalance the sin,"[435] which involves a certain degree of suffering that a person must endure to purify himself of the pleasure he derived from sin. In this case, the brothers had to suffer to rectify their having overcome their innate brotherly love and compassion to harm Yosef.

Yosef first demanded of them, וְאֶת אֲחִיכֶם הַקָּטֹן תָּבִיאוּ אֵלַי — "*Bring me your youngest brother*,"[436] striking their hearts with the first pangs of fear for Binyamin's welfare, while meanwhile awakening their feelings of love and brotherhood for him. It was then that they first said, אֲבָל אֲשֵׁמִים אֲנַחְנוּ עַל אָחִינוּ — "*We are guilty of harming our brother.*" They had begun to recognize the atrocity of their sin in severing the bonds of brotherhood by selling Yosef as a slave.

By admitting their mistake, they had taken the first step in their path toward *teshuvah*. Their second step was taken when they offered themselves together in slavery in payment for the theft of the cup, וְגַם אֲנַחְנוּ נִהְיֶה לַאדֹנִי לַעֲבָדִים — "*We shall also be slaves to our master*."[437] By resolving to face their difficulties as a group, they had reached the admirable recognition that all Jews are truly responsible for one another.[438]

The completion of their *teshuvah* was finally attained when Yehudah declared his willingness to become Yosef's slave in place

---

434. *Bereishis* 42:21.
435. See *Orchos Tzaddikim: Shaar HaTeshuvah.*
436. *Bereishis* 42:20.
437. Ibid. 44:9.
438. *Shevuos* 39a.

of Binyamin. The highest expression of love for another human being is when one is willing to accept suffering in his stead, as we find expressed in the Mishnah, "R' Yishmael said: Let me be the atonement for Bnei Yisrael."[439] Rav Ovadiah MiBartenura explains that in R' Yishmael's great love for the Jewish people, he prayed that any misfortune intended for Bnei Yisrael should befall him instead.

Only after Yosef saw that his plan had come to fruition, and the solid foundations of brotherly love had indeed been laid in Klal Yisrael, was he at last able to reveal himself and express to them the great love that he felt toward them: וַיֹּאמֶר יוֹסֵף אֶל אֶחָיו גְּשׁוּ נָא אֵלַי וַיִּגָּשׁוּ וַיֹּאמֶר אֲנִי יוֹסֵף אֲחִיכֶם אֲשֶׁר מְכַרְתֶּם אֹתִי מִצְרָיְמָה ... וְהִנֵּה עֵינֵיכֶם רֹאוֹת וְעֵינֵי אָחִי בִנְיָמִין כִּי פִי הַמְדַבֵּר אֲלֵיכֶם — "Then Yosef said to his brothers, 'Come close to me, if you please,' and they came close. And he said, 'I am Yosef your brother — it is me, whom you sold into Egypt ... Behold! Your eyes see as do the eyes of my brother Binyamin that it is my mouth that is speaking to you.'"[440]

Rashi explains that after Yosef revealed his identity, he saw his brothers draw backward in dismay. He sympathized with their shame and soothed their hearts with soft, warm supplications to draw close to him in brotherhood. He assured them that just as he had no grievances against Binyamin, who took no part in their crime, he had no grievance against them either.[441] Their sin against him had been atoned and the bonds of brotherhood were fully restored.

May we also merit to mend the rifts in our families and communities, drawing together in love and brotherhood, and so merit the fulfillment of Moshe Rabbeinu's prophecy: וַיְהִי בִישֻׁרוּן מֶלֶךְ בְּהִתְאַסֵּף רָאשֵׁי עָם יַחַד שִׁבְטֵי יִשְׂרָאֵל — "He shall be King in Yeshurun, when the heads of the nation gather together, and the Tribes of Israel are united."[442]

Hashem's Kingship will be revealed upon us when at long last we unite together in peace and brotherhood.[443]

---

439. *Negaim* 2:1.
440. *Bereishis* 45:4,12.
441. *Rashi.*
442. *Devarim* 33:5.
443. *Rashi.*

The Greatest Consideration

THE OHR HACHAIM ASKS WHY YOSEF FAILED TO CONtact his father during the entire time that he served as steward of Potiphar's house and viceroy of Egypt. Surely Yosef could imagine his father's overwhelming misery, languishing under the false impression that his favorite son has been killed. For that entire period of twenty-two years, Yaakov was bereft of his *ru'ach hakodesh* (Divine inspiration), it only being restored to him after he learned that Yosef still lived, as the verse states, וַתְּחִי רוּחַ יַעֲקֹב אֲבִיהֶם — *"And the soul of Yaakov was revived."*[444] The Rambam explains that prophecy can only rest upon a person in a state of joy.[445] Yaakov's pervasive unhappiness regarding Yosef's demise thus prevented him from experiencing Hashem's closeness.[446]

Why did Yosef not send word to Canaan that he was alive and well, and thus allay his father's grief? The Ohr HaChaim explains that if Yosef had informed Yaakov that he still lived, he would have been compelled to explain what had happened to him. His brothers' crimes against him, and their false information that "a wild animal had devoured him," would be revealed to Yaakov, causing them untold humiliation.[447]

Yosef was thus forced into the unenviable position of having to choose between the suffering of his father and the humiliation of his brothers. In light of our Sages' warning that it is better to be thrown into a fiery furnace than to embarrass another person in public,[448] Yosef chose to remain silent and let his father grieve until the time came when he was forced to reveal himself.

We are all well aware of the importance of respecting one another's feelings, yet sometimes we take other considerations into account and imagine that for our own best interests, or perhaps even for the public good, we are justified in embarrassing someone

---

444. *Bereishis* 45:27, *Targum Yonasan.*
445. *Shabbos* 30b.
446. *Shemoneh Perakim,* Chapter 7.
447. *Bereishis* 45:26.
448. *Berachos* 43b.

else. However, from Yosef's example we learn the true importance of guarding the honor of our peers, such that Yaakov had to endure twenty-two years of misery so that his sons would be spared from embarrassment.

Our Sages thus exhort us, "Let the honor of your peer be like the reverence of your teacher, and the reverence of your teacher like the awe of Heaven."[449] In Tanna D'Vei Eliyahu we learn:

HaKadosh Baruch Hu said to Bnei Yisrael, "My sons, there is nothing that I failed to give you. And what do I ask in return? I ask only that you love one another, respect one another, fear (to offend) one another, and that there never be found among you sin, theft, or disreputable deeds, only in order that you might never come to disgrace, as it is written, "[Hashem] tells you, man, what is good, and what Hashem demands of you: only to act justly, love kindness, and walk humbly with your God."[450,451]

---

449. *Pirkei Avos* 4:15.
450. *Michah* 6:8.
451. *Tanna D'Vei Eliyahu Rabbah* 26.

פרשת ויגש
Parashas Vayigash

The Moment of Truth

וַיֹּאמֶר יוֹסֵף אֶל אֶחָיו אֲנִי יוֹסֵף הַעוֹד אָבִי חָי וְלֹא יָכְלוּ אֶחָיו לַעֲנוֹת
אֹתוֹ כִּי נִבְהֲלוּ מִפָּנָיו.

*And Yosef said to his brothers, "I am Yosef! Is my father
still alive?" But his brothers could not answer him because
they were left disconcerted before him.*[452]

ABBA KOHEN BARDELA SAID: WOE TO US, FOR THE DAY
of judgment! Woe to us, for the day of rebuke! ... Yosef was
younger than his brothers, yet they could not stand before
his rebuke ... When HaKadosh Baruch Hu will come to rebuke each
person according to what he is, how much more so.[453]

The giants of *mussar* have often asked, what rebuke was inherent in Yosef's revelation to his brothers? He did no more than proclaim his true identity, and inquire after his father's welfare. Why
was this considered an "astonishing" rebuke, which his brothers
were unable to withstand?[454]

---

452. *Bereishis* 45:3.
453. *Bereishis Rabbah* 93:10.
454. **AN IMPORTANT NOTE:** The character and deeds of Yaakov's sons, the

The most effective *mussar* does not involve scathing criticism, harsh rebuke, or terrifying descriptions of the horrors of Gehinnom. The best *mussar* is nothing more than the revelation of the inescapable truth, which is so startlingly obvious, that it cannot possibly be denied.

Rather than confronting the truth and dealing with it, man often prefers to flee from it. He flees from Hashem; he flees from himself; and he flees from the still small voice in his heart, which gently whispers to him that he must change. Rather than heed this voice, he rushes headlong into endless delusions of fancy, in frantic escape from the truth — yet his flight is futile, since ultimately, the truth is inescapable. The truth will give him no peace, by day or by night. It will cut off him off at every exit. The small voice in his heart will grow and grow, until it becomes a thundering roar that cannot possibly be ignored. Only then, with nowhere else to run, man will finally turn to confront the truth, and then bury his head in shame for what he has done.

Yosef's brothers had taken a defenseless youth, and sold him into slavery. They turned a deaf ear to his pleas for mercy. They caused untold pain and misery to their poor father. After the deed was done, they buried any feelings of gnawing guilt deep within their hearts, and turned, each one of them, to his occupations. Yet Hashem would not allow them to forget. He gathered them all together, on the pretense of descending to Egypt, to bring food for their families. Then, with no warning at all, the truth suddenly surfaced. They were at long last confronted with the severity of their crime. "'I am Yosef! Does my father yet live?' And his brothers could not answer him, for they were astonished by him." The moment of truth had arrived, and they were struck speechless, unable to utter even one word in their own defense.

---

founders of the Twelve Tribes of Israel, are not subject to our criticism. It would be an inexcusable impudence for us to dare criticize them in any way. They were surely prompted by lofty motives, which are far beyond our grasp. Nevertheless, the commentaries that preceded us interpreted the events of their lives according to their superficial appearance, in order that we learn important lessons of *mussar* from them. We follow their example in this essay, without any intention to cast aspersions on our holy forefathers, *chas v'shalom.*

The same is true in our own lives. We flee from the truth, never taking a moment to hear the still small voice that calls to our heart, saying, "Return to Hashem." Deep down, we know that it is a crooked path we walk, yet we pay no heed, until Hashem stops us, and thrusts the truth in our faces. Then, no word of rebuke is necessary. It is painfully obvious. Woe to us for this most terrible rebuke of all. Woe to us for the day of judgment.

━━━━•━━━━

Sometimes, the ego entrenches itself behind a barricade of excuses, to justify even the most horrendous behavior. Man convinces himself that he is righteous in all his ways, and there is nothing that needs to be rectified. Yet all his fortifications of defense will melt in an instant, like sand castles swept into the sea, when the wave of truth washes over it. Man is then rendered defenseless before the shocking truth. At that moment, he feels as if the world has collapsed around him.

When Yosef's brothers threw him in the pit and then sold him into slavery, they did not do so out of unbridled anger. They were all great *tzaddikim*, the progenitors of the Tribes of Israel, and the bearers of the legacy of the *Avos*.

Rather, our Sages offer several possible explanations for their actions. Some explain that the brothers viewed Yosef as a dangerous foe, who must be eliminated to protect their lives. Others explain that they presumed Yosef to be a false prophet, making him liable for the death penalty. Still others explain that they regarded him as a rebel against Yehudah, their rightful king.

In any case, Yosef's brothers had their justification. Their defenses were prepared, and no words of rebuke could possibly break through, since in their own estimation they were perfectly correct. When Yosef put Shimon in jail, and demanded that they return with Binyamin, pangs of misgiving began to stir in their hearts. Yet they still did not admit that they were wrong. "We are guilty regarding our brother, since we saw the distress of his soul when he pleaded with us, but we did not listen. Therefore, this trouble has befallen us," they said.[455] They admitted their guilt in

---

455. *Bereishis* 42:21, see *Ramban*.

ignoring his pleas for mercy, but they still did not admit that they were wrong in selling him. Nothing could pry from their hearts the conviction that they were right, until suddenly the unimaginable occurred. Yosef himself stood before them and said, "I am Yosef! Does my father yet live?", and their defenses suddenly crumbled before their eyes. Yosef's dreams were at long last fulfilled. They found themselves bowing before him, as he had long ago said they would. They had despised and hounded him for his dreams. They had made sure that his dreams could not possibly be fulfilled. And yet, without warning, the dreamer returned, and his dreams became reality. Yosef did not need to utter even one word of rebuke. Their error was revealed for all to see.

So too, each and every one of us is convinced in his own way that he is right, he is faultless, and he is just in all his deeds. His, and only his, opinion is correct, and it absolutely pointless to reconsider. One surrounds himself with moats and walls of self-justification to protect his unriskable ego. He will crush anyone who dares offer a dissenting opinion. The ego will defend itself from rebuke at all cost. Thus, it spends all its days, lost in a fog of delusion, unreachable, unchallengeable, and unchangeable. So much greater is its fall, when the day of judgment comes, and the winds of truth scatter the fog, leaving the ego utterly defenseless. Not a word of rebuke need be uttered. Man will hang his head in shame, recognizing his fatal error at long last, and having nothing at all to say in his own defense. Woe to us, for this most bitter of all rebukes: the sudden confrontation with inescapable truth.

We have no choice but to take the time to inspect our deeds each day, weighing our every action on the scales of justice, with humble recognition of our own shortcomings, and with an earnest desire to mend what is broken, and to improve our character. "Do not believe in yourself until the day of your death,"[456] our Sages warn us. Let us take up the candle of truth, and cast light into the dark recesses of our hearts. Only then can we hope to hold our heads up, when the day of judgment arrives.

———•———

---

456. *Pirkei Avos* 2:5.

Another important point in this discussion can be seen by comparing two similar Midrashim. In *Yalkut Shimoni*, the Midrash states: R' Shimon ben Elazar said, "Woe to us, for the day of judgment! Woe to us, for the day of rebuke! Yosef was younger than his brothers, yet they could not stand before his rebuke, since they were astounded before him. When HaKadosh Baruch Hu arrives to rebuke each person for his deeds, how much more so.[457]

This Midrash is identical in every respect to the Midrash cited above, except for one important distinction. Above, the Midrash stated that Hashem will rebuke each person for what he is (״לְפִי מַה שֶהוּא״). Here, the Midrash states that Hashem will rebuke each person for his deeds (״לְפִי מַעֲשָׂיו״).

This distinction can also be found in this week's *parashah*. When Yosef told his brothers, "I am Yosef your brother, whom you sold to Egypt,"[458] he rebuked them for their deeds: for throwing him into a pit, for selling him into slavery, for dipping his coat into blood and claiming that he had been killed, and for the terrible lie that they told their father.

When he told them, "I am Yosef! Does my father yet live?"[459], he rebuked them, not for their deed, but for who they were, and for the character traits that they had displayed. "*My* father," he said; not, "*Our* father." This was a subtle but biting rebuke to them, for having been so cold and heartless toward their father. For twenty-two years, they had stood at their father's side, and seen him mourn inconsolably for his lost son. Why had they never before sought to ease his pain, by searching for Yosef, and returning him to Yaakov's side? What sort of children were they? This was perhaps the harshest rebuke of all. The recognition of fault in one's very character can be much more shocking than the recognition of a faulty deed, no matter how terrible it was.

Hence, we must also make careful inspection, not only of our deeds, but also of our very character: our attitude, and our relationship with others. May Hashem grant us, for the sake of His holy Name, that we may merit to correct our deeds and our characters, to serve Him with wholehearted love.

---

457. *Yalkut Shimoni, Vayigash* 152.
458. *Bereishis* 45:4.
459. Ibid. 45:3.

The All-Consuming Love

וַיֶּאְסֹר יוֹסֵף מֶרְכַּבְתּוֹ וַיַּעַל לִקְרַאת יִשְׂרָאֵל אָבִיו גֹּשְׁנָה וַיֵּרָא אֵלָיו וַיִּפֹּל עַל צַוָּארָיו וַיֵּבְךְּ עַל צַוָּארָיו עוֹד.

Yosef harnessed his chariot and went up to meet Yisrael his father in Goshen. He appeared before him, fell on his neck, and he wept on his neck excessively.[460]

WHEN THEY WERE AT LAST REUNITED AFTER SO MANY years, Yosef cried upon his father's shoulder, but Yaakov did not cry upon Yosef's. Rashi explains that instead Yaakov was reciting *Shema*.

It is amazing to consider Yaakov's self-control at this poignant moment. Yosef was his favorite son, whom he had presumed dead for twenty-two years. All that time, he refused to be consoled, insisting that he would descend to his grave in misery over the loss of his son. When he first heard that his son still lived, we can almost sense the outburst of emotion in the verse, "How great! My son Yosef still lives! I shall go and see him before I die."[461] Words cannot express the wonderful joy and excitement he must have felt. And yet when he finally saw his son, he was not overcome by emotion. He did not embrace and kiss his long-lost son. He did not even utter one word of greeting. He merely recited *Shema*; the same *Shema* we each recite twice each day.

The difference is that for Yaakov, *Shema* was no simple mechanical routine; no chore or religious duty to be dispensed with before we can get on with our day. For him, it was an outpouring of emotion, even more powerful than his reunion with his son. For him, the words, *"You shall love Hashem your God with all your heart,"* were not just ideological conviction, but a very real, powerful emotion.

The Sefer HaChinuch comments on the mitzvah to love

---

460. *Bereishis* 46:29.
461. Ibid. 45:28.

Hashem: A person should focus all his thoughts and desires on the love of Hashem. He should constantly ingrain in his heart that all the pleasures of this world, including wealth, family, and honor, are all meaningless and worthless compared to the love of Hashem. He should always strive for the wisdom to recognize this, and train his thoughts to revolve around the awareness of Hashem's Unity, until not even one moment by day or by night passes, without him thinking about his love for his Master, which consumes his entire heart.[462]

Yaakov's love for Hashem was the single dominant motivation in his life. Therefore, all other emotions paled in comparison. The Maharal adds that Yaakov's love for Hashem was inspired to even greater heights when he was granted the wish for which he had never dared hope. The Maharal writes:

When Yaakov saw his son ruling over Egypt, his heart was overcome with love and awe of Hashem. He was struck by the recognition of how many acts of kindness Hashem had done for him, and how He so generously rewards those who serve Him. Such is the way of the pious, who are inspired by the happy events of their lives to draw closer to Hashem due to the good and the truth that He does with them.

It was only fitting that Yaakov recite *Shema* when he was finally reunited with Yosef. He had suffered much pain during Yosef's absence. Now that he saw Yosef as king, he felt love for Hashem Who had brought this about. Therefore, Yaakov recited *Shema*, to accept Hashem's sovereignty and declare his love and awe of Him.[463]

Yaakov lived a hard life, in which he had to contend with one misfortune after another. He was hounded by his twin brother, abused by his deceitful father-in-law, and bereaved by the loss of Yosef for twenty-two tragic years, in which the *Shechinah* was hidden from him. Yet in the end of his life he merited a period of joy and *nachas* the likes of which he had never known. The *Shechinah* had returned to rest upon him, and his happiness knew no bounds.

The Tanna D'Vei Eliyahu describes this last stage of Yaakov's life: Hashem's mercy was extended toward Yaakov, and He granted

---

462. *Sefer HaChinuch* 418.
463. *Gur Aryeh.*

him seventeen good years with which to conclude his life. Yaakov Avinu had seventeen good years at the end of his life, and thus it became as if his entire life had been good, as it is written, "And Yaakov lived in the land of Egypt."[464]

The Tanna D'Vei Eliyahu interprets the expression "Yaakov lived," to mean that he lived a content, fulfilled life, the likes of which he had never known. He was surrounded by his beloved family, all of them toiling in Torah study, with his successful and righteous son caring for all their needs. Therefore, he saw this as the most appropriate opportunity to express his love for Hashem, and his gratitude for all that Hashem had done for him. He finally merited to see an end to his suffering, and to realize that all his hardships had been for the best.

The Name "Hashem" refers to His attribute of mercy, while the Name "Elokim" refers to His attribute of strict justice. Sometimes our eyes deceive us, making it seem as if His justice is unmerciful. For this reason, the Klausenberger Rav *zt"l* taught that we cover our eyes when we say, "*Hashem Elokeinu, Hashem Echad,*" to affirm that His mercy and justice are inseparable, even though we cannot always see how this is true.

It was this realization that was perfectly evident to Yaakov, as he merited to see his son alive and well, and all his hardships vanish into thin air. Therefore, it was only fitting that he choose that moment to recite *Shema*.

Years of Life

WHEN YAAKOV AVINU FIRST MET PHARAOH, AND Pharaoh asked him his age, Yaakov answered with a most peculiar complaint: וַיֹּאמֶר פַּרְעֹה אֶל יַעֲקֹב כַּמָּה יְמֵי שְׁנֵי חַיֶּיךָ. וַיֹּאמֶר יַעֲקֹב אֶל פַּרְעֹה יְמֵי שְׁנֵי מְגוּרַי שְׁלֹשִׁים וּמְאַת שָׁנָה מְעַט וְרָעִים הָיוּ יְמֵי שְׁנֵי חַיַּי וְלֹא הִשִּׂיגוּ אֶת יְמֵי שְׁנֵי חַיֵּי אֲבֹתַי בִּימֵי מְגוּרֵיהֶם — "*Pharaoh said to Yaakov, 'How many are the days of the years of your life?'*

---

464. *Bereishis* 47:28; *Tanna D'Vei Eliyahu Rabbah* Ch. 6.

Yaakov answered Pharaoh, 'The days of years of my sojourns have been a hundred and thirty years. Few and bad have been the days of the years of my life, and they have not reached the life spans of my forefathers in the days of their sojourns.'"[465]

What was Yaakov Avinu trying to say? Why did he not just answer directly, that he was one hundred and thirty years old? What did he mean by "the years of my sojourns," and why did he mention at all the lives of his forefathers, in which Pharaoh had expressed no interest?

Although we are inspired by the heights of greatness that Yaakov Avinu achieved, he held himself inadequate despite the magnitude of his accomplishments. "קָטֹנְתִּי מִכֹּל הַחֲסָדִים — *"I have been made small by all Your kindnesses,"* he said to Hashem.[466] He felt himself to be unworthy of the kindness that Hashem had shown him.

When asked by Pharaoh how long his life had been, his heart plumeted. He thought to himself, *What is my life? Am I alive at all?* The wicked even in their lifetimes are considered as dead.[467] The Rambam writes that for the wise, and for those who pursue wisdom, life without Torah study is tantamount to death.[468] *Can the days of my existence truly be considered life at all, considering my inadequacies?* he thought. Therefore, he did not answer that he had lived for one hundred and thirty years, but rather that the "the years of his sojourns" had been one hundred and thirty — as if to say that he had existed for one hundred and thirty years, but how long had he actually *lived* with Torah and mitzvos? "Few and bad have been the days of the years of my life, and they have not reached the days of years of the lives of my forefathers."

He compared his own sorry state to the glorious achievements of his forefathers, who had truly lived their lives. "Avraham was old and come of days."[469] He had utilized the days of his life to their utmost potential. The same was true of Yitzchak. Their days had been full of Torah and *yiras Shamayim*. Hence, Yaakov referred to

---

465. *Bereishis* 47:8-9.
466. Ibid. 32:11.
467. *Berachos* 18b.
468. *Hilchos Rotzeiach* 7:1.
469. *Bereishis* 24:1.

their years as "years of life." His own years were merely "years of sojourn," whereas his years of real life had been "few and bad."

With this we can understand why the Torah writes of Adam, וַיִּהְיוּ כָּל יְמֵי אָדָם אֲשֶׁר חַי תְּשַׁע מֵאוֹת שָׁנָה וּשְׁלֹשִׁים שָׁנָה וַיָּמֹת — *"And it was, that all the days that Adam had lived were nine hundred and thirty years, and he died."*[470] The Torah stresses that these were the days that he had actually lived, since he had utilized his life in the pursuit of Torah and mitzvos. The same was true of Avraham Avinu: וְאֵלֶּה יְמֵי שְׁנֵי חַיֵּי אַבְרָהָם אֲשֶׁר חָי — *"These were the days of the life of Avraham that he had lived."*[471] He had lived his life to the fullest. However, regarding Yishmael, the Torah states only וְאֵלֶּה שְׁנֵי חַיֵּי יִשְׁמָעֵאל — *"These were the years of the life of Yishmael."*[472] The Torah does not add the words *"that he had lived,"* since he had squandered his years on meaningless frivolities, that gave no meaning to his life. In his great humility, Yaakov Avinu thought that his own life had likewise not fulfilled its potential.

This was Yaakov's estimation of himself, but the Torah paints a very different portrait of his life. וַיְהִי יְמֵי יַעֲקֹב שְׁנֵי חַיָּיו שֶׁבַע שָׁנִים וְאַרְבָּעִים וּמְאַת שָׁנָה — *"And the days of Yaakov, the years of his life, were one hundred and forty-seven years."*[473] The Torah testifies that just like his forefathers before him, Yaakov brought life to the years of his existence, by utilizing them to their fullest, and thus giving eternal significance to all his days.

---

470. *Bereishis* 5:5.
471. Ibid. 25:7.
472. Ibid. 25:17.
473. Ibid. 47:28.

פרשת ויחי

Parashas Vayechi

The Legacy of Torah

IN THIS WEEK'S *PARASHAH*, WE LEARN ABOUT THE PASSING of Yaakov Avinu:

וַיְכַל יַעֲקֹב לְצַוֹּת אֶת בָּנָיו וַיֶּאֱסֹף רַגְלָיו אֶל הַמִּטָּה וַיִּגְוַע וַיֵּאָסֶף אֶל עַמָּיו. וַיִּפֹּל יוֹסֵף עַל פְּנֵי אָבִיו וַיֵּבְךְ עָלָיו וַיִּשַּׁק לוֹ. וַיְצַו יוֹסֵף אֶת עֲבָדָיו אֶת הָרֹפְאִים לַחֲנֹט אֶת אָבִיו וַיַּחַנְטוּ הָרֹפְאִים אֶת יִשְׂרָאֵל. וַיִּמְלְאוּ לוֹ אַרְבָּעִים יוֹם כִּי כֵּן יִמְלְאוּ יְמֵי הַחֲנֻטִים וַיִּבְכּוּ אֹתוֹ מִצְרַיִם שִׁבְעִים יוֹם.

When Yaakov finished instructing his sons, he drew his feet onto the bed; he expired and was gathered to his people. Then Yosef fell upon his father's face; he wept over him and kissed him. Yosef ordered his servants, the physicians, to embalm his father; so the physicians embalmed Yisrael. His forty-day term was completed, for such is the term of the embalmed; and Egypt bewailed him for seventy days.[474]

Taken at face value, it seems that Yaakov Avinu actually died. However, the Gemara tells us that this is not so:

R' Yochanan said, "Yaakov Avinu never died."

"Then why was he eulogized, embalmed, and buried?" asked his peers.

---

474. *Bereishis* 49:33-50:3.

"I learn this from a *pasuk*," R' Yochanan explained. "As it is written, 'And you, do not fear, My servant Yaakov, says Hashem, and do not tremble, Yisrael, for I will rescue you from afar, and your descendants from the land of their captivity.'[475] The *pasuk* equates him to his descendants. Just as his descendants live on, so too does he."[476]

The Maharsha explains that R' Yochanan's peers could not understand whether he referred to a physical death or a spiritual one. R' Yochanan could not have meant that Yaakov's body never died, since Yaakov was embalmed and buried. Nor could he have meant that Yaakov's soul never died, since this was also true of Avraham and Yitzchak, and therefore R' Yochanan had no need to make special mention of Yaakov.

R' Yochanan then explained that Yaakov was distinguished among the *Avos*, since "just as his descendants live on, so too does he." Whereas Avraham fathered the wicked Yishmael, and Yitzchak fathered the evil Eisav, Yaakov was unique in that all of his children were perfectly righteous. By continuing Yaakov's mission of spreading light and wisdom in the world, his sons made his presence felt even after his body had died.

A parallel to this can be found elsewhere in the Gemara:

Why does the *pasuk* state regarding David's passing that "he rested" (שְׁכִיבָה), whereas regarding Yoav's passing, it states that "he died" (מִיתָה)? ... Since David left behind a son of his stature, he is said to have rested. Yoav, who did not leave behind a son of his stature, is said to have died.[477]

———◆———

From the hands of the Mighty Power of Yaakov, from there, he shepherded the stone (אֶבֶן) of Yisrael.[478]

This was part of Yaakov's final blessing to Yosef. Rashi explains that the word "אֶבֶן" is used here as an acronym for "אָב וּבֵן," which means "*father and son*." The unique strength of Yaakov lay in his

---

475. *Yirmiyahu* 30:10.
476. *Taanis* 5b.
477. *Bava Basra* 116a.
478. *Bereishis* 49:24.

ability to pass on the tradition in an unbroken chain from one generation to the next. Before he left the world, he gathered his sons together. The Gemara describes their final meeting:

Yaakov wished to reveal to his sons what would occur at the end of days, but the Divine Presence left him. "Perhaps, *chas v'shalom*, there is an imperfection in my bed [a reference to his line of descent], just as Avraham had Yishmael, and my father Yitzchak had Eisav."

His sons then said in unison, "*Shema Yisrael, Hashem Elokeinu, Hashem Echad* — Just as your heart is solely devoted to the One Hashem, so too are our hearts."

At that moment, Yaakov Avinu declared, "*Baruch Sheim Kavod Malchuso L'Olam Va'ed* — Blessed is the Name of the Glory of His Kingship for all eternity."[479]

When Yaakov realized that the Divine Presence had left him, he feared that this was because his sons harbored inclinations toward idolatry. He expressed his concern, and they reassured him that their hearts were solely devoted to Hashem. Why did Yaakov suspect them of idolatry in particular, rather than any other sin, which might have caused the Divine Presence to leave him?

The Zohar states that Adam's sin of eating from the Tree of Knowledge encapsulated the three most heinous sins: idolatry, illicit relations, and murder.[480] Similarly, the Gemara states that Adam leaned toward idolatry, and that he attempted to undo his Bris Milah — a sin akin to illicit relations.[481] Adam was also considered a "murderer" to some extent, since he brought death to the world by eating from the Tree. The Midrash states that he should have been killed immediately for this sin, but since it was inadvertent he was instead sentenced to exile from Gan Eden, just as an unintentional murderer is exiled to one of the cities of refuge.[482] These sources support the Zohar's assertion that Adam was guilty of the three most heinous sins.[483]

---

479. *Pesachim* 56a.
480. *Zohar*, end of *Parashas Behar*.
481. *Sanhedrin* 38b.
482. *Midrash Tanchuma, Parashas Massai*.
483. **DISCLAIMER**: When discussing the sins of our forefathers, the spiritual giants who preceded us, we must always bear in mind that they

By corrupting his own soul, Adam corrupted the entire world. It was then the mission of the *Avos* to purify the world, by purifying their own souls, which were included in Adam's own, and therefore were party to his sin. Just as gold is refined by isolating and removing undesirable impurities, so too the *Avos* purified their souls, and the souls of their descendants, by isolating and rejecting the three basic impurities.

Avraham Avinu began this task by isolating the trait of illicit relations, and passing it on to Yishmael. Yishmael was then cast aside, and Yitzchak was born free of any inclination toward this sin.

Yitzchak then isolated the trait of murder, by passing it on to Eisav (who "lived by the sword"[484]) and casting him aside. Thus, there remained only the trait of idolatry against which Yaakov had to struggle.

When the Divine Presence departed from Yaakov, he feared this was a sign that the trait of idolatry still existed among his sons. If so, he would be forced to cast aside one of his sons, to isolate the trait of idolatry, in order to create a pure lineage for generations to come. Then, when all his sons recited *Shema* together, he realized that he had succeeded in purifying the souls of all his children, without having to sacrifice any of them. Therefore, this was surely not the reason that the Divine Presence had departed.

This explanation is clearly supported by the *Targum Yerushalmi*:

Yaakov Avinu told his sons, "My grandfather Avraham had an imperfection (in his lineage); namely, Yishmael and the sons of Keturah. My father Yitzchak also had an imperfection; namely, my brother Eisav. I fear that there might also be among you one whose heart is divided from his brothers, who will go to worship false gods."

---

were righteous and holy individuals, who were held accountable for the most minute transgression, as if it was the most heinous sin. Therefore, sources such as these should not be interpreted literally. Even when they are meant to be taken literally, we do not always understand the context that surrounds them. Specifically in the case of Adam, Rabbeinu Chananel explains that he did not really lean toward idolatry, or attempt to undo his Bris Milah (see source). However, this essay takes the Gemara at face value, in an attempt to draw from them the moral lessons that are relevant to our own lives.

484. See *Bereishis* 27:40.

The founders of the Twelve Tribes of Yaakov then answered as one, "Hear us, our father Yisrael. Hashem is our God, Hashem is One."

"Let His great Name be blessed forever and ever," said Yaakov.[485]

How did Yaakov succeeded in purifying his life from idolatry, without having to sacrifice any of his children? The Zohar states that the world rests on three pillars: Torah, personified by Yaakov, *Avodah* (prayer, or the service of the Beis HaMikdash), personified by Yitzchak, and acts of kindness, personified by Avraham.[486]

When using the Torah to purify the faults in creation, and the faults in one's own character, one need not "separate the impurities" as done when refining gold. Torah has the power to take the impurities themselves and transform them into good. Hashem implores us, "If they would only abandon Me, but not abandon My Torah, the light of the Torah would draw them back to goodness."[487] Torah is so powerful that not only can it illuminate the darkness, it can take the cloak of darkness itself, and transform it into radiant light. Since Yaakov personified the pillar of Torah study, he was able to create a legacy of perfect goodness for the generations that followed him, such that none of his sons were lost to the darkness of idolatry.

On Wings of Angels

BEFORE YAAKOV AVINU DIED, HIS SONS GATHERED around him and said, "*Shema Yisrael, Hashem Elokeinu, Hashem Echad* — Hear, Yisrael, Hashem is our God, Hashem is One," to which he responded, "*Baruch Sheim Kavod Malchuso L'Olam Va'ed* — Blessed is the Name of the Glory of His Kingship for all eternity." What is the significance of Yaakov's response?

The Gemara cites a seeming contradiction between two *pesukim*, both of which describe the appearance of the *seraphim* (fiery angels). Yeshayahu described them as having six wings, while

---

485. *Targum Yerushalmi, Bereishis* 49:1-2.
486. *Zohar* I, 146b.
487. *Eichah Rabbah*, introduction, 2.

Yechezkel described them as having only four. The Gemara explains that Yeshayahu described them as they appeared while the Beis HaMikdash stood — then they appeared with six wings. Yechezkel described them as they appeared after the Beis HaMikdash had been destroyed — when they appear with only four wings.[488]

The Arizal explains that the six words, *"Baruch Sheim Kavod Malchuso L'Olam Va'ed,"* correspond to the six wings of the *seraphim*. The Vilna Gaon adds that since the destruction of the Beis Ha-Mikdash, the two middle wings of the *seraphim* have been folded and concealed behind their backs. The two middle wings correspond to the two middle words, *"Kavod Malchuso,"* which mean, "the Glory of His Kingship." As long as the Beis HaMikdash lies in ruins, the Glory of Hashem's Kingship is hidden. We pray in Yom Tov davening, "גַּלֵּה כְּבוֹד מַלְכוּתְךָ עָלֵינוּ" — *Reveal the Glory of Your Kingship upon us,"* in hope that the middle wings of the *seraphim* may soon be extended, that the Beis HaMikdash be rebuilt, and that the Glory of Hashem's Kingship may once again be revealed for all the world to see.

The *pasuk* from *Ashrei* states, כְּבוֹד מַלְכוּתְךָ יֹאמֵרוּ וּגְבוּרָתְךָ יְדַבֵּרוּ — *"They shall speak the Glory of Your Kingship, and tell of Your might."*[489] The Ben Ish Chai explains that in the future, everyone will speak of the mighty deeds that Hashem will perform. Then, the wings corresponding to *"Kavod Malchuso"* will be extended, and the Glory of Hashem's Kingship will once again be revealed.[490]

In the meantime, the Glory of Hashem's Kingship is still hidden. Perhaps for this reason, we say, *"Baruch Sheim Kavod Malchuso L'Olam Va'ed"* quietly when reciting *Shema.*[491] The time has not yet come for our declaration of Hashem's Glory to resonate throughout the world.

---

488. *Chagigah* 13b.
489. *Tehillim* 145:11.
490. *Ben Yehoyada, Chagigah,* ibid. The Oheiv Yisrael (*Vayeishev*) argues that the wings corresponding to *"L'OlamVa'ed — for all eternity"* were concealed when the Beis HaMikdash was destroyed. However, he cites his own Rebbe, R' Elimelech of Lizhensk *zt"l,* as agreeing to the Vilna Gaon's interpretation, that the wings corresponding to *"Kavod Malchuso"* were concealed. Their difference seems to be based on the debate between the Amoraim in the Gemara (ibid.), over whether the wings that covered the *seraphim's* feet, or the wings with which they sing, were concealed.
491. *Shulchan Aruch, O.C.* 61:13.

Our Sages offer two other reasons why we recite this verse softly. According to the Gemara, when Moshe taught Bnei Yisrael to say *Shema*, he did not add "*Baruch Sheim Kavod Malchuso L'Olam Va'ed.*" However, when Yaakov Avinu first heard his sons say *Shema*, he responded, "*Baruch Sheim Kavod Malchuso L'Olam Va'ed.*" Were we to say this loudly, it would be an affront to Moshe. Were we to omit it entirely, it would be an affront to Yaakov Avinu. As a compromise, we say it softly.[492]

Another explanation, found in the Midrash, is that when Moshe Rabbeinu ascended to Heaven to receive the Torah, he heard the angels saying, "*Baruch Sheim Kavod Malchuso L'Olam Va'ed.*" When he returned to earth, he taught Bnei Yisrael this praise, but cautioned them to say it quietly, in order not to incite the envy of the angels. This is comparable to a thief who stole a priceless jewel from the palace of the king, and gave it to his wife to wear, warning her only to wear it in private, so no one would discover that he stole it. Therefore, only on Yom Kippur, when we become like angels, do we say, "*Baruch Sheim Kavod Malchuso L'Olam Va'ed,*" out loud.[493]

The soul of a Jew longs throughout the year to call out, "*Baruch Sheim Kavod Malchuso L'Olam Va'ed,*" to publicize Hashem's Glory throughout the world. How can we contain our fervor to sanctify Hashem's holy Name?

Perhaps for this reason our Sages tell us that we should call out in a loud voice, "*Yehei Shmei Rabba M'Vorach L'Olam Va'ed* — May His Great Name be Blessed for all eternity,*" during *Kaddish*. If a person does so, any harsh decrees that have been written against him will be rescinded.[494]

This phrase from *Kaddish* parallels "*Baruch Sheim Kavod Malchuso L'Olam Va'ed*" from *Shema*. Both have precisely the same meaning. In fact, the *Targum Yerushalmi* on our *parashah* states that Yaakov responded, "*Yehei Shmei Rabba M'Vorach L'Olam Va'ed,*" upon hearing his sons recite *Shema*, whereas the Gemara states that he responded, "*Baruch Sheim Kavod Malchuso L'Olam Va'ed.*" We see from here that their meaning is one and the same.

---

492. *Pesachim* 56a.
493. *Devarim Rabbah, Parashas Va'eschanan,* cited in *Tur, O.C.* 619.
494. *Shabbos* 119b.

Since we are as yet unable to say "*Baruch Sheim Kavod Malchuso L'Olam Va'ed*" out loud, as is our hearts' desire, we must instead say, "*Yehei Shmei Rabba M'Vorach L'Olam Va'ed*" — the Aramaic equivalent. Since angels do not understand Aramaic (or, according to some opinions, they pay it no heed[495]) there is no concern that we might incite their envy by reciting this Aramaic rendition of their prayer.

We hope and long that the day may soon come, when Hashem's Glory will at last be revealed for all the world to see.

Parting With Bereishis

THE RAMBAN CALLS *SEFER BEREISHIS* "THE BOOK OF Creation," since it begins with the creation of the world, and continues with the creation of the Jewish nation: the deeds of our forefathers, which were the foundation of our nation. From *Sefer Bereishis,* we proceed to *Sefer Shemos,* which the Ramban calls "the Book of Exile and Redemption." As we conclude *Bereishis* and begin *Shemos,* we look back to the stories of our forefathers, with hope and prayer that their merit may accompany us into the Exile, and that in their merit we may soon be redeemed.

The link between *Bereishis* and *Shemos* can be understood by way of a parable to a young child who leaves his home for the first time, to start his first day at school. He enters the world of the unknown, with no little trepidation, and looks back toward his parents, who stand from afar, smiling and waving to him, giving him the courage he needs to continue onward. So too, we look back toward the merit of our forefathers, to give us strength and courage in this bitter and terrible Exile that we must face.

As we have frequently noted, our Sages tell us that, "Man must ask himself, *When will my deeds reach the deeds of my forefathers?*[496] The question is often asked: How could we possibly aspire to reach the towering heights of greatness that the *Avos* achieved? Rebbe Yisrael of Ruzhin explained that we cannot expect to equal them in

---

495. See *Shabbos* 12b; *Raavad, Tamim Dei'im* 184.
496. *Tanna D'Vei Eliyahu Rabbah*, Ch. 23.

greatness, but we must at least strive to "reach" their deeds, that is, to have some kind of connection to them, by emulating them to the best of our ability.

However, we can also explain that we are in fact able to ascend to their heightened level, by following the trail that they blazed before us. When our own strength falters, they descend to help us, taking us by the hand and leading us along the way. As our fathers, it is part of their task to make sure that we can follow them to the spiritual greatness that is the destiny of our nation.

As we learned in a previous essay, our Sages tell us that the world rests on three pillars: Torah, *Avodah* (prayer, or the service of the Beis HaMikdash), and *gemilus chassadim* (acts of kindness).[497] These three pillars were personified by the *Avos*.[498] Avraham excelled in performing acts of kindness, welcoming wayfarers into his home, and the like. Yitzchak excelled in *Avodah*, and was himself offered as a sacrifice on the *Mizbei'ach*. Yaakov excelled in Torah. He was known as a "simple man, who dwelt in the tents (of Torah study),"[499] and spent fourteen years in uninterrupted study in the academies of Sheim and Ever.[500]

It is interesting to note that the Mishnah in *Avos* lists these three pillars in the order of Torah, *Avodah*, and *gemilus chassadim*; whereas the *Avos* who personified these attributes appeared in exactly the opposite order. First Avraham (*chesed*), then Yitzchak (*Avodah*), then Yaakov (Torah). What are we meant to learn from this?

The *Avos* saw it as their task to draw the people of their generation toward the service of Hashem. In influencing a person to come close to Hashem, the first step must always be *chesed* — acts of kindness. Before discussing ideas of spirituality, such as Torah and *Avodah*, one must first establish a bond of love, and true concern for the other person's welfare. Only then can he be drawn close to Hashem.

This is very true in our own generation, in which many of our brethren have become estranged from the tradition of our forefathers. It is preposterous to assume that these people can be drawn back to Torah with harsh words of reproach. Our only hope is to

---

497. *Pirkei Avos* 1:2.
498. *Zohar* I, 146b.
499. *Bereishis* 25:27.
500. See *Rashi, Bereishis* 28:11.

forge a loving and compassionate relationship with them. We must show them the love that Hashem, their Father in Heaven, has for them, and thereby draw them back to His embrace.

The last of the *Avos* was Yaakov Avinu. Whereas a relationship with Hashem begins with *chesed*, it reaches its zenith through Torah study, which is the ultimate expression of attachment to the Creator. Before Yaakov descended to Egypt, he sent Yehudah ahead to establish yeshivos in which his family could study Torah during their exile. Thereby, he laid the foundation for Klal Yisrael in *Galus* throughout the generations to remain faithful to Hashem and retain their holy stature, in the merit of Torah study which would guide and protect them. Only the light of the Torah has the power to drive back the darkness of *Galus*, and let us retain our national integrity until Mashiach's arrival.

Of all the episodes discussed in *Sefer Bereishis,* Yosef's is surely related at the greatest length and is the most detailed. The story of his dreams, his conflict with his brothers, his slavery and imprisonment, his rise to power, and the reuniting of his family span the course of four *parshiyos*, almost one third of the *Sefer*. In contrast, the lives of the *Avos* themselves are described in far less detail.

Surely, this is because Yosef's story has the greatest relevance to our own lives. It was the senseless hatred between the brothers that ultimately led to their descent into Egypt, where their children were enslaved and tortured for hundreds of years. Many generations later, punishment was again exacted, when R' Akiva and nine fellow Tannaim were executed by the Romans, to atone for the sin of the ten brothers, who sold Yosef into slavery. Although we cannot claim to understand the depth of Hashem's judgment, or His ultimate plan for His nation, it is quite clear that the direct cause of our suffering, both now and throughout our history, is the unjustifiable strife and bickering among us.

We conclude *Sefer Bereishis,* and the narrative of the lives of the *Avos*, with this one crucial message, which calls out to each and every one of us. The senseless bickering among us is the cause of our troubles. Only by bridging the gaps between our hearts can we hope to be redeemed, may it be soon and in our days.

ספר שמות

SEFER SHEMOS

Introduction to
Sefer Shemos

"For it is dearer in my eyes to teach a basic tenet of religion and faith than anything else I may teach."

Rambam, in his commentary on the Mishnah,
end of *Maseches Berachos*

"... and also there are many other commandments similar to these that serve as a remembrance of the Exodus from Egypt. And all these commandments serve to be a testimony for us through all the generations regarding the wonders performed in Egypt, that they not be forgotten ... It is through the big and public miracles that a person comes to acknowledge the hidden miracles, which are the foundation of the whole Torah; for a person has no portion in the Torah of Moshe Rabbeinu unless [he] we believe that everything that happens to us is miraculous and in no way "natural" or simply "the way of the world."

Ramban, end of *Parashas Bo*

The Natural Miracle

THE RAMBAN ILLUMINATES A WAY TO UNDERSTAND THE secret of the miracles and wonders that Hashem performed for Bnei Yisrael in Egypt. These miracles were not done for Bnei Yisrael solely for that time and place, but to light the way for us in the darkness of exile and to infuse within our hearts a clear consciousness that even in times, actions, and matters that appear to us as "natural," circumstances where Hashem's hand is not clearly visible to all, we must see and feel Hashem's protection over us. These miracles were performed for the Jews so that through them we can thank our Father in Heaven and praise His Great Name for every breath, as our Sages instructed us: עַל כָּל נְשִׁימָה וּנְשִׁימָה צָרִיךְ אָדָם לְקַלֵּס לְבּוֹרֵא — *"for every breath a person must praise the Creator."*[1]

What, in fact, is the meaning of a *"nes,"* a miracle? In common parlance, *"nes"* and *"pele,"* miracle and wonder, respectively, are linked. There is an assumption that the two are synonymous. Thus we say in davening, עַל הַנִּסִּים וְעַל הַנִּפְלָאוֹת — *"upon the miracles and upon the wonders,"* thanking Hashem for the miracles and wonders. But in Scripture, the actual meaning of נֵס is a flag or a banner, as we see in the *pasuk,* כִּנְשֹׂא נֵס הָרִים תִּרְאוּ וְכִתְקֹעַ שׁוֹפָר תִּשְׁמָעוּ[2] — *"you will see when the banner is hoisted up upon the mountains, and when the shofar sounds you will hear."* Similarly, אֶל חוֹמֹת בָּבֶל שְׂאוּ נֵס[3] — *"Hoist up a banner against the walls of Babylon."* In davening as well we say וְשָׂא נֵס לְקַבֵּץ גָּלֻיּוֹתֵינוּ — *"and raise the banner to gather our exiles."* One would think the word נֵס has two distinct meanings — miracle and banner — but in fact they are one and the same, for this is the purpose of God's miraculous and supernatural mode of operation: to serve as a banner proclaiming that "nature" is also run by God. Just like a flag symbolizes and proclaims ownership and leadership over a country, a city, or a fortress atop which it flies, so too does a miracle, a נֵס, stand in proclamation of God's Lordship over the world and all of creation, so that we, as the Ramban says, *"believe that all that happens to us is miraculous and nothing is 'natural' or 'the way of the world.'"*[4]

The Rama writes that if one forgot to say עַל הַנִּסִּים in bentching, one can say, הָרַחֲמָן הוּא יַעֲשֶׂה לָנוּ נִסִּים וְנִפְלָאוֹת כַּאֲשֶׁר עָשָׂה לַאֲבוֹתֵינוּ — *"The compassionate One! May He perform for us miracles and wonders as He performed for our forefathers."* The Acharonim question

---

1. *Bereishis Rabbah* 14:9.
2. *Yeshayahu* 18:3.
3. *Yirmiyahu* 51:12.
4. *Rambam, Shemos* 13:16.

this ruling. The Gemara[5] states that if a man prays for his expectant wife to have a boy, his prayer is in vain (since she is already expecting, and obviously the gender has already been determined). Our Sages also say[6] that אֵין מַזְכִּירִין מַעֲשֵׂה נִסִּים — *"do not bring proofs from miracles,"* since we do not pray for a miracle.[7]

But according to what we have stated above, certainly it is permissible to daven for a miracle that will fulfill its intended destiny: to be a flag, serving as a banner and a sign of God's sovereignty over the world, just like the miracles done for our forefathers, through which God's Name was sanctified. It is unquestionably a great mitzvah to daven that God's Name be sanctified in His world, and this is the whole purpose of our existence: to profess the Oneness of God and to sanctify His Name. But a miracle that will not bring about a proclamation of God's Oneness and power in His world is a miracle in vain and therefore davening for such a meaningless miracle is truly for naught. Someone who davens for his wife to have a boy is davening in vain because if his prayer were answered and his wife gave birth to a boy, even the person to whom this miracle happened would never know the magnitude of this miracle. One should not daven for such a miracle, since it will never serve as a banner sanctifying God's Name.

The Gemara[8] tells of a man whose wife died, leaving him with a nursing infant for whom the man could not afford to hire a wet nurse. A miracle was performed and the man himself was able to nurse his son. Said R' Yosef, "Come and see how great this man was, for such a miracle was performed on his behalf!" Abaye answered him, "On the contrary. How inferior is this man for whom the natural order was changed on his behalf!" The *Tosafos Yeshanim* asks, How is this different from the Medrash that states that this same miracle happened to Mordechai who was able to nurse Esther? Based on what we have previously learned, we can say that this miracle is different than that which occurred to Mordechai. In the case of Mordechai and Esther, it was a miracle in a string of miracles that in the end brought about a tremendous קִדּוּשׁ ה', a sanctification

---

5. *Berachos* 54a.
6. Ibid. 60a.
7. For further insight, see *Yeshuos Yaakov* there, 100:2.
8. *Shabbos* 53b.

of God's Name, and with such a miracle, one that achieves its lofty goal, no one could say regarding Mordechai, "How inferior is this person."(Clearly in his case, natural order was not changed on behalf of an individual but rather to sanctify God's Name in the world.) This is indeed the end goal of all the great and well-known miracles that happened to Bnei Yisrael: to profess God's Name and serve as a flag emblematic of God's sovereignty and guidance of the world.

A story is told of a boy who, upon hearing his father speak extensively about the miracle of the splitting of the Red Sea, asked his father, What was so great about this miracle after all? God created the sea and so what is the profundity of Him being able to split it? The father answered with the following parable: There was a certain sculptor, a supremely gifted artist of inimitable talent. One day the sculptor sculpted a horse from marble and placed the horse in the city street so that people would see the work of art and marvel at the artistry of this sculptor. A long time passed, but no one noticed the sculptured horse and no one commented on its magnificence. The artist was heartbroken and humiliated that people were not appreciating his fine sculpture and recognizing its beauty. The sculptor's friends comforted him by saying that the sculpture is so perfect that people think it's a real horse standing on the side of the road and therefore they do not marvel at the sculpture. The sculptor asked, What then can I do? To make a horse that does not resemble a real horse would damage my reputation as a sculptor. His friends advised him to take the horse he sculpted and cut it in half and anyone walking past will marvel at this never-before-seen phenomenon — a horse split in half and still standing on its legs. When the people will look closer at this wonder, they will see that it's not a real horse but in fact a glorious creation, a brilliant artistic work of a great and talented artist.

This is how the father answered his son as to the significance of the splitting of the Red Sea. Would we be worthy of a pure heart, a soul that yearns and a mind that is thirsty and desires to know God and to be close to Him, there would be no need for God to split the sea to make us believe in Him and love Him. We would see in the sea itself, as in all of creation, the handiwork of God, Creator of the world, and our mouths would be filled like the breadth of the sea with gratitude and praise to God's Name, like Yeshaya HaNavi

שְׂאוּ מָרוֹם עֵינֵיכֶם וּרְאוּ מִי בָרָא אֵלֶּה הַמּוֹצִיא בְמִסְפָּר צְבָאָם לְכֻלָּם בְּשֵׁם said,[9] יִקְרָא מֵרֹב אוֹנִים וְאַמִּיץ כֹּחַ אִישׁ לֹא נֶעְדָּר — *"Raise your eyes on high and see Who created these [things]! He brings forth their legions by number; He calls to each of them by name; by the abundance of His power and by vigor of His strength, not one is missing!"* And as Dovid HaMelech said,[10] כִּי אֶרְאֶה שָׁמֶיךָ מַעֲשֵׂי אֶצְבְּעֹתֶיךָ יָרֵחַ וְכוֹכָבִים אֲשֶׁר כּוֹנָנְתָּה. מָה אֱנוֹשׁ כִּי תִזְכְּרֶנּוּ — *"When I behold Your heavens, the work of Your fingers, the moon and the stars that You have set in place, [I think,] what is frail man that You should remember him?"*

The Rambam writes,[11] *"What is the path to loving God and to fearing Him? When a person looks at all His deeds and all His great and wondrous creations and through them is able to see the immeasurable and infinite wisdom of God, he immediately comes to love God and praise Him and desires to know God."*

But the lethargy born of habit dulls our feelings and hardens our hearts to the point where we, human beings who pass to and fro through the world, do not notice the work of God and all of His wonders that surround us. This is why God split the sea for us, so that we look not only at the split sea but at the sea *itself* and at the whole of Creation. This look at all of Creation enables us to see God's mighty hand, His constant supervision and great kindness in every matter and at every moment, and we come to praise His Name for every breath we take.

Concerning the era of Mashiach it is written:[12] כִּי מָלְאָה הָאָרֶץ דֵּעָה אֶת ה' כַּמַּיִם לַיָּם מְכַסִּים — *"for the earth will be as filled with knowledge of Hashem as water covering the seabed."* The purpose of God splitting the sea was to strengthen Bnei Yisrael's faith for generations to come, to enable us to see God's guardianship over the laws of nature. Perhaps we can expound homiletically on this verse and say that in the future, God's hand in the world will be so revealed and the whole land will be filled with knowledge of God that even when nature takes its natural course — כַּמַּיִם לַיָּם מְכַסִּים — *"as water covering the seabed,"* our knowledge of God and our faith in Him will be so

---

9. *Yeshayahu* 40:26.
10. *Tehillim* 8:4-5.
11. *Rambam, Hilchos Yesodei HaTorah* 2:2.
12. *Yeshayahu* 11:9.

powerful that there will no longer be a need for God to perform great miracles such as splitting the sea in order to instill faith in our hearts.

It is not merely in the wonders of nature and its beautiful phenomena that we can see the hand of God and His supervising of the whole world, but even in every minor event and minute detail of our individual lives. Unlike people who turn to their Father in Heaven solely in times of trouble or when they are on the verge of making significant and far-reaching decisions, we must do as our Sages have instructed us: to thank Him for every breath. In his commentary to *Sefer Mishlei*, Rabbeinu Yonah bemoans the fact that we are not cognizant of God's involvement in the minutiae of everyday life. On the *pasuk* בְּכָל דְּרָכֶיךָ דָעֵהוּ — *"in all your ways know Him,"*[13] Rabbeinu Yonah advises:

"With each action that you wish to do, remember God and put your hope in Him that He enable you to succeed and place your trust in Him and turn your heart to Him, for the matter is not in your hand. This verse בְּכָל דְּרָכֶיךָ דָעֵהוּ *comes in addition to the previous verse of* בְּטַח אֶל ה' בְּכָל לִבֶּךָ — *"trust in Hashem with all your heart." There is a type of person who trusts Hashem in a general way and believes that everything is in the hands of Heaven. He relies on Him and not on man or his own might and intellect, but his trust in God is in a general way, for the big things, and not in the details of everything he does. This is what the verse* בְּכָל דְּרָכֶיךָ דָעֵהוּ *comes to add, that in every detail of all that you do, in every way of each action, remember Him… Know that there are people who turn their eyes to God concerning a big matter, for example if they wish to embark on a business journey, but they do not remember God in the small actions. Hence it says* בְּכָל דְּרָכֶיךָ דָעֵהוּ, *know Him in all matters large and small. One must remember God in everything, because all actions are dependent on God and any success is due to His kindness."*

These words are a lesson for us, a way of life and *mussar* as to how one must incorporate faith and trust into everyday life.

Rabbi Nachman of Breslov would instruct his followers to daven to Hashem in their own colloquial language, like a child turns to his mother, because trusting Hashem and davening to Him for everything is the sign — indeed, the cornerstone — of faith.

---

13. *Mishlei* 3:6.

The Gemara states[14] that יֶזה הַסּוֹמֵךְ גְּאוּלָה לִתְפִלָּה מוּבְטָח לוֹ שֶׁהוּא בֶּן עוֹלָם הַבָּא — "anyone who joins the blessing of redemption [which is recited after the Shema] to the prayer of Shemoneh Esrei can trust that he is worthy of the World to Come." The commentators ask, Why is such a great reward given for such a small detail concerning the halachos of davening? Rabbeinu Yonah quotes from his teacher, responding to this question:[15]

"… because when a person mentions Yetzias Mitzraim and then immediately davens, he is demonstrating that he trusts Hashem in davening for all his needs. Someone who doesn't trust Hashem won't be asking Him for anything. Just like the Midrash Rabbah states in Parashas Bo that when Bnei Yisrael saw the miracles and supernatural wonders that the Creator was doing for them, they trusted Him and that is why it says 'Bnei Yisrael saw the great hand that Hashem inflicted upon Egypt; and the people revered Hashem and they had faith in Hashem and in Moshe, His servant.' When a person mentions this redemption, where our forefathers trusted Hashem and He saved them, and then he immediately davens, he is demonstrating that he too trusts that Hashem will answer him just like He answered Bnei Yisrael because of their faith in Him, and this is why he merits a place in the World to Come."

We see from these words that the main part of faith is to strengthen our trust in Hashem in asking Him to fulfill our needs in every single thing. The verse in *Yirmiyahu* states: אָרוּר הַגֶּבֶר אֲשֶׁר יִבְטַח בָּאָדָם[16] — "cursed is the man who trusts in a person," yet one who trusts Hashem is blessed as it states further:[17] בָּרוּךְ הַגֶּבֶר אֲשֶׁר יִבְטַח בַּה׳ — "blessed is the man who trusts in Hashem." And when a person makes an effort to grow in this characteristic, he is guaranteed assistance from Heaven. As the Rambam writes,[18] God imbued every Jewish soul with faith in Him like it says,[19] וְגַם בְּךָ יַאֲמִינוּ לְעוֹלָם — "they will also believe in You forever."

Observing these miracles that Hashem did for Bnei Yisrael

---

14. *Berachos* 4b.
15. Ibid.
16. *Yirmiyahu* 17:5.
17. Ibid. 17:7.
18. *Iggeres Teiman.*
19. *Shemos* 19:9.

endows a person with love and fear of God and strengthens his faith and trust to the point where he accepts the yoke of Heaven upon himself with love. As Rabbeinu Yonah says:[20] The whole purpose of *Yetzias Mitzraim* was accepting the yoke of Heaven and God's kingship over us, to be His servants as the verse states כִּי עֲבָדַי הֵם אֲשֶׁר הוֹצֵאתִי אֹתָם מֵאֶרֶץ מִצְרָיִם[21] — *"for they are My servants whom I have taken out of the land of Egypt."* When a person links redemption to davening, he proves that by virtue of his mentioning the Exodus from Egypt, he accepts upon himself the yoke of serving God, as our Sages state,[22] אֵיזוֹ הִיא עֲבוֹדָה שֶׁבַּלֵּב זוֹ תְּפִלָּה — *"which service [of God] is in the heart?. . .this is prayer."* Therefore a person merits life in the World to Come, and this is the purpose of mentioning and examining the miracles of *Yetzias Mitzraim*.

The Rambam asserts that it is a mitzvah to mention *Yetzias Mitzraim* every day and night.[23] This is based on the words of Ben Zoma in the Gemara.[24] Yet the Rambam does not list this as a mitzvah in his סֵפֶר הַמִּצְוֹת. The Acharonim ponder why the Rambam does not count this as one of the 613 mitzvos.[25] It would seem that according to the Rambam, the obligation to remember the Exodus is not a mitzvah of its own, but rather is part of the mitzvah of reciting *Shema*. This warrants explanation: What does mentioning the Exodus have to do with reciting *Shema*, whose main focus — as the Mishnah states[26] — is accepting the yoke of heaven and the mitzvos?

According to the above it seems that remembering the Exodus from Egypt is a prerequisite to accepting the yoke of heaven, because through remembering the Exodus a person is aware of his servitude to God, which was the whole purpose of the Exodus. Once he is cognizant of this, he is now ready to accept upon himself the yoke of Heaven, like a slave accepting upon himself the yoke of the master.

---

20. *Berachos* 2b.
21. *Vayikra* 25:42.
22. *Taanis* 2b.
23. *Rambam, Hilchos Krias Shema* 1:3.
24. *Berachos* 12b.
25. See also *Tzelach, Berachos* 12b and *Ohr Same'ach Hilchos Krias Shema* 1:3.
26. *Berachos* 13a.

Torah as a Means
of Acquiring Faith in God

THERE IS ANOTHER WAY OF ATTAINING FAITH IN GOD and a love and fear of Him, aside from observing all His wonders: through examining and toiling in Torah study. The Rambam writes:[27] *"Hashem in His love has commanded us to think about and examine His commandments, His words, and His acts till we grasp Hashem and can internalize it fully to the point of ecstasy. This is the love that is incumbent upon us."*

We see from the words of the Rambam that there are two paths which lead to love of God. Actually it is possible that the Rambam is discussing two ways, or two different aspects, of loving God, not merely two pathways to achieving that love. In *Sefer HaMitzvos* the Rambam discusses a love that is intellectual, deriving pleasure from understanding. But in *Hilchos Teshuvah*[28] the Rambam writes: *"... and what is the proper love? That one love God a great love that is so powerful that his very soul is bound with the love of God, such that he is constantly contemplating this love as though he were a lovesick person who doesn't have the capacity to think of anything other than [the object of his love] and he is constantly thinking about [it], wherever he may be, while he is eating or drinking. Even more than that form of lovesickness we are obligated to love God like we were commanded "with all your heart and with all your soul." This is what Shlomo HaMelech refered to when he wrote, שֶׁחוֹלַת אַהֲבָה אָנִי*[29] *— 'that I am sick with love.' In fact, all of Shir HaShirim is an allegory for this love."*

We see from here that love of God is in the realm of the emotional; a love that burns in the heart of a person till he becomes lovesick.

It seems that the two ways of attaining love of God are referring to the two aspects of this love. Attaining an intellectual love

---

27. *Sefer HaMitzvos;* Mitzvah 3.
28. *Hilchos Teshuvah* 10:3.
29. *Shir HaShirim* 5:8.

of God is achieved through learning Torah, and attaining the emotional love of God is achieved through looking at His wonders in the world. It would seem from the words of the Rambam that the former aspect of loving God is the primary commandment, while the latter is not so much a commandment but a desirable mode of behavior. The Rambam writes זֹאת הִיא הָאַהֲבָה הַמְחוּיֶּבֶת, *this is the love that is **required***, and therefore he includes this in *Sefer HaMitzvos* which deals with the commandments in the Torah. But in *Hilchos Teshuvah* the Rambam writes that love in the heart, the emotional type of love, is the הָאַהֲבָה הָרְאוּיָה, *the **befitting** love*, which would indicate that although this is a desirable mode of love, it is not a commandment, and therefore the Rambam wrote about this in *Hilchos Yesodei HaTorah,* where he discusses character development in addition to discussing the commandments.

We find two approaches in the Rishonim concerning the first *pasuk* of *Shema* where we accept upon ourselves עוֹל מַלְכוּת שָׁמַיִם, *the yoke of heaven.* The *Sefer HaChinuch*[30] writes that accepting upon ourselves the yoke of heaven is the mitzvah of believing in God's Oneness, and that in saying *Shema* we accept, know, and believe that Hashem our God is One. According to the *Sefer HaChinuch*, the crux of accepting the yoke of Heaven is in saying ה' אֶחָד, *Hashem is One*. But the *Avudraham*[31] writes in the name of the *Riva* that the crux of accepting *Ol Malchus Shamayim,* the yoke of Heaven, is not merely in accepting God's Oneness but in accepting His Kingship over us, as he writes,

> *"There are ten positive commandments in this Parashah [Shema], one of them is accepting the yoke of heaven as it says 'Hashem our God,' and the second, the Oneness of God, as it says 'Hashem is One.'"*

Thus we see that accepting the yoke of heaven is manifest in "ה', אֱלֹקֵינוּ," and belief in One God is sourced in "ה' אֶחָד."[32]

Taking these two opinions into consideration, there are really two aspects to the core of our belief: ה' אֱלֹקֵינוּ, that *God is our King*, that He chose us from all the nations and that we accept

---

30. Mitzvah 417.
31. *Seder Shacharis shel Chol.*
32. See also *Rabbeinu Yonah, Shaar HaAvodah,* pp. 23-24.

His Kingship over us, and אֶחָד 'ה, that *He is One and the only One,* Ruler of the world. The way to achieve complete faith in terms of ה' אֱלֹקֵינוּ is through learning and toiling in Torah that was given to *us* as an inheritance and to no other nation — מוֹרָשָׁה קְהִלַּת יַעֲקֹב — *"the heritage of the Congregation of Jacob,"* and this is what the Rambam refers to in *Sefer HaMitzvos* as mentioned earlier. The way to achieve perfection in terms of אֶחָד 'ה is through looking at the wonders of creation and through these see that God is the only God in the world and wonder that His wisdom is infinite and beyond measure, and this is what the Rambam refers to in *Hilchos Yesodei HaTorah.*

Similarly the two *berachos* of *Shema* refer to these two principles. בִּרְכַּת הַמְּאוֹרוֹת, *the blessing of the luminaries,* which speaks of the wonders of God's creations, parallels the אֶחָד 'ה aspect, alluded to in the Rambam in *Hilchos Yesodei HaTorah,* and the *berachah* of *Ahavah Rabbah,* the *berachah* on Torah study,[33] parallels the 'ה אֱלֹקֵינוּ aspect alluded to in the Rambam in *Sefer HaMitzvos.* The two *berachos* of *Shema* parallel the two ways of achieving a love of God, which in turn parallel the two principles of accepting God's sovereignty over us.

I heard from my Rebbe, the Rebbe of Sanz Klausenberg *z"tl,* that anyone who is fortunate enough to learn Torah can attain all the levels of ה' אַהֲבַת, *love of God,* by learning Torah, and does not need to observe the wonders of nature. Our Sages tell us[34] that הַמְהַלֵּךְ בַּדֶּרֶךְ וְשׁוֹנֶה וּמַפְסִיק מִמִּשְׁנָתוֹ וְאוֹמֵר, מַה נָּאֶה אִילָן זֶה וּמַה נָּאֶה נִיר זֶה, מַעֲלֶה עָלָיו הַכָּתוּב כְּאִלּוּ מִתְחַיֵּב בְּנַפְשׁוֹ — *"One who walks on the road while reviewing [a Torah lesson] but interrupts his review and exclaims, 'How beautiful is this tree! How beautiful is this plowed field!' Scripture considers it as if he bears guilt for his soul."* The Rebbe explained the reason for this as follows: Because he is a *talmid chacham,* reviewing a Torah lesson, he needs to attain his love of God through his study and not through the beauty of nature.

---

33. As explained in *Berachos* 9b.
34. *Pirkei Avos* 3:9.

Natural Order
and Supernatural Order

I T IS IMPORTANT FOR US TO KNOW THAT NOT ONLY IS nature comprised of Divine Providence and God's hidden miracles, but furthermore, as the Rishonim teach us, the main point of Creation — its whole foundation — is premised on a miraculous order to the world. As the *Akeidas Yitzchak* writes,[35] up until Adam's sin, the world was governed by miraculous law, and the laws of nature were subject to this system affected by Adam's morality. The whole world was subjugated to do man's will so that he, in turn, could do God's will, as our Sages teach us,[36] *the ministering angels would roast his meat and strain his wine.* (The Zohar writes[37] that if not for Adam's original sin, he would have had control over the ministering angels.) The earth sprouted only trees and fruits that benefitted man, and only after he sinned did the earth produce thorns and thistles. Once Adam had distanced himself from his intended purpose, namely, to serve his Creator, the world became distanced from its original intention of serving man. Therefore man is called *Olam Kattan*, a small world, because the whole world is directed by him.

Man's impact on the world continues even after he sinned; every action that a person does influences the nature of the world. The whole of creation was put into effect for man to do God's will, and man in turn executes his influence on the world. As our Sages teach,[38] לֹא נִבְרָא כָּל הָעוֹלָם כּוּלוֹ אֶלָּא לְצַוֵּות לָזֶה — *"the entire world was created only as an accompaniment for this person."*[39] Similarly Rashi teaches[40] that the world was created for the Torah and for Bnei

---

35. *Parashas Noach, Shaar 12, Maamar Niggun HaOlam.*
36. *Sanhedrin 59b.*
37. *Zohar Chadash 14.*
38. *Shabbos 30b.*
39. "לְצַוֵּות" in this context can also mean *command;* namely, the entire world is there at the behest of man.
40. *Bereishis 1:1.*

Yisrael, both called רֵאשִׁית, the *first* or *primary*.[41] Says the Ramban,[42] *When Bnei Yisrael keep the mitzvos as they should, Eretz Yisrael will be as it was prior to man's sin, no animal or beast will kill or harm man....*

...the principle is that when Bnei Yisrael are complete and numerous, they are not governed by nature at all, not physically, not concerning their land, not collectively as a nation, nor individually. God will bless their bread and water, will remove any sickness from among them such that they will not even need a doctor nor seek out medicinal remedies, as the verse says, אֲנִי ה' רֹפְאֶךָ[43] — *"I am Hashem, your Healer."*

This concept can be explained by the Mishnah:[44] *R' Shimon ben Elazar says: "Have you ever seen an animal or a bird that has a trade? Yet they sustain themselves without travail, though they were created only to serve me, whereas I was created to serve my Master. Does it not follow that I certainly should be able to sustain myself without difficulty? However, I have corrupted my deeds and thereby forfeited my sustenance."*

We see from here that had man not sinned he would have received his sustenance without any trouble and toil, just like the animals and the birds.

Livelihood is not the only thing influenced by man's actions; rather, the whole world, all of nature, is influenced by man's actions. As the Mishnah states,[45] בַּעֲשָׂרָה מַאֲמָרוֹת נִבְרָא הָעוֹלָם. וּמַה תַּלְמוּד לוֹמַר? ... אֶלָּא לְהִפָּרַע מִן הָרְשָׁעִים שֶׁמְּאַבְּדִין אֶת הָעוֹלָם שֶׁנִּבְרָא בַּעֲשָׂרָה מַאֲמָרוֹת, וְלִתֵּן שָׂכָר טוֹב לַצַּדִּיקִים שֶׁמְּקַיְּמִין אֶת הָעוֹלָם שֶׁנִּבְרָא בַּעֲשָׂרָה מַאֲמָרוֹת — *"With ten utterances the world was created. What does this come to teach us? ... This was to exact punishment from the wicked who destroy the world that was created with ten utterances, and to bestow goodly reward upon the righteous who sustain the world that was created by ten utterances."*

Man's actions are what maintain or destroy, elevate or degrade the universe. This correlation between man's actions and the world

---

41. For further insight, see *Rambam, Moreh Nevuchim.*
42. *Vayikra* 26:6.
43. *Shemos* 15:26.
44. *Kiddushin* 82a.
45. *Pirkei Avos* 5:1.

is not just on a collective level but on an individual level as well. Any individual who has perfected himself and elevated himself to levels of holiness and purity has the whole world subjugated to him and designed to serve him so that he, in turn, can serve God — all because he is doing God's will. We can now answer the difficulty with Abaye's words in the Gemara:[46] *"How inferior is this person for whom the natural order was changed."* For does it not seems strange that a person for whom natural orders change is called inferior? But according to the above we can understand. In every generation God planted righteous people who affected salvations and through whom many great wonders were performed, as we see with R' Chanina ben Dosa in the Gemara in *Berachos*.[47] Even in more recent generations God had mercy on His children and placed righteous people among them through whom great miracles were performed. Would anyone say about these righteous individuals, "How inferior these people are, for whom the laws of Creation have changed"? Clearly not. For concerning these righteous and holy people there was no change in the laws of nature, but a return to the real, original intention of the world — to subjugate the laws of nature to the will of these righteous individuals who deserve this, because their whole life — their whole essence — is dedicated to God and His Torah. But the Gemara that discussed the natural orders being changed referred to average people, people for whom a man being capable of nursing a child is truly a change in the laws of nature. Thus we can answer the question of the Tosafos Yeshanim on Mordechai and Esther as well, for the Gemara was discussing average people. But with regard to Mordechai and Esther there was no change in the laws of nature. In this case nature was returning to the original intention of the world: that of subjugating the laws of nature to the will of the righteous.

This is what is meant by our Sages' words that the Exodus from Egypt was not orchestrated through an angel but by God alone. Because Bnei Yisrael were not yet deserving of the laws of nature changing for them, the redemption needed to be brought about

---

46. *Shabbos* 53b.

47. See, for example, the episode with R' Chanina ben Dosa cited on *Berachos* 34b and *Taanis* 24b-25a.

by God Himself so that He could change nature for them. This is what R' Yose of Yukras said to his son,[48] אַתָּה הִטְרַחְתָּ אֶת קוֹנְךָ לְהוֹצִיא תְּאֵנָה פֵּירוֹתֶיהָ שֶׁלֹּא בִּזְמַנָּהּ יֵאָסֵף שֶׁלֹּא בִּזְמַנּוֹ — *"You troubled your Creator to make the fig tree bring forth its fruit when it was not its time, let [that person] be taken from the world when it is not yet his time."* Any change in the laws of nature is done by God Himself, not through an angel or any messenger. Thus we find in *Hallel* the *pasuk,* "מַה לְּךָ הַיָּם כִּי תָנוּס — *"What ails you, O sea, that you flee?"* At that point Bnei Yisrael were not deserving of the laws of nature being suspended for them, and therefore the Psalmist wonders, *What ails you, O sea, that you flee?*

Seeing the Sounds

ON A DEEPER LEVEL, GOD'S REVELATION THROUGH open and revealed miracles has the ability to affect man's view and understanding of the world, to heighten his outlook on the world around him and his relationship to it. Our Sages say,[49] שֶׁהָיוּ רוֹאִין אֶת הַנִּשְׁמָע וְשׁוֹמְעִין אֶת הַנִּרְאָה — *"they were able to see the sounds and hear the sights."* They were also able to point at God and say, זֶה קֵלִי וְאַנְוֵהוּ — *"This is my God and I will glorify Him."*

A deep concept is gleaned from this. The Nefesh HaChaim explains[50] that of all the senses with which man has been blessed by God, sight is the most accurate. Anything which a person has seen with his own eyes, he has not even a shadow of a doubt in his heart as to the authenticity of that thing's existence. With other senses — hearing, for example — a person might hear something but not be absolutely certain as to what it is he heard, or its authenticity. Our Sages say,[51] לֹא תְהֵא שְׁמִיעָה גְּדוֹלָה מֵרְאִיָּה — *"the hearing should not be greater than the sighting."* But Bnei Yisrael, children

---

48. *Taanis* 24a.
49. *Mechilta, Parashas Yisro.*
50. *Nefesh HaChaim, Shaar* 3, Ch. 11, in a note.
51. *Rosh Hashanah* 25b.

of God who cling to the faith of their fathers, know that eyesight is not what determines the truth of something's existence. Even God, *because of Whom all things in existence in the heavens and the earth and in between is in existence solely because of His existence,*[52] said, כִּי לֹא יִרְאַנִי הָאָדָם וָחָי — *"for no human can see Me and live."* Thus, our eyes do not even see the essence of the ultimate Existence!

What really does man amount to, if not the soul that resides within him, the soul that his Creator breathed into him — and the soul is not even visible! Our eyes cannot see the ministering angels who are carrying out God's will in His world, or the demons and spirits who hover in space. We know these things to exist because our fathers have told us so, and we have received the tradition from our holy teachers in each generation.[53] The *Sefer HaChinuch* writes in his introduction that the basis of our faith is the tradition that has been passed down from father to son, generation to generation, even though these things are not visible to the human eye.

When our forefathers stood at Har Sinai they attained a level of spirituality whereby they were able to *see the sounds*, meaning that they believed that which they had heard as though they had actually *seen* it. They heard that which is seen, the whole physical world was so removed from their consciousness and feelings that it was as if it were only hearsay,[54] not truly verifiable.

Based on the above we can explain what is brought in the following Gemara:[55] *R' Yochanan once sat and lectured: The Holy One, Blessed is He, will one day bring precious stones and pearls which are thirty amos by thirty amos, and He will cut out from them an opening of ten amos by twenty amos, and He will place them at the gates of Jerusalem. A certain student mocked him for discussing such incredible occurrences. The student said: Now, we cannot find precious stones and pearls even the size of an egg of a small dove, can stones of such an immense size ever be found? After a time the student's ship set sail upon the sea, and he saw ministering angels sitting and*

---

52 *Rambam, Hilchos Yesodei HaTorah* 1:1.

53. For further insight see the *Ramban* on *Devarim* 4:9.

54. For further insight see the *Meshech Chachmah* on *Parashas Chukas* and the *Meor Einayim* on *Parashas Beshalach* where each of them writes that a person must ensure the power of hearing controls the power of seeing.

55. *Bava Basra* 75a.

sawing precious stones and pearls that were thirty amos by thirty amos, and ten amos by a height of twenty amos was cut from them. The student said to the ministering angels, For whom are these? They told him that the Holy One, Blessed is He, will one day place them at the gates of Jerusalem. The student came back before R' Yochanan and said to him, My Master! Continue to lecture! You are fit to lecture. Just as you said, so I saw. R' Yochanan said to him: You empty person! Had you not seen it yourself would you not have believed it? You are one who mocks the words of the Sages. R' Yochanan set his eyes upon him and the student became a heap of bones.

It is interesting to note that the student was not punished for mocking the words of his teacher R' Yochanan, but rather was punished when he returned to R' Yochanan to confirm what he had said. This warrants explanation, but based on what we've learned we can understand. When the student came back to R' Yochanan and expressed his amazement and excitement for what he saw, he said, "Just as you (R' Yochanan) said, so I saw." By saying this he showed that through his **seeing** with his own eyes he believed what R' Yochanan had **said,** and therefore he retracted his mockery of R' Yochanan's initial words to him. R' Yochanan grew angry with him and said, "You empty person! Had you not seen it yourself would you not have believed it?" R' Yochanan was rebuking his student for not believing the words of the Torah. Is it our **eyes** — what we see before us — that determine whether we believe something, or the Torah — which we hear with our **ears** — that determines what we believe? For this the student was punished, because someone of his stature (and surely he was of a great caliber — he had witnessed ministering angels and even conversed with them) should be able to "see the sound," to believe that which his ears hear, and know it to be true as if he had seen it.

The student's punishment was measure for measure, and in it we see a reminder of his transgression. To the naked eye, a human being is merely a heap of bones. Yet we know that his life comes solely from the power of his Divine soul that sustains him and makes him alive. Because the student valued only that which his eyes were able to see, he was turned into a heap of bones, measure for measure. This is why R' Yochanan said to him: You empty person! Do you not admit that you have a soul in you although it cannot be seen? Why can't you "see," i.e. believe, what is heard, instead of only "hearing," i.e. believing, what you see?

We find that it was characteristic of R' Yochanan to impart to his students that there is no truth like the truth of Torah, even when things appear to be in complete opposition to reality. Says the Gemara,[56] *[R' Yitzchak] said to [Rav Nachman]: Thus said R' Yochanan: Yaakov Avinu never died. [Rav Nachman] said to [R' Yitzchak]: Was it for naught that the eulogizers eulogized him and the embalmers embalmed him and the buriers buried him!? [R' Yitzchak] replied to [Rav Nachman]: I am expounding a verse etc ....*

Rashi explains that Yaakov really didn't die, but that to the embalmers and eulogizers he appeared dead. Expounding on a verse, R' Yochanan said that Yaakov Avinu didn't die, although this seems to contradict reality.

The Gemara[57] relates: *Rav Sheishes was full of light (i.e. blind). Everyone was going to greet the king. Rav Sheishes rose and went with them. A certain Sadducee met [Rav Sheishes], and said to him, "Whole pitchers go to the river. Where do broken [pitchers] go?" [Rav Sheishes] answered him, "Come and see that I know more about the king's procession than you do." The first troop passed. When it became loud, that Sadducee said to [Rav Sheishes], "The king has come!" Rav Sheishes said to him, "He is not coming." A second troop passed by. When it became loud, that Sadducee said to Rav Sheishes, "Now the king is coming!" Rav Sheishes said to him, "The king is not coming." A third [troop] passed by. When it subsequently grew quiet, Rav Sheishes said to him, "It is now certain that the king is coming." That Sadducee asked him, "How do you know this?" He answered him, "For the royalty of earth is a reflection of the royalty of Heaven. Hence I knew that the king would come when it grew quiet after three troops passed by because it is written regarding the royalty of Heaven: 'Go out and stand on the mountain before Hashem. And behold, Hashem was passing, and a great powerful wind, smashing mountains and breaking rocks, went before Hashem; Hashem was not in the wind. After the wind came an earthquake; Hashem was not in the earthquake. After the earthquake came a fire; Hashem was not*

---

56. *Taanis* 5b.
57. *Berachos* 58a.

in the fire. After the fire came a still, thin sound.' "[58] When the king finally came, Rav Sheishes began blessing him. That Sadducee said to him, "Someone you cannot see you are blessing!" What became of that Sadducee? Some say that his colleagues painted his eyes. And some say that Rav Sheishes set his eyes upon him and he became a heap of bones.

This, too teaches us a profound lesson, that what our eyes see does not determine the absolute truth; rather, what we hear. Rav Sheishes who was blind not only understood spiritual matters better than the Sadducee but understood earthly matters better than him too. When the Sadducee did not learn a lesson, remained set in his ways to value "seeing" as the uppermost sense and to disregard Rav Sheishes by asking him, "Someone you cannot see you are blessing!" he was punished measure for measure and his eyes were painted or became a heap of bones as mentioned above.

Based on this we can explain what the *pasuk* states,[59] אֶת קֹלְךָ שָׁמַעְתִּי בַּגָּן וָאִירָא כִּי עֵירֹם אָנֹכִי — "I heard the sound of You in the garden and I hid [i.e. was afraid] because I am naked." Adam did not merit seeing the voice of God but only heard it, and that is why he was afraid. But in future times we will merit כִּי עַיִן בְּעַיִן יִרְאוּ בְּשׁוּב ה' צִיּוֹן,[60] וְרָאוּ כָל בָּשָׂר יַחְדָּו כִּי פִּי ה' דִּבֵּר[61] — "with their own eyes they will see that Hashem returns to Zion, and all flesh together will **see** that the mouth of Hashem has **spoken**." וְהוּא יַשְׁמִיעֵנוּ בְּרַחֲמָיו שֵׁנִית לְעֵינֵי כָּל חַי — "and He will let us hear, in His compassion, for a second time in the presence of all the living."[62] We will once again be able to *see the sounds* when God *will let us hear in the presence of all the living.* Perhaps this is why we are commanded, ... הִשָּׁמֶר לְךָ פֶּן תִּשְׁכַּח אֶת הַדְּבָרִים אֲשֶׁר רָאוּ עֵינֶיךָ[63] — "beware for yourself ... lest you forget the things your eyes have **seen**," which it does not mention by remembering the Exodus or any of the other six constant remembrances.[64]

---

58. *I Melachim* 19:11-12.
59. *Bereishis* 3:10.
60. *Yeshayahu* 52:8.
61. Ibid. 40:5.
62. *Kedushah* of *Mussaf* for Shabbos and Yom Tov.
63. *Devarim* 4:9.
64. According to the *Ramban* this is a negative commandment. Also see

Everything That God Does Is for the Good

THERE IS ANOTHER GREAT LESSON WE CAN LEARN FROM studying and examining the miracles that God performed for our forefathers; namely, that these miracles are a mighty and powerful expression of God's Attribute of Mercy and kindness. God changed the set order of creation and suspended the laws of the nature solely for the benefit and salvation of his beloved children, Bnei Yisrael. In this sense too, a miracle, a *"nes,"* serves as a banner demonstrating that God's measure of justice is inherent in His Attribute of Mercy and stems from it for, מִפִּי עֶלְיוֹן [65]לֹא תֵצֵא הָרָעוֹת — *"from the mouth of the most High evil does not emanate."* Even though at times we do not see the mercy in the judgment, we must believe and proclaim that כָּל דְּעָבִיד רַחֲמָנָא לְטַב עָבִיד — *"everything that God does is for the good."* Even when a person thinks that God's attribute of judgment has targeted him, he must toil to see and feel God's mercy inherent in the judgment. The *pasuk* states: בָּנִים אַתֶּם לַה׳ אֱלֹקֵיכֶם לֹא תִתְגֹּדְדוּ וְלֹא תָשִׂימוּ [66]קָרְחָה בֵּין עֵינֵיכֶם לָמֵת — *"you are children to Hashem, your God — you shall not cut yourselves and you shall not make a bald spot between your eyes for a dead person."* The Ibn Ezra comments on this,[67]

You must know that you are children of God and that he loves you more than a father loves a child, [and therefore] do not mutilate yourselves for anything that He does because anything that He does is for the good and if you do not understand it, [it is like] young children who do not understand the actions of their father but they trust him. So should you do.[68]

A story is told of a person who came to the great Maggid of Mezeritch, and asked the Maggid to teach him how to keep what our Sages have taught us: חַיָּיב אָדָם לְבָרֵךְ עַל הָרָעָה כְּשֵׁם שֶׁמְּבָרֵךְ עַל

Iggeres Teiman of the *Rambam*.
65. *Eichah* 3:38.
66. *Devarim* 14:1.
67. Ibid.
68. For further insight see *Ramban* ibid.

[69]הַטּוֹבָה — "*a person is obligated to bless God for the bad just as he blesses God for the good.*" The Maggid instructed him to go to Reb Zusha of Hanipoli, who could teach him how this is done. The man went to speak with Reb Zusha whose countenance indicated that he was poor and destitute, dressed in rags and suffering terribly. He told Reb Zusha that the Maggid had instructed him to come to Reb Zusha to get instruction as to how to thank God for the bad as well as the good. Reb Zusha responded in amazement, "Surely you are mistaken. I truly do not know how to thank God for the bad, because never in my life have I experienced anything bad. I've been happy with my lot, and from my youth to the present day God has bestowed only goodness and kindness upon me."

This was the modus operandi of the Sages in the Talmud. The Gemara[70] tells of R' Chanina ben Dosa,

And another thing happened concerning R' Chanina ben Dosa, who went to study Torah from Rabban Yochanan ben Zakkai, and Rabban Yochanan ben Zakkai's son fell ill. [Rabban Yochanan ben Zakkai] said to him: "Chanina , my son! Seek Divine mercy for him that he might live." So R' Chanina lay his head between his knees and sought Divine mercy for him and he lived. Whereupon Rabban Yochanan ben Zakkai said: "Had Ben Zakkai [i.e. myself] stuck his head between his knees all day long they would not have paid any attention to him in the Heavenly Court." His wife said to him: "Is Chanina then greater than you?" He said to her: "No; rather he is like a servant before the King, who comes and goes freely and is on intimate terms with Him, while I am like an important officer before the King, appearing in the palace only on important occasions, and am therefore on less intimate terms with Him."

Rav Levi Yitzchak of Berditchev explains [71]that a servant is not like an officer. A servant serves the king but does not understand the royal plans and tactics of the kingdom. He does not know its edicts and mores, and does not participate in shaping the laws of the kingdom. This is what Rabban Yochanan ben Zakkai meant when he said he is like an officer before the King. He meant he

---

69. *Berachos* 54a.
70. Ibid.
71. *Kedushas Levi, Parashas Chukas.*

knew how and why God operates in certain ways, and that all of God's measures are merciful and kind, and therefore his prayer for the salvation and healing of the destitute is not as accepted. But R' Chanina ben Dosa was like a servant before the king and when he witnessed the suffering of the Jewish people he was shaken to the core of his soul, and his prayer for their salvation was pure and unequivocally accepted.

There was another such "officer," and that was R' Akiva ben Yosef who instructed us to say, כָּל דְּעָבִיד רַחֲמָנָא לְטַב עָבִיד — "everything that God does is for the good," on every calamity that befalls us. The Gemara [72] tells how with each tragedy R' Akiva thanked God and saw His mercy and kindness even in the midst of the tragedy.[73] Not only in his own suffering did R' Akiva see the hand of God but even in others' suffering. The Gemara tells us[74] regarding when his great teacher, R' Eliezer ben Hurkinus, fell ill, *When R' Eliezer took ill, his students came in to visit him. [R' Eliezer] said to them: "There is great anger in the world!" [All but one of the students] began to weep, but R' Akiva laughed. [The other students] said to him: "Why do you laugh?" [R' Akiva] said to them: "But why are you weeping?" They said to him: "Is it possible that a Torah scroll dwells in pain and we do not weep?" [R' Akiva] said to [the other students]: "For that [very reason] I am laughing! Indeed, as long as I saw my master, R' Eliezer, prospering — for his wine does not ferment into vinegar, his flax is not smitten by hail or blight, his oil does not turn rancid and his honey does not spoil, I said to myself, 'Perhaps, God forbid, my master has already received his world' (i.e. the full measure of reward for his righteous deeds in this world). But now that I see my master in pain, I rejoice."*

The Gemara proceeds to tell us that when R' Eliezer took ill, four sages came in to visit him. They were R' Tarfon, R' Yehoshua, R' Elazar ben Azariah, and R' Akiva. After the first three praised their teacher at length, comparing him to the orb of the sun, a drop of rain and a father and mother, R' Akiva spoke up and said, "Precious

---

72. *Berachos* 60b.
73. See also *Yerushalmi Berachos* 9:5 and *Yerushalmi Sotah* 5:5 that even when the Romans arrested him for studying Torah and they were about to execute him, he was still happy (brought in *Tosafos Sotah* 31).
74. *Sanhedrin* 101a.

are sufferings!" We see that R' Akiva saw the kindness and mercy of God even in the suffering of his master, R' Eliezer ben Hurkenus.

R' Akiva saw God's attribute of kindness not only in individual human suffering, but also in a larger, collective context: the exile of the Jewish people and the destruction of the *Beis HaMikdash*. The Gemara tells us,[75] *And once, after the destruction of the Temple, Rabban Gamliel, R' Elazar ben Azariah, R' Yehoshua, and R' Akiva were traveling on the road, and they heard the sound of the Roman crowds in the plaza of [Rome] one hundred and twenty mil [away], and they started to weep. But R' Akiva was laughing. They asked him: "For what reason are you laughing?" He replied to them: "And you, for what reason are you weeping?" They answered him: "These heathens who bow down to idols and burn incense to idolatry live in security and in calm, and as for us, the house that is the footstool of our God (i.e. the Temple) is consumed in fire, should we not weep?" He said to them: "For this very reason I am laughing! For if such is the reward for those who transgress His will, that they dwell in such security and calm, then for those who do His will, how much more so; how much greater reward can they expect!"*

On another occasion they were coming up to Jerusalem after the destruction of the Temple. When they came to the Temple Mount they saw a fox emerging from the Holy of Holies, and they started to weep. But R' Akiva laughed. They said to him: "For what reason are you laughing?" He replied to them: "For what reason are you weeping?" They said to him: "A place about which it is written 'the non-Kohen who approaches shall die,' and now foxes prowl over it! Should we not weep?" He said to them: "For this very reason I am laughing... now that the prophecy of Uriah has been fulfilled, and Jerusalem and the Temple Mount are totally desolate, it is certain that the prophecy of Zechariah will be fulfilled."

We see from here that R' Akiva was an officer of God, who saw the light shining in the darkness, the good inherent in the seemingly bad, not only on an individual level but on a national level as well. He saw the lights of redemption rising and shining from the darkness of exile and destruction.[76]

---

75. *Makkos* 24a.
76. Heaven forbid that we foolishly think that R' Akiva was naturally jolly,

Perhaps now we can explain the Midrash[77] that Moshe said to God, שְׁלַח נָא בְּיַד תִּשְׁלָח בִּידֵי רַבִּי עֲקִיבָא — "Send through whomever You will send [to redeem Your people] through R' Akiva." At first glance, Moshe's suggestion is bewildering. The Medrash[78] teaches us that God showed Moshe every generation and its leaders, and if so, Moshe saw all the judges of the Jewish people, all the kings, the prophets, the men of the Great Assembly and their students — could he not find anyone suited for this task of redeeming the Jewish people and serving as their savior in their times of woe, other than R' Akiva?[79]

We find that after Bnei Yisrael sinned with the Golden Calf and Moshe begged God for forgiveness, he said to Him הוֹדִיעֵנִי נָא אֶת[80] דְּרָכֶךָ — "make Your way known to me." The Gemara[81] says that when Moshe asked God this question, what he was really asking was: *What is the reason why there are righteous people for whom things are good, and there are righteous people for whom things are bad? And there are wicked people for whom things are good, and wicked people for whom things are bad.* Moshe's question seems incongruent with his agenda of asking for forgiveness for Bnei

---

laughed easily and never cried. The Gemara (*Kiddushin* 1:1) says: "Her husband has revoked [her vows] and Hashem will forgive her." When R' Akiva would reach this verse he would weep. He would say: Now if someone who intended to eat pork but instead lamb's meat came into his hand the Torah nevertheless says [such a person] is in need of atonement and forgiveness, then someone who intended to eat pork and indeed pork came into his hand, how much more so is he in need of atonement and forgiveness! The Gemara continues that R' Akiva would likewise cry when he reached the verse "... and he did not know, he is guilty and must bear his iniquity." We see that this same R' Akiva who laughed when his friends cried would cry when others saw no reason to do so. (See *Sanhedrin* 65a for another example of this.) It is clear that the character traits of Chazal didn't stem from their natural personalities rather from the depth of their holy understanding, according to their individual souls, their specific purpose in life. See further *Ohr Yisrael* Ch. 28.

77. *Midrash Osios D'Rabbi Akiva Os* 90.
78. *Bamidbar Rabbah* 23:5.
79. See further *Menachos* 29b where the Gemara describes how when Moshe saw R' Akiva and his Torah, he said to God, "You have such a candidate, and You are giving the Torah through me?"
80. *Shemos* 33:13.
81. *Berachos* 7a.

Yisrael's sin — what does this question have to do with the Golden Calf? It's most probable that the deeper meaning of Moshe's question was with regard to Bnei Yisrael's fate as a result of their sin. Moshe saw what was going to happen to this people whom God had chosen and already at their outset they sin and are punished by sword and plague. God showed Moshe all future generations, each generation and its leaders, and Moshe saw the future of the Jewish people, all their suffering and travails, and that is why he asked this question about a righteous person who suffers and a wicked person who has it good.[82] It follows that when Moshe saw R' Akiva, how he saw the fox roaming where the Holy of Holies once stood, how he heard the clamor of Rome, and nevertheless said *everything that God does is for the good,* Moshe said *this* is the person that is deserving of being the leader of the Jewish people, because he is the most appropriate candidate suited for the task. R'Akiva, more than any other person, knows how to bear suffering and see the good inherent in it.

In answer to his question, God told Moshe: וְרָאִיתָ אֶת אֲחֹרָי וּפָנַי לֹא יֵרָאוּ — *"you will see My back but My face may not be seen."*[83] The Gemara there tells us that God showed him the knot of His *tefillin.* The knots of the *tefillin* form the Name שׁ־ד־י, and there are two explanations as to what this particular Name of God represents. One is אֲנִי הוּא שֶׁאָמַרְתִּי לָעוֹלָם דַּי — *"I am the One Who told the world 'enough,'"* i.e., that the world unfurled till God told it to cease.[84] The other explanation is שֶׁאֵין הָעוֹלָם וּמְלוֹאוֹ כְּדַאי לֵאלֹקוּתִי — *"the whole world cannot contain My Godliness."*[85] This Name represents constriction (He told the world to stop) which stems from the Attribute of דִּין, *Judgment.* It also represents a spreading out (the world cannot contain His Godliness), which stems from the Attribute of Mercy. We see that these two attributes are inextricably linked and even the Attribute of Judgment stems from God's mercy. This is one of the basic tenets of our faith, as our Sages have taught us. The *Tiferes Shlomo* explains the *pasuk* לְהַגִּיד בַּבֹּקֶר חַסְדֶּךָ וֶאֱמוּנָתְךָ בַּלֵּילוֹת — *"to*

---

82. See further in the aforementioned Gemara for the argument as to whether Moshe's request was granted or not.
83. *Shemos* 33:23.
84. *Chagigah* 12a.
85. *Bereishis Rabbah* 26:3. See further *Sefas Emes Parashas Vaeira.*

relate Your kindness in the dawn and Your faith in the nights," that the main test of faith is at night; namely, times of *hester panim,* when God is not visible, when the darkness covers the land and it seems as though the Attribute of Judgment has taken over the world. This is the main reason that the obligation of eating in the *succah* and eating matzah is on the first **night** of Yom Tov, for these mitzvos indicate a basic principle of faith; they are in remembrance of the Exodus from Egypt.

In this vein we can explain what the Medrash says[86] that when R' Yishmael Kohen Gadol was being executed, the ministering angels screamed out, ‏זו תּוֹרָה וְזוֹ שְׂכָרָהּ?!‏ — *"This is Torah and this is the reward for Torah study?!"* God responded to them that if they do not keep still, He will return the world back to ‏תֹהוּ וָבֹהוּ‏, the void and emptiness that was before Creation. The Ramban explains ‏תֹהוּ וָבֹהוּ‏ as the two cornerstones of the world that were created on the first day and from which all of Creation emanated.[87] But if God threatened to destroy the world and turn it back into ‏תֹהוּ וָבֹהוּ‏, why not destroy even the ‏תֹהוּ וָבֹהוּ‏, the two cornerstones? What use are the cornerstones of Creation if God doesn't want the world to be in existence at all?

We can explain this with the following *mashal*: A man goes to an expert tailor and orders a fancy garment. The tailor takes his measurements and tells him to bring him fabric of a specified length and width. After a few days the tailor shows him a beautifully crafted garment. Upon seeing the garment, he takes out a tape measure, measures the garment on all sides, and sees that the garment doesn't measure up to the original length and width of the fabric he gave the tailor. He demands that the tailor return the "stolen" fabric. The tailor responds that the man cannot truly understand where all the fabric went because he is not an expert at tailoring, but if he insists, he can take apart the garment and show him that all the pieces add up to the original size of the fabric, and he'll see that nothing was stolen. But would he really want the tailor to undo a beautifully crafted garment?

So too with God. We cannot comprehend God's thoughts because they are so removed from us, *as high as the heavens over the earth, so are My ways higher than your ways, and My thoughts*

---

86. *Midrash Eilah Ezkerah* and the *Piyut* in *Mussaf* for Yom Kippur.
87. *Rambam, Bereishis* 1:2.

than your thoughts,[88] and no living creature can fully understand the secrets of creation. As God said to Iyov, *"Where were you when I laid the earth's foundation? Tell, if you know understanding! Who sets its dimensions? — if you know — or who stretched a [surveyor's] line over it? Into what are its bases sunken, or who laid its cornerstone?"*[89] If I undo the "garment," if I return the world back to nothingness so you see all the secrets of creation, you will see that *The Rock! - perfect is His work, for all His paths are justice; a God of faith without iniquity, righteous and fair is He,*[90] and all his actions are great acts of merciful kindness.

I once heard from the Rebbe of Sanz זצוק״ל (and other Chassidic commentators explain this as well) that this is why we cover our eyes when we say *Shema*, when we accept upon ourselves the yoke of heaven.[91] When we accept upon ourselves the yoke of heaven by saying *Shema*, we say, ה׳ אֱלֹקֵינוּ ה׳ אֶחָד — *"Hashem our God, Hashem is One"*; namely, that the Attributes of Mercy and Judgment (represented by the Names הַוָיָה and אֱלֹקִים, respectively) are one and even the measure of judgment is contained within the realm of God's mercy. Even though it may appear to as though the Attribute of Judgment is at hand, we cover our eyes to demonstrate and proclaim that our belief that *everything God does is for the good* is untarnished.

In this vein the Kol Aryeh[92] explains the *pasuk* אַל תִּירָא מֵרְדָה מִצְרַיְמָה כִּי לְגוֹי גָדוֹל אֲשִׂימְךָ שָׁם. אָנֹכִי אֵרֵד עִמְּךָ מִצְרַיְמָה וְאָנֹכִי אַעַלְךָ גַם עָלֹה וְיוֹסֵף יָשִׁית יָדוֹ עַל עֵינֶיךָ[93] — *"Have no fear of descending to Egypt, for I shall establish you as a great nation there. I shall descend with you to Egypt, and I shall also surely bring you up; and Yosef shall place his hand on your eyes."* Yaakov was fearful of going down to Egypt — a spiritual wasteland — and God told him that even if initially the decree to go down to Egypt appears to be harsh, in the end it will be clearly revealed that it was for the good. Just like the selling of Yosef, which at first appeared as though the Attribute of דִין had

---

88. *Yeshayahu* 55:9.
89. *Iyov* 38:4-6.
90. *Devarim* 32:4.
91. See *Berachos* 13a and *Tur Orach Chaim* 61.
92. Introduction to *Shu"t Kol Aryeh, Pesach Tov*, 7.
93. *Bereishis* 46:3-4.

targeted Yaakov — his son being thrown into a pit and then sold to the Ishmaelites; in the end it became clear that God had sent Yosef down to Egypt to ensure their sustenance during the famine. This is why the *pasuk* says, וְיוֹסֵף יָשִׁית יָדוֹ עַל עֵינֶיךָ — *"and Yosef shall place his hand on your eyes,"* just like we do when we say *Shema*, to show that we are confident in our faith that inherent in the *din* is abundant mercy; we just haven't merited seeing the mercy as of yet. The Zohar alludes to this and states on this *pasuk,* דָּא הִיא רָזָא דִקְרִיאַת שְׁמַע — *"this [the story of Yosef being sold and Yaakov going down to Egypt] is the secret of saying Shema."*

The Kol Aryeh[94] also quotes the Chasam Sofer who explains the *pasuk,*[95] וְרָאִיתָ אֶת אֲחוֹרָי וּפָנַי לֹא יֵרָאוּ — *"and you will see My back, but My face may not be seen."* It is not within our power to see the inner kindnesses of God, inherent in the judgment, בִּרְאִיַּית פָּנִים, meaning, prior to the events happening. Rather, וְרָאִיתָ אֶת אֲחוֹרָי — *"and you shall see My back,* from behind — in *hindsight* — we and future generations see clearly the extent of God's goodness. We can now understand God's answer to Moshe when Moshe, upon seeing the horrible torture and death of R' Akiva, asked זוֹ תּוֹרָה וְזוֹ שְׂכָרָהּ?! — *"Is this Torah and is this its reward?!"* God said to him, שְׁתוֹק! כָּךְ עָלָה בְּמַחֲשָׁבָה לְפָנַי[96] — *"Quiet! This is part of My greater plan to which you are not privy."* It is only in hindsight — and if we merit it — that we see the mercy inherent in the judgment and the goodness in the bad, but not in the present of the harsh reality.

In the future, when the Gates of Wisdom open and *the earth will be as filled with Godly knowledge of Hashem as water covering the sea,*[97] then will our eyes see and our hearts rejoice when we understand that all the exiles we have had to endure, all the tragedies and calamities that have befallen us in this world were all merciful kindnesses from God and the key to our redemption. As the *pasuk* states,[98] הַזֹּרְעִים בְּדִמְעָה בְּרִנָּה יִקְצֹרוּ הָלוֹךְ יֵלֵךְ וּבָכֹה נֹשֵׂא מֶשֶׁךְ הַזָּרַע בֹּא יָבֹא בְרִנָּה נֹשֵׂא אֲלֻמֹּתָיו — *"Those who tearfully sow will reap in glad song. He who bears the measure of seeds walks along weeping, but*

---

94. Loc. cit.
95. *Shemos* 33:23.
96. *Menachos* 29b.
97. *Yeshayahu* 11:9.
98. *Tehillim* 126:5-6.

will return in exultation, a bearer of his sheaves." The exiles are like bearing measures of seeds and sowing, and the redemption is likened to reaping the wheat that was planted during the exile. When we merit the redemption, we will see how the exile dissipates like a bad dream, and [99] הָיִינוּ כְּחוֹלְמִים — "we will be as dreamers." The pasuk states, [100] אַל תִּשְׂמְחִי אוֹיַבְתִּי לִי כִּי נָפַלְתִּי קָמְתִּי כִּי אֵשֵׁב בַּחֹשֶׁךְ ה' אוֹר לִי — "Do not rejoice over me, my enemy, for though I fell, I will rise! Though I sit in the darkness, Hashem is a light unto me!" Chazal explain:[101] had I not fallen, I would not have risen, had I not sat in the darkness, I would not have had light. For the roots of redemption are entrenched in the exile, and in the future we will see how had we not fallen, we never would have risen. This is why we end the kinnos on Tishah B'Av with a kinnah in which the exile is compared to labor pains. אֵלִי צִיּוֹן וְעָרֶיהָ כְּמוֹ אִשָּׁה בְּצִירֶיהָ — "Wail, O Zion and her cities, like a woman suffering from birth travail." Just like the pains of birth are necessary and through them new life is brought into the world, so too the lights of redemption shine from the darkness of the exile.

Perhaps now we can explain the words of the Gemara:[102] "And Hashem will become King of all the earth, on that day Hashem will be One and His Name will be One." Is He not One today?! What does the verse mean by saying Hashem will be One on **that** day? R' Acha bar Chanina said: The World to Come is unlike this world. In this world, upon hearing good tidings one says: בָּרוּךְ הַטּוֹב וְהַמֵּטִיב, Blessed are You, Who is good and Who does good; and upon hearing bad tidings one says: בָּרוּךְ דַּיַּן הָאֱמֶת, Blessed are You, the true Judge. But in the World to Come, all of [the blessings] will be: בָּרוּךְ הַטּוֹב וְהַמֵּטִיב, Blessed are You, Who is good and Who does good. It seems from the Gemara that the change from this world to the next is only in terms of the blessing but not in terms of reality, meaning that the nature of things will not change, only our response to them. Our Sages did not say that this world has good and bad within it and the Next World has only goodness. Rather, our Sages said that man's relationship to events and his blessing on them will change in the Next World. In other words, in the Next World we will make the blessing of הַטּוֹב

---

99. See *Taanis* 23a.
100. *Michah* 7:8.
101. *Yalkut Shimoni, Tehillim, Remez* 628.
102. *Pesachim* 50b.

וְהַמֵּטִיב retroactively on all the "bad" things we experienced in this world, things for which we have already recited the blessing of בָּרוּךְ דַּיָּן הָאֱמֶת. In the future our mouths will fill with laughter and our tongues with joyous song for all the terrible things that happened to us in this world. We will see clearly how all the things we thought were catastrophic are actually the goodness and magnanimity of God, such that we will be able to make the blessing of הַטּוֹב וְהַמֵּטִיב retroactively for all the suffering we experienced in this world.

Our Sages teach us[103] that just as the nation was punished two-fold (as the *pasuk* states:[104] כִּי לָקְחָה מִיַּד ה' כִּפְלַיִם בְּכָל חַטֹּאתֶיהָ — *"for she has received double for all her sins from the hand of Hashem"*) so too will we merit being comforted twofold, as it says, נַחֲמוּ נַחֲמוּ[105] עַמִּי יֹאמַר אֱלֹקֵיכֶם — *"Comfort, comfort My people, says your God."* Perhaps we can explain that Bnei Yisrael have suffered twofold in their exiles. The actual trials and afflictions they suffered in the hands of their enemies and torturers, and God hiding His face giving the oppressors the opportunity to taunt them saying, "Where is your God?" Rashi's teaches[106] that a miracle had occurred for Yosef when he was sold to the Ishmaelites. Usually Ishmaelite caravans would transport crude oil, but the traders to whom Yosef was sold were carrying perfumes. The purpose of this miracle, say the *Baalei Mussar*, was to show Yosef that God was being merciful toward him even at this moment of distress,[107] עִמּוֹ אָנֹכִי בְצָרָה — *"I am with him in distress."* Throughout this hard exile, as the Jews have been cast in desolation, they haven't always merited seeing a sign from heaven, a sign of God's mercy. The הֶסְתֵּר פָּנִים, God hiding His face, is also twofold, as the *pasuk* states:[108] אָנֹכִי הַסְתֵּר אַסְתִּיר פָּנַי בַּיּוֹם הַהוּא — *"but I will surely have concealed My face on that day,"* using a double expression. With God hiding His face Bnei Yisrael have been punished twofold, and in the future we will be comforted twofold, when God will say "enough" to our trials and we will merit an era that is all goodness. We will be comforted when we see that all

---

103. *Yalkut Shimoni, Yirmiyahu, Remez* 312.
104. *Yeshayahu* 40:2.
105. Ibid.
106. *Bereishis* 37:25.
107. *Tehillim* 91:15.
108. *Devarim* 31:18.

our travails were for our benefit, and we will see that God has not abandoned us even for a moment.

Following the same line of thought, we can explain what our Sages teach us,[109] that in future times all the festivals will be canceled except for Purim. Why? When we take a closer look at the miracle of Purim, we see that Purim is very different from all the other festivals. All the other festivals are in essence a reminder and a testimony to God's revelation and His acting with us in a way that was miraculous, in ways that transcend the laws of nature. In the future, God's presence will be revealed to such a supernatural degree that it will not be necessary to have these reminders of God's miracles, and therefore all the festivals will be nullified. Whereas Purim is not merely a reminder of God's miracles, but a lesson for us to know that all of God's decrees are actually rooted in mercy, like the lots Haman drew to annihilate the Jewish people and God switched the outcome around, or the tree which Haman prepared on which to hang Mordechai, and where ultimately Haman and his sons were hanged. The Bnei Yissaschar explains that the name Purim differs from the names of other festivals. All the other festivals have names which attest to the miracles: פֶּסַח, Passover, because שֶׁפָּסַח הקב"ה עַל בָּתֵּי אֲבוֹתֵינוּ בְּמִצְרַיִם — "God passed over the houses of our forefathers in Egypt [when He struck the Egyptians]"; סֻכּוֹת is reminiscent of the Clouds of Glory that sheltered and protected us in the desert; חֲנוּכָּה, for the חֲנוּכַּת הַמִּזְבֵּחַ, the renewed inauguration of the Altar in the Temple. Purim is named not for the salvation but for the decree; it is called Purim for the פּוּר, the ballots that Haman cast. On Purim we commemorate not only the miracles, but the fact that the harsh decrees themselves turned out to be the keys to the redemption and salvation, and therefore the days of Purim will never be nullified, even in the future; for in the future we will see that all the exiles and all the harsh decrees were in actuality hidden kindnesses.[110]

The Gemara[111] asks where we find an allusion to the story of Esther in the Torah, and answers that the allusion is in the *pasuk*

---

109. *Yalkut Shimoni, Mishlei* 9:12 (944). Also brought down in the *Yotzer L'Shabbos Zachor.*
110. *Tzelach* on *Pesachim* (ibid.) writes that he heard this explanation in his youth from R' Efraim Reisheve, Maggid of Brod.
111. *Chullin* 139b.

וְאָנֹכִי הַסְתֵּר אַסְתִּיר פָּנַי בַּיּוֹם הַהוּא — *"but I will surely have concealed My face on that day."* This is not merely a play on the name אסתר and the words of the *pasuk* הַסְתֵּר אַסְתִּיר. Rather, the story of Esther is a lesson in how to cope with times of הֶסְתֵּר פָּנִים, God's hiding Himself. It would seem that this is the reason why we do not recite *Hallel* on Purim, rather we fulfill this obligation through the Megillah reading as the Gemara says, *Reading the Megillah on Purim is equivalent to reciting Hallel.* Even if one doesn't read the Megillah, one doesn't recite *Hallel.* The *Hallel* on Purim is also hidden just as the whole essence of the day is not revealed but concealed (though the *Meiri* comments that if one does not read the Megillah one recites *Hallel* instead[112]).

It is brought down[113] that Haman wanted to hang Mordechai at the time of קְרִיאַת שְׁמַע. God engineered this to show that Haman's evil schemes ultimately revealed God's kindness. As was mentioned earlier, דָּא רָזָא דִקְרִיאַת שְׁמַע[114] — *"this is the secret of saying Shema,"* that judgment is rooted in mercy and the two Names corresponding to judgment and mercy — הַוָיָה and אֱלֹקִים are one — ה׳ אֱלֹקֵינוּ ה׳ אֶחָד.

Accordingly, we can now explain what our Sages say,[115] that Haman was hanged on Pesach. The miracle of Purim is a great paradigm of the faith and trust we should have; it complements the faith and trust inherent in remembering the Exodus from Egypt.

Our Sages tell us,[116] *A Baraisa was taught in R' Meir's name: Why was the Torah given to Israel? Because they are strong willed. A Baraisa was taught in the school of R' Yishmael: The verse states: "from His right hand, He presented the fiery law to them."[117] The Holy One, Blessed is He, declared: "These people are fit that the fiery law be given to them."*

Rashi there writes, **because they are strong willed** — *therefore the Torah was given to them for them to toil in, for it will weaken them and humble their hearts.*

---

112. *Meiri*, the first chapter of *Megillah*.
113. *Midrash Talpios, Achashverosh.*
114. *Zohar, Bereishis* 46:4.
115. *Megillah* 15a.
116. *Beitzah* 25a.
117. *Devarim* 33:2.

The commentators have a difficulty explaining Rashi's words; according to what he says, it seems as though the Torah was given to Bnei Yisrael because they are deficient. Yet according to the above it seems that Bnei Yisrael were chosen from all the nations *because* of this "deficiency": the inner strength to stand firm with their forefathers' belief, even during the terrible הֶסְתֵּר פָּנִים throughout the darkness of exile. As the Kuzari writes,[118] Bnei Yisrael are the chosen nation from among all people, elite in their creation and genealogy. Only Bnei Yisrael who are tough have the power to sanctify God's Name throughout the long exile and darkness of destruction, and therefore they were chosen from all the nations and were given the Torah.

The Ramban explains[119] that the words of the *pasuk* מִימִינוֹ אֵשׁ דָּת לָמוֹ — *"His right hand presented the fiery Torah to them,"* illustrate how the Attribute of Judgment is enveloped in mercy, for the right always represents mercy as our Sages say:[120] לְעוֹלָם תְּהֵא שְׂמֹאל דּוֹחָה וְיָמִין מְקָרֶבֶת — *"the left hand should push away, but the right hand should draw close,"* and fire represents the Attribute of Judgment. Thus we can read the *pasuk* מִימִינוֹ — *from His right hand*, namely from His Attribute of Mercy — אֵשׁ דָּת לָמוֹ, comes the "fire," the Attribute of Judgment. Therefore, says the Ramban, the Torah was given to Bnei Yisrael, because only they, with עַזּוּת דִּקְדוּשָׁה, the spiritual resoluteness, can accept and endure the harsh judgment of exile and recognize how it stems from God's mercy.

Faith and Trust in Times of God's Concealment

THROUGHOUT THE AGES, SPANNING THE LENGTH OF OUR exile, during hard times of הֶסְתֵּר פָּנִים, of God hiding His face, Bnei Yisrael have strengthened themselves through their faith, trusting God and awaiting His salvation. The Gemara[121] tells

---

118. *Kuzari, Maamar* 1 *Os* 95.
119. *Ramban, Devarim* 33:2.
120. *Sotah* 47a.
121. *Avodah Zarah* 18a.

us: *the Romans found R' Chanina ben Tradyon sitting engaged in Torah studies and convening gatherings in public for its dissemination and a Torah scroll was resting in his lap, in open violation of their edicts. They therefore brought him and wrapped him in a Torah scroll, encircled him with bundles of vine shoots, and set them on fire. They brought tufts of wool, soaked them in water and placed them on his heart so that his soul would not depart quickly. His students said to him, "Rabbi, what do you see?" He told them, "The parchment is burning but the letters are taking flight.".*

Tosafos[122] asks as to the nature of the question they asked R' Chanina, "What do you see?" Why did the students ask this; what made them think he saw something? Perhaps we can say that their question did not pertain to sight with the *eyes*, but rather to the real eyesight; namely, the eyes of the mind and heart. Those days were times of anger and fury, overshadowed by death, harsh decrees, and annihilation, where nary a day came whose curse wasn't greater than the previous day. Here stood R' Chanina, the leader of the generation in whose presence the students sought shelter, and they were witnessing his execution. When they, brokenhearted and despairing, asked "Rabbi, what do you see?" what they were really seeking was some sort of answer as to their future. Is there hope for them, now that they are being abandoned like sheep without a shepherd?

To this R' Chanina answered them, Do not despair, there is hope for you and there is reward for your actions. The "parchment is burning" — the evil Romans can burn our bodies, but "the letters are taking flight" — the soul of the Jewish nation can never be destroyed. Every Jew is compared to a Torah scroll, as the Gemara explains:[123] *one who stands by a dead person at the time of the departure of the soul is obligated to rend his garments. To what is this analogous? To a Torah scroll that was burned, where the one who witnesses it must rend his garments.* The body is likened to the parchment of the Torah scroll,[124] and the souls of Bnei Yisrael are

122. Ibid.
123. *Shabbos* 105b.
124. Introduction to *Beis HaLevi* Vol. 1.

bound to the letters of the Torah.[125] The *Pnei Yehoshua*[126] quotes from the *Zohar,* that the name יִשְׂרָאֵל is an acronym for יֵשׁ שִׁשִּׁים רִבּוֹא אוֹתִיּוֹת לַתּוֹרָה, *there are six hundred thousand letters in the Torah,* for each Jew is linked to one of the letters of the Torah.[127] Anyone witnessing the soul departing the body and ascending is as if he is witnessing a Torah scroll burning and the letters taking flight. But when God will desire it, the letters will return to their places and once again people will congregate by the masses for Torah study, for God has promised us that Torah will never be forgotten.

It is this supernatural mode of behavior, this devotion and willingness to die for the sake of Heaven, which transcends all logic, which brought the downfall of the Roman Empire and Bnei Yisrael's salvation. Tosafos states[128] in the name of the *Maaseh HaMerkavah* that the downfall of the Roman Empire came about because of what happened to R' Chanina ben Tradyon.

It is in the merit of Bnei Yisrael's willingness to sacrifice themselves for Torah study even in the darkest of times — when God is hidden — that they will merit God's revealing Himself in this world, redeeming them for all to see.

The Mishnah tells us,[129] *Regarding Nikanor, miracles occurred to his doors, and [the Sages] would recall them them with praise.*

The Gemara goes on: [130]*Therefore, all of the gates that were in the Temple were later rendered out of gold, except for the gates of Nikanor which were left in their original state because of the miracles that had occurred through them.*

There were many miracles that took place in the Beis HaMikdash. There were ten continuous miracles in the Beis HaMikdash as delineated in *Avos.*[131] The Gemara tells us[132] that the light of the sun never entered the Beis HaMikdash, rather the light of the Beis HaMikdash shone from the inside, miraculously illuminating the

---

125. *Nefesh HaChaim, Shaar* 4, Ch. 11; *Meor Einayim, VeEschanan; Kedushas Levi, Bamidbar.*
126. *Kiddushin* 30a.
127. For further insight see *Aish Dos* 7:3.
128. *Avodah Zarah* 2b s.v. *Romi.*
129. *Yoma* 37a.
130. Ibid. 38a.
131. 5:5.
132. *Menachos* 86b.

world on the outside. The Gemara tells us furthermore[133] that the Ark did not occupy space in the Holy of Holies, and elsewhere the Gemara[134] lists many other miracles that took place in the Beis HaMikdash. With all these miracles on a daily basis, what is so unique about Nikanor's copper gates that they did not exchange them for gates of gold, simply because of the miracle that took place with them?

The Gemara there teaches us what was the miracle with the copper gates of Nikanor.

They said: when Nikanor went to bring doors from Alexandria in Egypt, upon his return, a sea gale threatened to drown him. [The sailors] took one of [the doors] and threw it into the sea to lighten the load of the ship. But the sea still did not subside from its raging, and the ship remained in danger. [The sailors] sought to throw its companion door overboard. However, [Nikanor] stood up against them and hugged [the door]. He said to them, "You will have to throw me into the sea with it." Immediately, the sea subsided from its raging. [Nikanor] was then pained about the loss of [the door's] companion, which had been thrown overboard. As soon as he arrived at the port of Acre in Eretz Yisrael he saw [the first door] poking out from under the walls of the ship.

At first glance it seems that Nikanor's actions were a rash act of suicide. He knew that he would not be able to convince them to risk their lives to save the doors, and Nikanor did not even request of them to refrain from throwing the second door overboard, rather he said, "Throw me overboard with it." What would he gain by drowning with the gates?

Indeed, Nikanor taught us a great lesson. When a great wave comes to drown us, there is a need to sacrifice ourselves with utter dedication to God, dedication that transcends all logic and reason. This lesson is imperative for all generations, during times of God's anger and wrath. In times of darkness and the shadow of death, it seems to us that once again mighty waves will destroy us and drown the remainder of Bnei Yisrael. There are "clever" people who wish to lighten the load of our ship by throwing the doors

---

133. *Megillah* 10b.
134. *Yoma* 38a.

of the Beis HaMikdash — the Torah — overboard. Against these so-called clever individuals we must stand resolute and wrap ourselves around the doors of the *Mikdash* and say, "Throw us overboard with these, we are not leaving them behind," just as Nikanor had done. In order for us to remember this lesson, the gates of Nikanor were never exchanged for gates of gold.

This principle is incumbent on us during these trying times of God's hiddenness in the End of Days. The שַׁעַר הָעֲבוֹדָה, *the Gate of Service,* has been taken away from us with the destruction of the Beis HaMikdash. We must cling to the remaining gate, שַׁעַר הַתּוֹרָה, *the Gate of Torah,* with unyielding devotion, with a dedication so powerful that it transcends logic and reason, with a strong love and endless joy. Thus will we merit seeing the other lost door glistening in the stormy waters beneath our ship, and the words of the Navi Yeshayah will be fulfilled: וְנִגְלָה כְּבוֹד ה' וְרָאוּ כָל בָּשָׂר יַחְדָּו כִּי פִּי ה' דִּבֵּר[135] — *"the glory of Hashem will be revealed, and all flesh together will see that the mouth of Hashem has spoken."* Speedily in our days, Amen.

---

135. *Yeshayahu* 40:5.

פרשת שמות
Parashas Shemos

The Name of the Redeemer

וַיֹּאמֶר מֹשֶׁה אֶל הָאֱלֹקִים הִנֵּה אָנֹכִי בָא אֶל בְּנֵי יִשְׂרָאֵל וְאָמַרְתִּי לָהֶם אֱלֹקֵי אֲבוֹתֵיכֶם שְׁלָחַנִי אֲלֵיכֶם וְאָמְרוּ לִי מַה שְּׁמוֹ מָה אֹמַר אֲלֵהֶם: וַיֹּאמֶר אֱלֹקִים אֶל מֹשֶׁה אֶהְיֶ-ה אֲשֶׁר אֶהְיֶ-ה וַיֹּאמֶר כֹּה תֹאמַר לִבְנֵי יִשְׂרָאֵל אֶהְיֶ-ה שְׁלָחַנִי אֲלֵיכֶם.

Moshe said to God, "Behold, when I come to Bnei Yisrael, and say to them, 'The God of your forefathers has sent me to you,' and they say to me, 'What is His Name? — what shall I say to them?" God answered Moshe, "I-Shall-Be-as-I-Shall-Be." And He said, "So shall you say to Bnei Yisrael, 'I-Shall-Be has sent me to you.' "[136]

HASHEM *YISBARACH* IS KNOWN BY MANY NAMES, AS found throughout *Tanach*. Each Name describes a different attribute by which He reveals Himself, in His interactions with His world. Some Names represent Hashem's Attribute of Mercy. Others represent His strict justice. Some represent His lovingkindness. Still others represent His supreme might.[137] This particular Name of אֶהְיֶ-ה is found nowhere else in *Tanach*. What is the significance of the Name אֶהְיֶ-ה? Which attribute of Hashem does it represent?

---

136. *Shemos* 3:13-14.
137. See *Shemos Rabbah* 3:6.

In order to answer these questions, we peruse the writings of the Rishonim, who discuss the Name of אֶהְיֶ-ה.

1. The Ineffable Names of Hashem

There is a debate among the Rishonim, over whether or not אֶהְיֶ-ה is one of the true Names of Hashem, which may not be erased. The Rambam writes:

Anyone who destroys one of the holy and pure Names by which HaKadosh Baruch Hu is known is liable for lashes by Torah law, as the *pasuk* states regarding idolatry, "And you shall destroy their names from that place. Do not do so to Hashem your God."[138]

There are seven Names: the Name written with the letters יו"ד ק"א וא"ו ק"א (which is called "the Explicit Name") or the Names written ten קל, אלו ק, ואלקים, ואלקי, ושדי, וצב אות. Anyone who erases even one letter from these Names is liable for lashes.[139]

The Kesef Mishneh commentary on the Rambam explains that this ruling is based on the Gemara, which lists the Names that may not be erased. However, he notes that the Rambam apparently bases his ruling on a different version of the Gemara, since in our version, there is a different list of Names, which includes the Name אֶהְיֶ-ה. The Gemara states:

These are the Names that must not be erased: קל, אֱלֹקֶךָ, אֱלֹקִים, אֱלֹקֵיכֶם, אֶהְיֶ-ה אֲשֶׁר אֶהְיֶ-ה, אָלֶף דָּלֶת, וְיוּד הֵי, שַׁדַּ-י, צְבָ-אוֹת.[140]

Actually, the Gemara there does not list אֶהְיֶ-ה alone as one of the ineffaceable Names of Hashem, but אֶהְיֶ-ה אֲשֶׁר אֶהְיֶ-ה, seeming to imply that the three words together comprise a single Name of Hashem. A support for this can be found in Onkelos's Aramaic translation of *Chumash*. Rather than translating the Hebrew word "אֲשֶׁר" into Aramaic, he leaves it in the original Hebrew, seeming to imply that this is not merely a grammatical conjunction, but part of Hashem's proper Name.[141]

---

138. *Devarim* 12:3.
139. *Rambam, Yesodei HaTorah* 6:1-2.
140. *Shevuos* 35a.
141. This inference is admittedly problematic. Although it is true according to our version of the Targum Onkelos, the Ramban seems to have had a different version, from which he quotes the translation אֱהֵא עִם מַאן דְּאֱהֵא translating all three words into Aramaic; perhaps this version implies just the opposite, that אֶהְיֶ-ה is not a proper Name at all.

2. The Meaning of the Name

Rashi explains that when Hashem told Moshe אֶהְיֶ-ה אֲשֶׁר אֶהְיֶ-ה, He meant to say that He would be with Bnei Yisrael in future exiles, just as He was with them in Egypt. Moshe suggested that their current suffering was difficult enough, and there was no need for them to be concerned about future exiles. Hashem conceded, and instructed him to just say אֶהְיֶ-ה שְׁלָחַנִי אֲלֵיכֶם.

According to this, we can explain that Hashem first intended to reveal Himself with the three-word Name of אֶהְיֶ-ה אֲשֶׁר אֶהְיֶ-ה, and then agreed, based on Moshe's suggestion, to use only the one-word Name of אֶהְיֶ-ה. This seems to support the Kesef Mishneh's understanding, that on its own אֶהְיֶ-ה is the Name by which Hashem is known, not אֶהְיֶ-ה אֲשֶׁר אֶהְיֶ-ה.

On the other hand, if we interpret אֶהְיֶ-ה according to Rashi's understanding, perhaps it is not a Name at all, but an assurance that Hashem will always be by our side to assist us. As such, neither אֶהְיֶ-ה nor אֶהְיֶ-ה אֲשֶׁר אֶהְיֶ-ה are proper Names of Hashem, as is evident from the Rambam, cited above.

The Ramban expands on Rashi's explanation:

When Moshe said to Hashem that Bnei Yisrael would ask His Name, he meant that they would want to know the Name by which His Presence and Providence are evident. HaKadosh Baruch Hu answered that they did not need to know this Name as a proof of Moshe's claims, since Hashem would be with them throughout all their hardships. Whenever they would call out to Him, He would answer. This would be the greatest proof that Hashem is close to us whenever we call, and there is indeed a God Who judges the earth.

The Ramban also offers an alternate explanation of אֶהְיֶ-ה אֲשֶׁר אֶהְיֶ-ה:

I shall be with you to the same extent that you are with Me. If you open your hand to give *tzedakah* [to the poor], I will also open My hand [to deal kindly with you].

This explanation likewise does not clarify whether אֶהְיֶ-ה is actually a Name of Hashem, or a warning that His kindness toward us is contingent on our kindness toward others.

Quoting Rav Saadiah Gaon, the Ramban then offers a third explanation of אֶהְיֶ-ה, that Hashem has never been absent, nor will

He ever be absent, since He was the first Being, Who existed before the world was created, and the last Being, Who will continue to exist even after the world comes to an end. Rambam[142] offers a similar explanation that אֶהְיֶ-ה אֲשֶׁר אֶהְיֶ-ה means, הַנִּמְצָא אֲשֶׁר נִמְצָא — "*The Presence Who Is Present.*" In other words, Hashem is the only Being Whose existence is essential, whereas the existence of all other beings is dependent on Hashem. According to this explanation, it seems that אֶהְיֶ-ה is a Name of Hashem, which implies that He is the first and last Being, Whose existence is essential.

We now have three different explanations of the Name אֶהְיֶ-ה, each with its own halachic implications.

3. The Promise of Redemption

The Rashbam explains that the Name אֶהְיֶ-ה (I-Shall-Be) is a variation of י-הוה which means He-Shall-Be. We refer to Hashem in the third person form, whereas Hashem refers to Himself in first person. Accordingly, we can well understand why the Name אֶהְיֶ-ה is found nowhere else in *Tanach*. Normally, the Torah refers to Hashem in third person, as יו"ד ק"א וא"ו ק"א. In this case, Hashem declares His own Name in first person, אֶהְיֶ-ה.[143]

The Name י-הוה refers to Hashem's Attribute of Mercy.[144] The same is true of אֶהְיֶ-ה. This Name is the key to our redemption. The Name אֶהְיֶ-ה was first revealed during *Yetzias Mitzrayim*, yet it will be fully revealed only when the Final Redemption arrives. Hashem told Moshe Rabbeinu to inform Bnei Yisrael, "אֶהְיֶ-ה sent me to you," assuring them that despite the terrible darkness of their servitude, they must not despair. They would not have to carry the burden of slavery forever. The redemption was imminent — "אֶהְיֶ-ה sent me to you."

---

142. *Moreh Nevuchim* I, 63

143. The Rashbam makes passing note of the fact that the third letter, "*yud,*" in the Name אֶהְיֶ-ה is exchanged for the letter "*vav*" in י-הוה. This is a grammatical adaptation which is found elsewhere in *Tanach*, such as in the *pasuk* כִּי מֶה הֹוֶה לָאָדָם בְּכָל עֲמָלוֹ — "*What does man have from all his labors?*" (*Koheles* 2:22). Here, the usual spelling of "היה" is exchanged for "הוה." The significance of this adaptation in the Name of Hashem is beyond our grasp.

144. *Shemos Rabbah*, 3:6.

This same message is a beacon of hope for us in our present *Galus*. It has given us strength to persevere through these thousands of years of hardship and affliction, as we wander from one county to another, subject to the derision and abuse of the nations that surround us. Yet we stand proud in our faith in Hashem and the assurance that He will be with us throughout all our hardships. We raise our eyes to Him with hope and faith that He will soon redeem us, and we pray to Him three times each day that the *Shechinah* may soon return to Tzion with mercy.

We recognize that the *Galus* is a decree from Heaven. The righteous are not meant to know tranquility in this world. Yet, there will be an end to our travails. Hashem is with us, as He was with our forefathers in Egypt. "I-Shall-Be as I-Shall-Be," as Rashi explains: "I shall be with them in future exiles, as I was with them in Egypt."

The Jewish people find strength in this knowledge, and in the clear recognition that this world is like a fleeting dream, like dust scattered by the wind. It is only a vestibule, which leads into the palace that awaits us in the World to Come. Therefore, the suffering of *Galus* in this world cannot cast us into despondency.

4. The End of Days

Before Yaakov Avinu died, he summoned all his sons to reveal to them the date of their redemption. "Gather and I will tell you what will occur to you at the end of days," he said.[145] Rashi explains that He wished to reveal to them the end (קֵץ) but the *Shechinah* left him, and he was unable to reveal their destiny.

Rabbi Shimshon of Ostropole explained that Yaakov realized that the exile of his children in Egypt was a punishment for their sale of Yosef,[146] which had caused a blemish in Hashem's Name אֶהְיֶ-ה. Only nine brothers were involved in the sale, since Reuven and Binyamin did not take part. Therefore, Yaakov multiplied the number nine by the *gematria* (numerical equivalent) of the Name אֶהְיֶ-ה (which is 21), and reached the result of 189. Therefore, he assumed that they would be forced to endure 189 years of exile, and

---

145. *Bereishis* 49:1.
146. As discussed in the *Zohar* and the writings of the Arizal. See *Ohr HaChaim, Parashas Vayechi*.

they would be redeemed in the 190th year (the gematria of קץ). This is what Rashi meant, that Yaakov wished to reveal to them the קֵץ.

However, Yaakov did not realize that the nine brothers required a *minyan* of ten, in order to impose a *cheirem* (ban of excommunication) on anyone who would expose their sale. Therefore, they included the *Shechinah* as the tenth member of their group. Thus, their exile would be for 10 times 21 years, a total of 210. This is what Rashi meant, that the *Shechinah* departed from Yaakov. He was unaware of the *Shechinah's* involvement in Yosef's sale.

Years later, when Moshe was instructed to herald the redemption, he also erred in his calculations. He realized that there were ten participants involved in Yosef's sale, but he thought that they had caused a blemish in the Name י-הוה, instead of אֶהְיֶ-ה. Therefore, he calculated that Bnei Yisrael would be in *Galus* for 10 times 26 years (the gematria of י-הוה), for a total of 260 (the gematria of the word סר). Moshe was amazed when Hashem revealed to Him that the redemption was imminent, since according to his own calculations there should be another 50 years of *Galus*. This is the meaning of the *pasuk*, וַיַּרְא ה׳ כִּי סָר לִרְאוֹת — "*Hashem saw that Moshe had turned to see.*" The basic meaning is that Moshe turned to see the amazing spectacle of the burning bush. However, on a deeper level, it also means that Hashem saw that Moshe had erred in his calculation, presuming that the *Galus* would last for 260 (סר) years. Therefore, He informed Moshe that the *Galus* of Bnei Yisrael in Egypt was not meant to rectify the Name י-הוה, but rather the Name אֶהְיֶ-ה. He revealed to Moshe the Name אֶהְיֶ-ה, and with this Name informed him that the time for the redemption had come, since their 210 years of exile had been completed.

5. The Prayers of the *Avos*

There seems to be a discrepancy in the *pesukim* that describe Hashem's promise to redeem us:

Elokim spoke again to Moshe, saying: "So shall you say to Bnei Yisrael: Hashem the God of your forefathers, the God of Avraham, the God of Yitzchak, and the God of Yaakov, sent me to you. This is My Name forever, and this is My remembrance from generation to generation."

"Go and gather the elders of Israel and say to them: Hashem the God of your forefathers appeared to me, the God of Avraham, Yitzchak, and Yaakov, saying: I have remembered you, and what has been done to you in Egypt." [147]

In the first *pasuk*, Hashem presents Himself as the God of our forefathers, each one individually: "The God of Avraham, the God of Yitzchak and the God of Yaakov." In the second *pasuk*, He presents Himself as the God of all three together: "The God of Avraham, Yitzchak, and Yaakov."

Perhaps we can explain this discrepancy, based on the following Gemara:

Eliyahu HaNavi would regularly attend the yeshivah of Rebbi (Yehuda HaNasi). Once on Rosh Chodesh, Eliyahu came late.

"Why did the master come late today?" Rebbi respectfully asked him.

"It took time for me to rouse Avraham, wash his hands, wait for him to finish praying, send him back to rest, and then do the same for Yitzchak and Yaakov."

"Why did you not just rouse all three at the same time?" asked Rebbe.

"I feared that if they would all daven together, their prayers would be so powerful that they would bring Mashiach before his proper time," Eliyahu explained. [148]

With this we can reconcile these two *pesukim*. The first *pasuk* refers to the Ultimate Redemption, which will occur with the arrival of Mashiach: "This is My Name forever, and this is My remembrance from generation to generation." Regarding the final redemption, Hashem is considered the God of each of the *Avos* individually, since they were never allowed to pray together to hasten the Final Redemption.

The second *pasuk* refers to the redemption from Egypt: "I have remembered you, and what has been done to you in Egypt." Regarding the redemption from Egypt, Hashem is considered the God of all three *Avos* together, since their prayers to bring about the redemption from Egypt had been accepted long ago. Therefore,

---

147. *Shemos* 3:15-16.
148. *Bava Metzia* 85b.

Moshe was instructed to gather the elders of Israel and tell them that they had nothing more to fear. The prayers of the *Avos* had been successful, and the redemption of Bnei Yisrael from Egypt was imminent.

As we study *Sefer Shemos*, and learn about the exile and redemption of our forefathers long ago, we lift our eyes in prayer to Hashem that He may hasten our own redemption from this dark and bitter *Galus*, through which we have suffered for so many years. May Eliyahu HaNavi rouse our forefathers to pray on our behalf, and may we once again hear the long-awaited proclamation of our deliverance, פָּקֹד פָּקַדְתִּי אֶתְכֶם — *"I have remembered you."*

May the prophecy of Michah HaNavi soon be fulfilled: כִּימֵי צֵאתְךָ מֵאֶרֶץ מִצְרָיִם אַרְאֶנּוּ נִפְלָאוֹת — *"As in the days when you left Egypt, I will show you wonders."*[149]

Amen.

---

149. *Michah* 7:15.

פרשת וארא
Parashas Va'eira

From Slavery to Freedom

לָכֵן אֱמֹר לִבְנֵי יִשְׂרָאֵל אֲנִי ה' וְהוֹצֵאתִי אֶתְכֶם מִתַּחַת סִבְלֹת
מִצְרַיִם וְהִצַּלְתִּי אֶתְכֶם מֵעֲבֹדָתָם וְגָאַלְתִּי אֶתְכֶם בִּזְרוֹעַ נְטוּיָה
וּבִשְׁפָטִים גְּדֹלִים. וְלָקַחְתִּי אֶתְכֶם לִי לְעָם וְהָיִיתִי לָכֶם לֵאלֹהִים
וִידַעְתֶּם כִּי אֲנִי ה' אֱלֹהֵיכֶם הַמּוֹצִיא אֶתְכֶם מִתַּחַת סִבְלוֹת מִצְרָיִם.

"Therefore, say to Bnei Yisrael, 'I am Hashem, *and I shall take you out from under the burdens of Egypt; I shall rescue you from their service; I shall redeem you with an outstretched arm and with great judgments. I shall take you to Me for a people and I shall be a God to you; and you shall know that I am* Hashem *your God, Who takes you out from under the burdens of Egypt.'"*[150]

THE FOUR CUPS OF WINE THAT WE DRINK ON SEDER night correspond to the four expressions of redemption stated in these *pesukim*: I shall remove (וְהוֹצֵאתִי); I shall rescue (וְהִצַּלְתִּי), I shall redeem (וְגָאַלְתִּי), and I shall bring (וְלָקַחְתִּי).[151]

Between the first three cups of wine, it is permitted to drink. However, between the third and fourth cups, it is forbidden to

---

150. *Shemos* 6:6-7.
151. *Pesachim* 99b, *Rashi* and *Rashbam*.

interrupt by eating or drinking. This comes to teach us an important lesson. Some people view the awaited redemption as no more than a national liberation, in which we will be freed from the oppression we suffer under the hands of the nations. In their opinion, the first three expressions of redemption are sufficient. They wish to be removed, rescued, and redeemed. However, they do not see the great importance of being brought to Hashem, as His holy nation. This does not play an important role in their vision of redemption.

In order to contradict their erroneous ideology, our Sages instructed us not to make any interruption before the fourth cup. Taking our place as Hashem's chosen nation is in fact the most crucial aspect of the redemption. This is the redemption of the *neshamah* from the hands of the *yetzer hara,* as it returns to draw close to Hashem. This is our true aspiration, to see the Beis HaMikdash rebuilt, and to see the *Shechinah* rest upon Klal Yisrael.

The Ramban[152] writes that the entire *Sefer Shemos* is one continuing story of redemption. It begins with the servitude of our forefathers and the miracles of *Yetzias Mitzrayim;* and it concludes with the resting of the *Shechinah* upon the Mishkan. This symbolized how Bnei Yisrael had finally reached the ultimate stage of redemption, in which the *Shechinah* once again rested upon us, as it had rested upon our forefathers. This crucial aspect of our awaited redemption cannot be overlooked.

"Therefore, say to Bnei Yisrael, 'I am HASHEM, and I shall take you out from under the burdens of Egypt; I shall rescue you from their service; I shall redeem you with an outstretched arm and with great judgments. I shall take you to Me for a people.'"

At times, a slave must suffer under the hand of a cruel and tyrannical master, who oppresses him without mercy. Such a slave is subject to incessant physical and mental abuse. However, even a slave with a merciful master usually suffers from the difficult labors imposed upon him. Some slaves are even more fortunate, and are only required to perform light household tasks. Nevertheless, they

---

152. Introduction to *Shemos.*

suffer from subjugation to the will of another, since they cannot lead their lives according to their own desire.

In describing the liberation of our forefathers from Egypt, the Torah addresses all these aspects of slavery. Pharaoh held Bnei Yisrael in an iron grasp of horrific wickedness. He subjected them to death, torture, and grueling labors. From all these harsh decrees, Hashem rescued us. He "removed us" from beneath the burden of cruel abuse. He "rescued us" from the difficult labors they imposed upon us. He "redeemed us" from the degradation of slavery. Yet paramount in significance, was the great kindness He showed us, by "bringing us" to Him, and making us into His nation.

Hashem's Hidden Kindness

ON SEDER NIGHT, WE CONDUCT OURSELVES IN THE manner of freed men, by drinking wine, leaning on one side as we eat, and having others serve us. All this is in order to focus our full attention on our immense debt of gratitude to Hashem, Who redeemed us, and brought us from slavery to freedom. Why then do we also eat *maror*, which is the very symbol of our bitter servitude? Does this not contradict the theme of liberty, which is celebrated on this holy night?

By eating *maror* on Seder night, we instill in our hearts a firm awareness that even those things that appear to us as unfortunate are in fact manifestations of Hashem's hidden kindness. Everything that Hashem does is for the best.

The *pasuk* states, "Your are children of Hashem your God. Do not cut yourselves, and do not shave between your eyes in mourning for the dead."[153] The Ibn Ezra comments that Hashem loves us more than any father could ever love his son. Therefore, we must not mourn excessively over the sorrows that befall us. Everything that happens to us is for our own best interest. We might not always understand Hashem's designs, just as a young child does

---

153. *Devarim* 14:1.

not always understand his father. Yet a child knows for certain that his father would never harm him, and so too must be our faith in Hashem.

This was the lesson of Rabbi Akiva, who would always say, "Everything the Merciful One does is for the best."[154] Even after he was imprisoned for teaching Torah, he laughed as he was led to his execution.[155] R' Akiva was able to see Hashem's benevolent hand at work, even when he witnessed the sickness and suffering of his beloved rebbi and mentor, R' Eliezer ben Hurkenas. When R' Eliezer was ill, Rabbi Akiva visited him and said, "Suffering is beloved" — since it encourages a person to do *teshuvah*.[156]

When Rabbi Akiva and his peers saw a fox wandering among the ruins of the Beis HaMikdash, his peers cried, but he laughed. He explained to them that just as the prophecy of destruction was fulfilled, so too would the prophecies of consolation and redemption.[157] Even in the most tragic event in the history of our people, the destruction of the Beis HaMikdash, Rebbe Akiva was able to see the good.

I once heard from *Mori v'Rebbe*, the Klausenberger Rav *zt"l*, that this is the reason we cover our eyes when reciting *Shema*.[158] In *Shema*, we declare, "הֹ׳ אֱלוֹקֵינוּ הֹ׳ אֶחָד." The Name הֹ׳ refers to Hashem's Attribute of Mercy. The Name אלקים refers to His Attribute of Strict Justice.[159] Yet both Names are in fact one, since even the Attribute of Judgment is nothing but a manifestation of Hashem's hidden kindness. Although His judgment might seem harsh by all outward appearances, we cover our eyes to ignore the superficial aspect of the judgment. With perfect faith we declare, "הֹ׳ אֱלוֹקֵינוּ הֹ׳ אֶחָד," firmly believing that everything He does is for our best.

In a similar vein, the Kol Aryeh[160] explains the *pasuk* in which Hashem tells Yaakov Avinu, "Do not fear to descend to Egypt ...

---

154. *Berachos* 60b.
155. *Talmud Yerushalmi: Berachos* 9:5; *Sotah* 5:5.
156. *Sanhedrin* 101a.
157. *Makkos* 24. See *Minchas Asher* on *Maseches Pesachim, Maamar Derech Emunah*, 4.
158. See *Berachos* 13a.
159. See *Shemos Rabbah* 3:6.
160. Introduction to *Teshuvos Kol Aryeh: Pesach Tov*, 7.

Yosef will place his hand over your eyes."[161] At first, Yaakov viewed his descent to Egypt as a terrible misfortune. However, Hashem assured him that in the end he would see that this was for the best. Hashem told him to take as an example Yosef's descent into slavery. This also seemed like a terrible misfortune at first, but in the end it was revealed to be another manifestation of Hashem's hidden kindness. As a result of his having been sold as a slave, Yosef eventually became the viceroy to Pharaoh, and was able to support Yaakov's family during the years of famine.

Hashem told Yaakov that Yosef would place his hands over Yaakov's eyes. This refers to the practice of covering one's eyes when reciting *Shema*. He reminded Yaakov that we must ignore the misleading evidence offered by our senses, and trust that Hashem's Attribute of Strict Judgment is in fact pure mercy. For this reason, the Zohar describes the incident of Yosef's sale to Egypt as "the secret of *Kerias Shema*."

The Kol Aryeh expands on this point by citing the Chasam Sofer, who explains the *pasuk*, וְרָאִיתָ אֶת אֲחֹרָי וּפָנַי לֹא יֵרָאוּ — *"You will see My back, but My face may not be seen."*[162] We cannot always see the face of Hashem and His kindness as tragedy descends upon us. However, many years later we can often see His kindness from behind, recognizing in retrospect that all was for the best.

With this we can understand the Gemara, which states as follows:

Rav Yehudah said in the name of Rav: When Moshe ascended to Heaven, he found HaKadosh Baruch Hu sitting and attaching crowns to the letters of the Torah. "Master of the Universe, who forces Your hand?" he asked. (Rashi — What is lacking in Your Torah, that You must add these crowns?)

"Many generations from now, there will be a man named Akiva ben Yosef, who will expound mountains upon mountains of rulings based on every point of every crown," Hashem answered.

"Master of the Universe, let me see him," Moshe asked.

"Take a step back (חֲזוֹר לַאֲחוֹרְךָ)," Hashem said.

(Moshe then found himself in the academy of R' Akiva), and sat

---

161. *Bereishis* 46:3-4.
162. *Shemos* 33:23.

at the back of eight rows of students (signifying his relative lack of importance). At first, he was upset that he could not understand what they were saying. Then, he was relieved to hear a student ask R' Akiva for the source of one of his teachings, to which R' Akiva replied that it was a tradition they had received from Moshe Rabbeinu.

Moshe then returned before HaKadosh Baruch Hu and said, "Master of the Universe, You have such a man as this, yet You choose to give the Torah through me?"

"Silence! This is My will (כָּךְ עָלָה בְּמַחֲשָׁבָה לְפָנַי)," Hashem said.

"Master of the Universe, You have shown me his Torah, now show me his reward," Moshe asked.

"Take a step back (חֲזוֹר לַאֲחוֹרֶךָ)," Hashem said. Moshe stepped back and saw R' Akiva's flesh being weighed in the butcher's market (after it was stripped from his body by the Roman executioners).

"Master of the Universe, this is Torah, and this is its reward?" Moshe asked.

"Silence! This is My will (כָּךְ עָלָה בְּמַחֲשָׁבָה לְפָנַי)," Hashem said.[163]

When Hashem allowed Moshe to gaze into the future, and see what he could not possibly understand, He told Moshe, "Take a step back (חֲזוֹר לַאֲחוֹרֶךָ)." Moshe was allowed only to see "אֲחֹרָי" the back of Hashem, so to speak, of which Hashem said, "וְרָאִיתָ אֶת אֲחֹרָי — *You shall see My back.*" From this perspective, Moshe could not understand why he was chosen as the emissary to deliver the Torah, rather than R' Akiva, who seemed superior. Nor could Moshe understand the terrible suffering R' Akiva was made to suffer.

To both of these questions, Hashem answered, כָּךְ עָלָה בְּמַחֲשָׁבָה לְפָנַי — "This is My will," which is literally translated as, "This is what ascended in thought before Me." In other words, these thoughts can only be understood from a perspective of "לְפָנַי", of which Hashem said, וּפָנַי לֹא יֵרָאוּ — *"My face may not be seen."* Human wisdom cannot possibly comprehend Hashem's infinitely benevolent design for His creation.

---

163. *Menachos* 29b.

The Gemara explains that the word *chasah* (lettuce used for maror) symbolizes how Hashem had mercy (*chas*) upon us.[164] So too, all the species of *maror* listed in the Gemara have deep symbolism. The Chasam Sofer explains the significance of another species, תַּמְכָא, the first letters of which spell out the words תָּמִיד מְסַפְּרִים כְּבוֹד אֵ-ל — "*Constantly proclaiming the honor of Hashem.*"[165] This teaches us, that in the most bitter and painful episodes of our lives, we must proclaim the honor of Hashem, in realization that His hidden kindness supports us in our hour of need.[166]

The Chasam Sofer's rebbi, R' Nosson Adler, invested much time and effort into identifying the vegetable known as *karpas*, which the Maharil had translated into the German dialect contemporary to his time as אפיא, the first letters of which spell out אֵ-ל פּוֹעֵל יְשׁוּעוֹת אַתָּה — "*You are God, Who performs salvations.*"

The acronyms of these species signify the important message they convey. Although we often fail to perceive the hidden kindness inherent in Hashem's plan for His creation, we must firmly believe that from our very misfortune will sprout our greatest benefit. As we say in *Selichos*, "From the wound itself, He prepares the remedy."

May we be worthy of witnessing Hashem's revealed kindness, when His ultimate plan for our benefit at last comes to fruition, with the coming of Mashiach, and the building of the Beis HaMikdash. May it be soon, and in our days, Amen.

---

164. *Pesachim* 39a.
165. From the *berachah* "*Yotzeir HaMe'oros*" recited before the morning recital of *Shema*.
166. *Teshuvos Chasam Sofer O.C.* 132.

פרשת בא

Parashas Bo

The Debt of Gratitude

OUR SAGES INFER FROM THE *PASUK*, לְמַעַן תִּזְכֹּר אֶת יוֹם צֵאתְךָ מֵאֶרֶץ מִצְרַיִם כֹּל יְמֵי חַיֶּיךָ — *"in order that you may remember the day you left Egypt, all the days of your life,"*[167] that we must recall the Exodus every day and night.[168] In addition, there is a special mitzvah to recall the Exodus on Seder Night, the anniversary of our liberation. The question has often been asked, What is the difference between these two mitzvos of remembrance? What need is there of a special mitzvah to remember the Exodus on Seder Night, if we are anyway commanded to remember it every night of the year?

Our debt of gratitude to Hashem for liberating us from slavery entails two distinct obligations. The Torah states, "For Bnei Yisrael are servants to Me. They are My servants, whom I have taken out of the land of Egypt."[169] And elsewhere, "I am Hashem, your God, Who took you out of the land of Egypt to be your God."[170] Rashi comments on this *pasuk*, "For this reason I redeemed you — in order that you shall accept My decrees."

---

167. *Devarim* 16:3.
168. *Berachos* 12b.
169. *Vayikra* 25:55.
170. *Bamidbar* 15:41.

This debt of servitude is the aspect of *Yetzias Mitzrayim* that we must recall twice each day, as part of the recitation of *Shema*. When we proclaim Hashem's Oneness and Sovereignty by reciting *Shema*, we make a special point of recalling how He liberated us from slavery, for which we are eternally indebted to His service.

In his listing of the 613 mitzvos, the Rambam seems to omit the mitzvah of recalling the Exodus every day and night. Some explain that the Rambam did not view this as a distinct mitzvah unto itself, but rather a subclause in the mitzvah to recite *Shema*. According to what we have discussed above, this is well understood. We recall the Exodus in order to remind ourselves of our debt of servitude to Hashem. This is an integral part of our recitation of *Shema*, since it adds dedication and sincerity to our acceptance of Hashem's Sovereignty.

The second obligation that *Yetzias Mitzrayim* requires of us is to praise and thank Hashem for His unparalleled kindness, in performing awesome miracles on our behalf, and avenging the atrocities we suffered at the hands of the Egyptians. The very word "*haggadah*" is translated into Aramaic by the Targum Yonasan as אוֹדִינוּן — *thanking*, whereas the Targum Yerushalmi translates it as אוֹרִינָן וְשַׁבְּחִינָן — *singing and praising*.[171] This insight highlights the special obligation of remembering the Exodus on Seder night: to thank Hashem and sing His praise, with all our hearts and all our souls, in the deepest and most profound appreciation for His having delivered us from slavery to freedom, from groaning to joy, from mourning to Yom Tov, from darkness to great light, and from subjugation to liberty. This is the underlying theme of the *Haggadah shel Pesach*, and the special obligation of recalling the Exodus, which is unique to Seder night.

With this we can understand the implication of the Poskim, that the mitzvah of recalling the Exodus on Seder night requires us to make special mention of the astounding miracles and wonders that were performed on our behalf. We must contemplate the immensity of Hashem's kindness, in order that our songs of praise may flow from the innermost depths of our hearts and souls. In contrast, the mitzvah of recalling the Exodus each day requires no more than

---

171. *Devarim* 23:6.

remembering that Hashem took us out of Egypt. This is enough to obligate us to accept His sovereignty as our God.

Searching the Recesses
of the Heart

וַיִּקְרָא מֹשֶׁה לְכָל זִקְנֵי יִשְׂרָאֵל וַיֹּאמֶר אֲלֵהֶם מִשְׁכוּ וּקְחוּ לָכֶם צֹאן
לְמִשְׁפְּחֹתֵיכֶם וְשַׁחֲטוּ הַפָּסַח.

*Moshe called to all the elders of Israel and said to them,
"Draw forth and buy for yourselves one of the flock for
your families, and slaughter the pesach-offering"[172]*

D RAW — YOUR HANDS AWAY FROM IDOLATRY"[173]
Before beginning the search for *chametz* on the night
of the 14th of Nissan, it is customary to take ten pieces of
chametz, and scatter them throughout the house.[174] In the course
of the search for overlooked *chametz*, these ten pieces are also
gathered, and burned together with any *chametz* that may be
found.

What is the purpose of this custom? *Bedikas chametz* is a search
for bypassed *chametz*. Why then do we deliberately hide new *chametz*, only in order to find and destroy it?

The Poskim make note of the unusual stringencies associated
with *chametz*, which are unparalleled by any other forbidden food.
The Radvaz (R' David ibn Zimra, the Torah leader of Tzefas in the
16th century, and author of over 10,000 responsa) writes as follows:

Why is the prohibition against *chametz* on Pesach different
from all the other prohibitions in the Torah, such that the Torah
requires us to search for, burn, and annul it; our Sages require us

---

172. *Shemos* 12:21.
173. *Shemos Rabbah* 16:2.
174. *Rema, O.C.* 432:2.

to search every crack and corner to eliminate *chametz* from our possession; we are subject to two prohibitions against owning it: *bal yira'eh* and *bal yimatzei*; and the tiniest trace of it will render any mixture forbidden, such that it does not become nullified (*batel*) in a mixture [other prohibitions are subject to being nullified when unwillingly mixed into mixtures many times the volume of the prohibited ingredient]. Such stringencies are not found in any other prohibition of the Torah.

After suggesting and rejecting several halachic distinctions that might be the cause of these unusual stringencies, the Radvaz finally reaches the following conclusion:

Therefore, I rely on the teaching of our Sages in the Midrash, that *chametz* on Pesach represents the *yetzer hara*, the proverbial "leavening of the dough." For this reason, we are required to search all the cracks and corners of our hearts to utterly destroy it. Not even the slightest trace of the *yetzer hara* is *batel*.[175]

A similar parallel was drawn by the Zohar, which compares *chametz* to idolatry. Both must be destroyed by fire. Both can be nullified by expressing disregard for them.[176]

When Bnei Yisrael were first commanded to offer the *korban Pesach*, this commandment was preceded by an instruction to "draw their hands" away from idolatry, turning away from the heathen practices they had known in Egypt, and embracing the service of the One true God. This process is renewed each year. On the holy days of preparation for Pesach, the search for *chametz* is accompanied by a search through the innermost recesses of our hearts, to root out and destroy the negative inclinations that are akin to idolatry, such as anger, falsehood, and arrogance.[177] Only then can we fully experience the liberation of the Pesach Seder, in which we are drawn close to Hashem's service.

The Ramchal writes that the holidays of the Jewish calendar are not mere anniversaries, that commemorate the events of our history. Rather, they are immensely significant points in the cycle of time, in which the miracles our forefathers experienced, and the

---

175. *Teshuvos Radvaz* III, 546.
176. *Zohar* II 40b, 182a. See also *Haggadah shel Pesach: Bris HaLevi*, by R' Shlomo Alkabetz Chs. 11-12.
177. *Shabbos* 105b; *Sanhedrin* 92a; *Sotah* 4b.

Divine light that shone upon them, are relived each year by their descendants, generation after generation.[178]

When our forefathers were liberated from Egypt, they were decidedly lacking in merit. So much so, that the angels objected to the drowning of the Egyptians in the Yam Suf and permitting the Jews to pass through unharmed, since they both worshiped idols.[179] Yet, despite their faults, Hashem displayed His infinite love and mercy for His children, carrying them on wings of eagles, and bringing them to Him. So too, the holiday of Pesach represents a unique opportunity to rise beyond our faults, and ascend "on wings of eagles," as it were, to draw close to Hashem.

In Kiddush, we say, "תְּחִלָּה לְמִקְרָאֵי קֹדֶשׁ זֵכֶר לִיצִיאַת מִצְרָיִם", which literally translates as, "the first calling to holiness, a remembrance of the Exodus from Egypt." Rebbe Naftali of Ropshitz explained that the first and foremost calling, that inspires a person to ascend in holiness, is the memory of the Exodus, and the great miracles that were performed for our forefathers, despite their having been entirely unworthy. They had reached the bottom of the darkest pit of sin and misery, having passed through the forty-ninth gate of impurity, and drawn close to the fiftieth gate, after which there could be no return. Yet in just a short time, they were elevated to a towering peak of holiness and glory. They were granted the holy Torah, and the *Shechinah* dwelled among them, in the Mishkan they constructed.

These thoughts can give us great encouragement, never to despair of our lowly state and our many shortcomings. Hashem can do miracles for us, as He did for our forefathers, and help us rise to lofty heights of Torah and *yiras Shamayim*.

In order to begin this process of climbing out of the darkness of iniquity, the first step is to rid our homes and our hearts of *chametz*. The Arizal said, based on the Zohar,[180] that if a person is scrupulously careful to rid his home of even the smallest trace of *chametz*, he will be protected from sin throughout the year. According to what we have explained above, this is well understood. *Chametz*

---

178. *Derech Hashem* 4:7. See also *Kedushas Levi, Shavuos.*
179. *Zohar* II, 170b.
180. Ibid. III, 282b.

on Pesach represents the *yetzer hara*. By ridding our homes of *chametz*, we free our hearts from the influence of the *yetzer hara*, and are thereby protected from sin.

Perhaps by deliberately spreading ten pieces of *chametz* about the house, we remind ourselves of a sad but true fact. Although we blame the *yetzer hara* for inciting us to sin, we are largely responsible for our own faults. With our own hands, we plant the seeds of darkness that sprout in our hearts. When we wantonly pursue our selfish pleasures, or give free rein to our anger, we nurture the negative character traits, the "*chametz*" of the heart, which we must later work so hard to destroy.

Rabbi Pinchas of Koretz writes that not only is uprooting *Avodah Zarah* (and the negative traits with which it is associated) included in the mitzvah of destroying *chametz*, it is in fact the primary focus of this mitzvah. For this reason, the *pasuk*, "חַג הַמַּצּוֹת תִּשְׁמֹר — "*observe the Festival of Matzos*," is found alongside the *pasuk*, אֱלֹהֵי מַסֵּכָה לֹא תַעֲשֶׂה לָּךְ — "*you shall not make metal gods for yourselves.*"[181] R' Pinchas adds that if all Klal Yisrael would destroy their *chametz* with the intention of also destroying *Avodah Zarah*, they would thereby make the *Galus* considerably easier to bear ("וואלט אויך גרינגער גיווען דער גלות").[182]

May we merit to rid our hearts of the "chametz" of selfishness, falsehood, and arrogance, and perfect ourselves with noble traits of generosity, kindness, and ahavas Yisrael. And may we soon merit to see the ultimate perfection of the world, with the coming of Mashiach and the rebuilding of the Beis HaMikdash, may it be soon and in our days,

Amen.

---

181. *Shemos* 34:17-18.
182. *Imrei Pinchas: Erev Pesach,* p. 132.

The Waxing and Waning
of the Moon

שֶׁהֵם עֲתִידִים לְהִתְחַדֵּשׁ כְּמוֹתָהּ.[183]

*Those [Bnei Yisrael] who are destined to renew themselves
like it [the moon]*

הַחֹדֶשׁ הַזֶּה לָכֶם רֹאשׁ חֳדָשִׁים רִאשׁוֹן הוּא לָכֶם לְחָדְשֵׁי הַשָּׁנָה — *"This
month shall be for you the beginning of the months, it shall be for you
the first of the months of the year."*[184]

The Medrash states,[185] *R' Levi in the name of R' Yose bar Ilai said
"It is appropriate that the bigger one count according to the bigger
and the smaller one to count according to the smaller. Esav counts
according to the sun which is bigger, and Yaakov counts according
to the moon which is smaller." R' Nachman said, "This is a good sign,
that Esav follows the sun [solar calendar] which is great. For just like
the sun rules at day but not at night, so too Esav has a portion in This
World, but none in the World to Come, [whereas] Yaakov follows
the moon [lunar calendar] which is small. Just like the moon rules at
night but also at day, so too Yaakov has a portion in This World and
in the World to Come.' R' Nachman said further, "As long as the light
of the bigger one exists, the light of the smaller one isn't visible. Once
the light of the bigger one fades, the light of the smaller one becomes
visible. So long as the light of Esav exists, Yaakov's light is not visible. But once Esav's light fades, Yaakov's light becomes visible, as the
pasuk states,* קוּמִי אוֹרִי כִּי בָא אוֹרֵךְ... כִּי הִנֵּה הַחֹשֶׁךְ יְכַסֶּה אֶרֶץ וַעֲרָפֶל לְאֻמִּים
וְעָלַיִךְ יִזְרַח ה' וּכְבוֹדוֹ עָלַיִךְ יֵרָאֶה[186] — *"Arise! Shine! For your light has
arrived... For behold! Darkness may cover the earth and a thick cloud
[may cover] the kingdoms, but upon you Hashem will shine, and His
glory will be seen upon you."*

The Rema states:[187] *It is common practice to say [at Kiddush
Levanah]* דָּוִד מֶלֶךְ יִשְׂרָאֵל חַי וְקַיָּם — *"David king of Israel is alive and
in existence,"* because the kingship of [David] is likened to the moon

---

183. *Kiddush Levahanah* prayer.
184. *Shemos* 12:2.
185. *Shemos Rabbah* 6:3.
186. *Yeshayahu* 60:1-2.
187. *Rema, Orach Chaim* 426:2.

and will be renewed in the future [like the moon is renewed]. The community of Israel will once again cleave to her husband, the Holy One Blessed is He, just like the moon renews [its relationship] with the sun, as the pasuk states, שֶׁמֶשׁ וּמָגֵן ה' — *"a sun and a shield is the Lord."*[188] *This is why we rejoice and dance at the sanctification of the new moon, which resembles the rejoicing at a wedding.*

The moon is substantially smaller than the sun, and even so, the nations of the world are likened to the sun whereas the Jewish people are likened to the moon. This is because the moon has a unique advantage over the sun in that she alone rules at night (whereas during the day, the sun's domain, the moon is often visible). Just like the sun, the nations of the world are great and numerous, but they rule only at day. Every nation has its heyday, so to speak, every empire has its zenith, but times change; their sun sets and they fall, sinking to the depths of oblivion and obscurity. They are relegated to the realm of the insignificant and soon forgotten. But Am Yisrael, the smallest of the nations, like the moon, rules at night as well. All through the long night of exile, through the terrible darkness of God hiding His face, Am Yisrael is still in existence, awaiting dawn. נַפְשִׁי לַה' מִשֹּׁמְרִים לַבֹּקֶר — *"I yearn for my Lord among those longing for the dawn,"*[189] and that dawn will come, שֶׁהֵם עֲתִידִים לְהִתְחַדֵּשׁ כְּמוֹתָהּ וּלְפָאֵר לְיוֹצְרָם עַל שֵׁם כְּבוֹד מַלְכוּתוֹ — *"those who are destined to renew themselves like it [the moon] and to glorify their Molder for the name of His glorious kingdom."*[190]

Rav Yaakov Emden writes:[191] *"I swear! When I look at our nation's existence throughout the exile, one sheep among seventy wolves, this miracle is greater in my eyes than all the miracles performed for our forefathers in Egypt, at the [Red] Sea, and in Eretz Yisrael."*

This gift that God has bestowed on the Jewish people—that we are likened to the moon which rules at night—represents the greatest miracle of all miracles. As He has promised, אָז יִבָּקַע כַּשַּׁחַר אוֹרֶךָ וַאֲרֻכָתְךָ מְהֵרָה תִצְמָח[192] — *"then your light will burst out like the*

---

188. *Tehillim* 84:12.
189. Ibid. 130:6.
190. *Kiddush Levanah*
191. *Sulam Beis E-l.*
192. *Yeshayahu* 58:8.

dawn and your healing will speedily sprout." This is why we say at Kiddush Levanah, דָּוִד מֶלֶךְ יִשְׂרָאֵל חַי וְקַיָּם — *"David, king of Israel, is alive and enduring,"* as the Rema writes that David's kingship is also compared to the moon. Even though kingship has ceased from Bnei Yisrael and their Temple has become desolate, nevertheless we await this future renewal, and even though He may tarry, nevertheless we anticipate every day that He will come and Mashiach ben Dovid will renew his kingship speedily.

In future times, the moon, too, will be renewed and once again God will make it large like it was initially at creation. But this is contingent on us and our actions. When we return to God and mend our ways and deeds, the moon too will return to its original glory.

Our Sages tell us,[193] *Reish Lakish said: "Why is the he-goat of Rosh Chodesh different from other mussaf he-goats in that it is stated regarding it לַה׳ (לְחַטָּאת), (atonement) for God? For by this expression, the Holy One Blessed is He said, "This he-goat shall be an atonement for that which I diminished the size of the moon."*

The K'sav Sofer asks[194] the following in the name of his father the Chasam Sofer: Why is the Rosh Chodesh atonement incumbent on Bnei Yisrael? It would seem to be God's responsibility, for having diminished the moon. He explains that were we to mend ourselves and our deeds, the moon would return to its original state, shining bright as the sun, and since it is due to our shortcomings and inadequacies, *we* are responsible to bring this atonement for the fact that the moon is still diminished. [195]

Rav Isser Zalman Meltzer says:[196] it is customary that one look at the tzitzis fringes after Kiddush Levanah. He says that although this may seem strange since nighttime is not the time to don or look at tzitzis [as it says וּרְאִיתֶם אוֹתוֹ וּזְכַרְתֶּם, *you will see it (tzitzis) and remember*, and at night one cannot adequately see], in the future, when the moon will return to its former glory, and nighttime will

---

193. *Shevuos* 9a.
194. *She'eilos U'Teshuvos K'sav Sofer, Orach Chaim* 74.
195. The printers of the Vilna Shas were wise to comment on the side of this Gemara in *Shevuos* 9a, that this Gemara has deeper kabbalistic meanings to it, and cannot be taken at face value to imply that God needs an atonement, Heaven forfend.
196. Cited in *Har Tzvi* 1:12.

be as bright as day, then nighttime will also be a time to don tzitzis. This is why we look at the tzitzis fringes after Kiddush Levanah, hoping, planning, and praying for the day when we will be able to observe the mitzvah of tzitzis even at night.

Those who are destined to renew themselves like it [the moon] and to glorify their Molder for the Name of His glorious kingdom.

[197] שָׂשִׂים וּשְׂמֵחִים לַעֲשׂוֹת רְצוֹן קוֹנָם — *"They are joyous and glad to perform the will of their Creator."*

Bnei Yisrael are compared to the moon. Though one may wonder why they are compared to the moon and not to the sun which is much larger, there is a deep reason for this. The sun is large, but it does not grow; it is static, whereas the moon is not; it wanes and waxes. What this represents is that it is not merely a question of how big a person is, but whether a person is a *growing* person.

The Maharsha writes[198] that although God diminished the moon, the moon is happy and joyous to do His will. Our Sages tell us[199] that God said to the moon, "Go and diminish yourself." This is a most difficult test; God did not diminish the moon Himself, rather He commanded *her* to diminish *herself*. Regarding this characteristic we say at Kidddush Levanah, שָׂשִׂים וּשְׂמֵחִים לַעֲשׂוֹת רְצוֹן קוֹנָם — *"they are joyous and glad to perform the will of their Creator."* We learn an important lesson from the moon. At times one must diminish or negate oneself, and do so happily.

An explanation is offered in the name of the Holy Rebbe Menachem Mendel of Riminov regarding the Mishnah וּמוֹרָא[200] רַבָּךְ כְּמוֹרָא שָׁמַיִם — *"and the reverence for your teacher [should be] like the reverence of Heaven."* He explains that we must learn from שָׁמַיִם, the heavenly bodies, the sun and the moon, how a student must behave toward his teacher. The moon does not have its own light; it merely reflects the light of the sun. It is truly a wonder that as the moon gets closest to the sun (when it is positioned between the earth and the sun), it does not reflect any light, whereas when it is furthest from the sun, when it is beyond Earth, it is a full moon shining brightly. So, too, must a student sometimes stand from a

---

197. *Kiddush Levanah.*
198. *Sanhedrin* 42a.
199. *Chullin* 60b.
200. *Pirkei Avos* 4:15.

distance, not get too close to the point where he is cavalier with his teacher, and only then, from a respectful distance, can he attain the wealth his teacher has to offer. *The reverence for your teacher [should be] like the reverence of Heaven.*

שֶׁהֵם עֲתִידִים לְהִתְחַדֵּשׁ כְּמוֹתָהּ וּלְפָאֵר לְיוֹצְרָם עַל שֵׁם כְּבוֹד מַלְכוּתוֹ[201] — "*Those who are destined to renew themselves like it, and to glorify their Molder for the name of His glorious kingdom.*"

זָכוֹר אֶת הַיּוֹם הַזֶּה אֲשֶׁר יְצָאתֶם מִמִּצְרָיִם[202] — "*Remember this day on which you departed from Egypt.*"

What is the distinction between the obligation to tell about the Exodus from Egypt at the Seder and the obligation to remember it every day and night of the year?

There are two aspects to remembering the Exodus from Egypt, and two distinct obligations incumbent upon us in this remembering. One is the obligation to accept the yoke of Heaven upon us, as our Sages say, "*It is not for naught that I have taken you out of Egypt, rather so that you accept Me as your King.*" We also see this from the *pasuk:* כִּי לִי בְנֵי יִשְׂרָאֵל עֲבָדִים עֲבָדַי הֵם אֲשֶׁר הוֹצֵאתִי אוֹתָם מֵאֶרֶץ מִצְרָיִם[203] — "*for the Children of Israel are servants to Me, they are My servants, whom I have taken out of the land of Egypt.*" Furthermore it states: אֲנִי ה' אֱלֹקֵיכֶם אֲשֶׁר הוֹצֵאתִי אֶתְכֶם מֵאֶרֶץ מִצְרָיִם לִהְיוֹת לָכֶם לֵאלֹקִים[204] — "*I am Hashem, your God, Who has taken you from the land of Egypt to be a God to you.*" The second is the obligation to tell the story of the Exodus from Egypt, to thank and to praise God for His abundant kindness, as the *pasuk* states, יוֹדוּ לַה' חַסְדּוֹ וְנִפְלְאוֹתָיו לִבְנֵי אָדָם[205] — "*Let them give thanks to Hashem for His kindness, and His wonders to the children of man.*" (We also find that the word הַגָּדָה, *Haggadah,* includes in it an obligation to thank and to praise. In *Parashas Bikkurim,* the gift of the first fruit, it says: וְאָמַרְתָּ אֵלָיו[206] הִגַּדְתִּי הַיּוֹם. *Targum Yonasan* translates this: *and you shall say to him, "I **thank** today."* The *Targum Yerushalmi* translates, *and you shall say to him, "I **thank** and I **praise** today."*

---

201. *Kiddush Levanah.*
202. *Shemos* 13:3.
203. *Vayikra* 25:55.
204. *Bamidbar* 15:41.
205. *Tehillim* 107:8.
206. *Devarim* 26:3.

Every day of the year there is an obligation to mention *Yetzias Mitzrayim*, the Exodus from Egypt, in order to accept upon ourselves the yoke of Heaven. This is why *Shema* is the prayer designated to fulfill this mitzvah, since its essence is accepting God as King. Mentioning the Exodus is a requisite component in accepting God as King. (Indeed, renowned commentators throughout the generations have been puzzled by the fact that the Rambam does not include the daily mentioning of the Exodus from Egypt as one of the 613 mitzvos. There are those who answer that the Rambam opines that this is not a mitzvah unto itself, rather a part of the mitzvah of saying the *Shema*. Based on what we have said, the rationale behind the Rambam's ostensible omission is clear.)

Remembering the Exodus at the Seder, however, is different. The purpose at the Seder is to thank and praise God, and therefore we say *Hallel* in the *Haggadah* Seder night. We can now understand why one has not fulfilled his obligation of discussing the Exodus from Egypt at the Seder unless he tells about the miracles and wonders God performed, whereas the rest of the year it is enough for a person just to mention that God took us out of Egypt. To remember that God took us out of Egypt is enough to obligate us to accept His kingship upon us. But the more we tell about the great miracles He did for us, the more our hearts swell with gratitude and our souls thank and exalt Him.

"Draw forth your hands away from idol worship"

(Preparing for Chodesh Nissan)

וַיִּקְרָא מֹשֶׁה לְכָל זִקְנֵי יִשְׂרָאֵל וַיֹּאמֶר אֲלֵהֶם מִשְׁכוּ וּקְחוּ לָכֶם צֹאן לְמִשְׁפְּחֹתֵיכֶם וְשַׁחֲטוּ הַפָּסַח.[207]

And Moshe called to all the elders of Israel and said to them, "Draw forth and take for yourselves a sheep for your families, and slaughter the Pesach-offering."

---

207. *Shemos* 12:21.

THE MIDRASH[208] ON THIS VERSE SAYS מִשְׁחוּ יְדֵיכֶם מֵעֲבוֹדָה זָרָה — *"draw forth your hands away from idol worship."*

It is customary that on the night of *Bedikas Chametz* we set out ten pieces of *chametz* for the sole purpose of finding them and fulfilling the mitzvah of *Bedikas Chametz*. The question is obvious: Is this really called "searching" for *chametz*? What is the point in putting out the pieces of *chametz* only to find them and remove them?

Perhaps we can explain this question based on the following: commentators throughout the ages have explained that eliminating the *chametz* is not merely getting rid of any leavened food, but also eliminating the *real chametz,* the Evil Inclination, which remains inside, in the very soul of man.

The Radvaz writes:[209] *I will answer what you have asked me, why chametz on Pesach is more severe than any other forbidden things in the Torah, to the point where we are obligated to search every hole and crevice and eradicate it. Not only is it forbidden to be eaten, but it cannot even be seen or found. Even the smallest amount of it is forbidden* (unlike other forbidden things which have a specified measurement, *kezayis,* for example), *and it is not nullified at all* (unlike other things which are *nullified in ratio of sixty to one*[210]). *We don't find such stringencies with any other prohibition in the Torah.*

Answers the Radvaz: *Our Sages tell us in the Medrash that chametz on Pesach alludes to the yetzer hara, the Evil Inclination. The yetzer hara is like the yeast in the dough, which, when not held in check, causes the dough to ferment and sour. Therefore, one is obligated to obliterate any trace of it, to remove it from oneself, and to search all the crevices of one's mind, for even the smallest amount of it is not nullified.*

We see that *chametz* represents the negative aspects of man, his evil inclinations. Similarly, the Zohar[211] juxtaposes what is written regarding *chametz* and what is written regarding *Avodah Zarah,* idol

208. *Midrash Rabbah* on *Shemos* 12:21.
209. *She'eilos U'Teshuvos* 3:546.
210. Something becomes nullified if it constitutes less than a sixtieth of the majority of the specified item.
211. Vol. 2, 40b and 182a.

worship. With regard to *chametz* the Torah states: וְלֹא יֵרָאֶה לְךָ[212]
שְׂאֹר — "*nor may leaven be seen in your possession,*" and concerning idol worship it says: [213] אֱלֹהֵי מַסֵּכָה לֹא תַעֲשֶׂה לָךְ — "*you shall not make yourselves molten gods.*" For this reason we find many similarities in the laws concerning *chametz* and *Avodah Zarah,* such as the obligation to burn it (as opposed to merely discarding it), and the criteria for its nullification (i.e. that it is not בָּטֵל, etc.), which we do not find elsewhere.[214]

Therefore, before the Bnei Yisrael were to take sheep for the *korban Pesach*, they first rid themselves of their internal *chametz*, i.e., the Evil Inclination— "*draw forth your hands away from idol worship*" — מִשְׁחוּ יְדֵיכֶם מֵעֲבוֹדָה זָרָה.

The Jewish festivals are not simply holidays enacted to commemorate historical events and miracles of the past. Rather they are days of renewal in the present, and the holy light that shone in the past during those events and miracles are reawakened each festival at its particular time. The days of Pesach are intended for us to get rid of the *chametz* inside us just as we get rid of the physical *chametz,* and to come closer to God. These days have a special סִיַעְתָּא דִּשְׁמַיָּא, *Divine assistance,* which enables us to come closer to God. When our forefathers left Egypt they did not deserve to be redeemed for they had sunk so low in Egypt, as the שַׂר שֶׁל יָם, *the angel governing the sea,* protested, הַלָּלוּ עוֹבְדֵי עֲבוֹדָה זָרָה וְהַלָּלוּ עוֹבְדֵי עֲבוֹדָה זָרָה — "*these (the Jews) are idol worshippers and these (the Egyptians) are idol worshippers,*" i.e. why should Bnei Yisrael be redeemed if they are in fact no better than the Egyptians? And yet, God in His mercy redeemed them and brought them closer to Him, on wings of eagles. Just as this took place many years ago, so too is this power prevalent nowadays. Each year when Pesach rolls around, there is a special power during this time and we are able to attain greater spiritual heights that ordinarily we are not capable of reaching.[215]

---

212. *Shemos* 13:7.
213. Ibid. 34:17.
214. For further insight see *Haggadah shel Pesach, Bris HaLevi,* by R' Shlomo Alkabetz, 11-12.
215. For further insight see *Derech Hashem* on *Moadim* and *Kedushas Levi* on *Shavuos.*

Rav Chaim of Sanz quotes his teacher Rav Naftali of Ropshitz[216] who expounds homiletically on the phrase recited in the Friday-night Kiddush: כִּי הוּא יוֹם תְּחִלָּה לְמִקְרָאֵי קֹדֶשׁ זֵכֶר לִיצִיאַת מִצְרָיִם — *"for that day is the prologue to the holy convocations, a memorial of the Exodus from Egypt,"* that תְּחִלָּה לְמִקְרָאֵי קֹדֶשׁ, the *prologue*, or *pre-requisite, for holiness* is זֵכֶר לִיצִיאַת מִצְרָיִם, remembering what happened to our forefathers at the Exodus from Egypt, how they were taken out from the depths and raised to loftiness. When we have this image in our minds, we can draw strength to pull ourselves up to great heights in Torah and fear of Heaven.

As the Ari *z"l* says, *anyone who is meticulous about getting rid of chametz on Pesach is guaranteed that he will not come to sin the entire year.* The source for his words is found in the Zohar[217] which states that destroying the *chametz* symbolically represents getting rid of the *yetzer hara*, and by nullifying the *yetzer hara*, sins and their resultant punishments are nullified as well.

We can now understand the reason for placing the pieces of *chametz* in order to find them and burn them. The *chametz* is the *yetzer hara* within us. We give the *yetzer hara* sustenance, and it's because of our sins that it festers and grows. It is therefore incumbent upon *us* to uproot it; *we* created that *"chametz"* and now we are responsible to look for it and get rid of it.

Rav Pinchas of Koritz, the noted student of the Baal Shem Tov, said:[218]

The main point of getting rid of the chametz is getting rid of the Avodah Zarah. Hence, regarding King Yoshiyahu, the king who cleansed the land of idolatry, it states:[219] for such a Pesach offering had not been celebrated... This is also the reason the pasuk[220] "You shall observe the festival of Matzos" follows the pasuk[221] "You shall not make yourselves molten gods." If all Bnei Yisrael would burn the chametz with this intention, namely, that they are burning the

216. See *Rav Asher Weiss on the Haggadah.*
217. *Zohar* III, 282b.
218 *Imrei Pinchas on Erev Pesach*, p. 132.
219. II *Melachim* 23:22.
220. *Shemos* 34:18.
221. Ibid. 34:17.

Avodah Zarah, the Evil Inclination, the exile would be easier to bear.[222]

Let us follow the path of our fathers, check the *chametz* that resides within us and burn away the idol worship from our hearts and in this way ease the yoke of exile, till we merit the rebuilding of the Beis HaMikdash where once again we will eat from the *korban Pesach*.

---

222. For further insight see *Sefer HaRoke'ach, Hilchos Pesach*, 271.

פרשת בשלח
Parashas Beshalach

Song of the Heart

THE MIDRASH ON THIS WEEK'S *PARASHAH* STATES AS
follows:

Az yashir Moshe — "**Then Moshe sang**": this is as the
pasuk states, "Your Throne has been established since 'then' (*az*)."[223]
R' Berachyah said in the name of R' Abahu, "Although You have
always existed, Your Throne had not been established, nor have
You been revealed in Your world, until Your children uttered song.
Therefore, the *pasuk* states, "Your Throne has been established
since then (*az*)" — (a reference to *az yashir*).

Alternatively: *Az yashir Moshe* — "**Then Moshe sang**": this is
as the *pasuk* states, "She opened her mouth with wisdom, and a
Torah of kindness is on her tongue."[224] From the day that HaKadosh
Baruch Hu created the world to the day Bnei Yisrael stood by the
banks of the sea, no man ever sang to HaKadosh Baruch Hu, until
Bnei Yisrael did. Hashem created Adam, but he did not utter song.
He rescued Avraham from the fiery furnace and from the kings,
but he did not utter song. He rescued Yitzchak from the sacrificial
knife, but he did not utter song. He rescued Yaakov from the angel,

---

223. *Tehillim* 93:2.
224. *Mishlei* 31:26.

from Eisav, and from the people of Shechem, but he did not utter song. When Bnei Yisrael came to the sea and it split before them, they immediately sang to HaKadosh Baruch Hu, as the *pasuk* states, "Then Moshe and Bnei Yisrael sang." To this the *pasuk* refers, "She opened her mouth with wisdom." HaKadosh Baruch Hu then said, "This is what I have been waiting for."[225]

What is the great significance of singing praises to Hashem, that throughout all the generations, Hashem waited longingly for this precious form of service? Furthermore, Rashi comments on the *pasuk Az yashir* — "Then Moshe sang," that when Moshe saw the great miracle of the splitting of the Yam Suf, "the thought arose in his heart to utter song."[226] What does Rashi mean to say? All of man's deeds and words are prompted by the thoughts that arise in his heart. Why did Rashi need to make note of this here, regarding *Shiras HaYam* (the Song of the Sea)?

The Maharal explains that Rashi was bothered by the future tense of the word "*yashir*," which literally means "he will sing." Rashi therefore comments that although the Torah describes a past event, it uses the future tense to describe the thought that arose in Moshe's heart to sing — in the future.

The Maharal then takes his question one step further, by asking why the Torah needs to tell us about Moshe's thoughts. Suffice it to say that Moshe sang, and we will realize that his song was preceded by the conscious decision to sing. The Maharal then offers a brilliant and beautiful insight into the nature of song, as follows:

The motivation for song stems from the heart. When joy touches the hearts of the righteous, they are inspired to sing. Undoubtedly, they sang and rejoiced with all their hearts. Therefore, the *pasuk* states, *az yashir* — "then they *will* sing," in the future tense, referring to the inspiration roused by the joy of experiencing a miracle. There was no conscious decision to sing, such as when a person's mind directs his body to act in a certain way. Had it been so, their song would not have been a song of joy. Rather, it began with a spontaneous awakening of joy in the heart, which flowed outward in song. For this reason, the Torah refers to

---

225. *Shemos Rabbah* 23:1,4.
226. *Shemos* 15:1.

their song in the future tense (referring to the joy of the heart that prompted it).[227]

It seems that song is more than just an expression of thanks; more than just a recognition of the miracle; and more than just words of praise. It is the spontaneous eruption of a heart ablaze with ecstatic joy. True song can not be uttered until the soul begins to soar high on wings of inspiration. When a person begins to contemplate the miracles of Hashem, and the great love that the Creator has for us, he realizes how close we really are to our Father in Heaven. The heart then pours forth an unquenchable outburst of joyous song. This is, as as we are taught, אֵין אָדָם שָׁר שִׁירָה אֶלָּא מִתּוֹךְ שִׂמְחָה וְטוּב לֵבָב — "Man can only sing when he is moved by joy and good heart."[228] The source for this is from the *pasuk*, הִנֵּה עֲבָדַי יָרֹנּוּ מִטּוּב לֵב — "Behold, My servants will sing from good-heartedness."[229]

Above, we cited the Midrash, which states that generation after generation passed, yet none of our forefathers ever sang to Hashem, until Bnei Yisrael sang *Shiras HaYam*. What was unique about the splitting of the sea, that it inspired joyous song, the likes of which the world had never before known?

When we merit to see the connection between the many subtle details of Hashem's Providence, the pieces of the puzzle are drawn together, and the "big picture" of His plan for us becomes clear. We then realize that we have seen not just one isolated miracle, but a vast framework of countless miracles, which have guided, supported, and protected us and our forefathers from generation to generation.

Adam HaRishon was amazed at the majestic beauty of creation, yet since the purpose of creation had not yet reached its fulfillment, he was not inspired to sing. Avraham was rescued from his adversaries, but he had not yet been established as a nation. Yitzchak's life was spared at the *Akeidah*, and Yaakov was given strength to overcome Eisav's angel. These were indeed momentous events, which left an eternal impact on the souls of their descendants forever, yet the saga of our nation had not yet reached its zenith.

---

227. *Gur Aryeh, Shemos* ibid.
228. *Rashi, Arachin* 11a.
229. *Yeshayahu* 65:14.

Bnei Yisrael witnessed many amazing miracles, throughout the Ten Plagues and the Exodus from Egypt. However, the "big picture" of Hashem's plan for salvation was still unclear to them. When the Egyptians chased them to the shore of the sea, they found themselves trapped, with the sea an impenetrable wall before them, murderous hordes of enemies behind them, snakes and scorpions encroaching from both sides, and the guardian angel of Egypt swooping down on them from above. They cried out to Hashem to save them, and then, suddenly, an unforeseeable avenue of escape opened before them. They passed through the Yam Suf on dry land, and their enemies drowned before their very eyes.

Only then did they have the peace of mind and clarity to look back and see the guiding hand that had been with them all along. Only then did they realize that the suffering they had experienced in Egypt was all part of Hashem's master plan for their ultimate good. Only then did the pieces of the puzzle come together. Hashem's kingdom became firmly established on that day, as He revealed us as His holy nation. Our destiny had at last been fulfilled, and our hearts burst forth in exultant song.

With this we can understand a subtle distinction made by the Ran, who asks why we say *Hallel* on Seder night, in apparent contradiction to the general rule that *Hallel* is recited only by day. The Ran explains that in the context of davening, *Hallel* is "recited" (קוֹרִין אֶת הַהַלֵּל). This is done only by day. On Seder night, however, *Hallel* is not just recited. It is sung as a spontaneous outburst of joy and enthusiasm, from the hearts of those who were redeemed on this holy night, and rejoice now as did their forefathers long ago.

הַשִּׁיר יִהְיֶה לָכֶם כְּלֵיל הִתְקַדֶּשׁ חָג — *"This song will be for you, on the night that the Festival is sanctified"* (Yeshayahu 30:29).

פרשת יתרו
Parashas Yisro

Na'aseh V'Nishma

URING THE COURSE OF THE LIBERATION OF BNEI
Yisrael from Egypt, we witnessed awesome miracles, the
likes of which the world had never seen. When we passed
through the Yam Suf, we saw even greater wonders. Our Sages
tell us that the prophetic revelations granted to even a simple
serving girl during Krias Yam Suf were greater than those seen by
Yechezkel, who envisioned the "*Merkavah*" — the Divine Chariot.[230]

Yet the greatest revelation of all was received at Har Sinai, when
the very Heavens were torn asunder, and Bnei Yisrael were able
to see with their own eyes, that throughout all the myriad worlds
Above, there was nothing else in all existence except for the One
True God, Whose majesty permeates everything that exists. Of this
revelation, Moshe Rabbeinu said, "אַתָּה הָרְאֵתָ לָדַעַת כִּי ה' הוּא הָאֱלֹהִים
אֵין עוֹד מִלְּבַדּוֹ — "*You have been shown, to realize, that Hashem is
Elokim, and there is nothing else beside Him.*"[231]

When they proclaimed, נַעֲשֶׂה וְנִשְׁמַע — "*We will do, and we will
listen,*"[232] they subjugated all their desires to the will of the Creator,

---

230. *Yalkut Shimoni* 244.
231. *Devarim* 4:35.
232. *Shemos* 24:7.

and were elevated to the level of angels.[233] They were purified from the "filth" of sinful inclination, with which the snake had defiled Chava;[234] and they were granted eternal life.[235]

Our Sages tell us that at the moment they made this declaration of perfect obedience, angels descended upon them, to crown each and every Jew with two crowns, one for "we will do," and one for "we will listen." What is the symbolism of these crowns, and what is their correlation to Bnei Yisrael's declaration of "we will do and we will listen"?

A person would normally hesitate to surrender his freedom, and obligate himself to a system of rules, without first understanding the commitment he is asked to undertake. Yet Bnei Yisrael willingly and joyfully accepted Hashem's mastery, committing themselves to do anything Hashem might ask of them. This sincere dedication to Hashem's will was expressed by the words "we will do and we will listen." At that point, Bnei Yisrael accepted upon themselves *ol malchus Shamayim* — "the yoke of the Kingdom of Heaven."

However, our Sages also tell us that Hashem suspended Har Sinai in the air over their heads, and warned the Jewish people that if they would not accept the Torah, they would be buried beneath the mountain.[236] Tosefos asks what need there was for this threat, since they had already said, *Na'aseh v'nishma* — "We will do and we will listen." Tosefos explains that Hashem was concerned that Bnei Yisrael would regret their decision, after seeing the fearsome fires, and the thunderous voice, which accompanied Kabbalas HaTorah. Therefore, He held Har Sinai over their heads, to warn them not to renege on their commitment.

Perhaps we can suggest another answer to Tosefos's question, by first noting that in light of the awesome miracles Bnei Yisrael had witnessed, and the lofty spiritual peak to which they were elevated, it is no wonder that they willingly accepted the Torah. In the course of the Ten Plagues and the splitting of the Yam Suf, they had seen Hashem upend the laws of nature. They had seen

---

233. *Shabbos* 88a.
234. Ibid. 146a.
235. *Avodah Zarah* 5a.
236. *Shabbos* 88a.

the fulfillment of Hashem's assurance, "And afterward, they will emerge with great wealth,"[237] each of them having left Egypt with no less than ninety donkeys, loaded with the plunder of Egypt.[238] Even greater were the riches they took from the Egyptian horsemen, who were drowned in the Yam Suf.[239] They traveled through a barren wasteland, filled with venomous snakes and scorpions, yet were nourished from manna, the "bread of angels,"[240] and quails sent by Heaven. They were led by a pillar of cloud by day, and a pillar of fire by night. Their clothes were miraculously laundered on their backs, and never wore thin. Having witnessed these miracles, which constantly surrounded them, was it any wonder that they willingly agreed to accept Hashem's commandments? Who would have refused?

Yet for this very reason it was necessary to hold Har Sinai over their heads. They had to realize that their acceptance of the Torah imparted upon them not only nobility, but also subjugation: subjugation to Hashem and his commandments, at all times, and under all circumstances. They were destined to endure thousands of years of hardship and sacrifice for the sake of the Torah, in which the glory and joy of Hashem's countenance would be hidden from them. By holding Har Sinai over their heads, Hashem showed them that their acceptance of the Torah must be absolute and uncompromised.

The Gemara states that when a gentile is converted into an *eved Canaani*,[241] he is immersed in a *mikveh* like any other convert. However, when he ascends from the water, a bucket of cement is balanced on his head, to immediately signify his new status as a slave, indentured to his master's service.[242]

The same was true at Har Sinai, when Bnei Yisrael were "converted" into Hashem's chosen nation. Har Sinai was held over our heads as a sign of subjugation. Bnei Yisrael realized this, yet they

---

237. *Bereishis* 15:14.
238. *Bechoros* 5b.
239. *Bamidbar Rabbah,* 13.
240. *Tehillim* 78:25.
241. Canaanite slave of a Jewish owner, who is obligated in mitzvos to the same extent as a Jewish woman.
242. *Yevamos* 46a.

still said *na'aseh v'nishma*, accepting this status as slaves of Hashem with love and joy. They saw that there is no greater privilege, and no status more noble, than to be vassals of the King of kings, Hashem. Tosefos cites from the Talmud Yerushalmi that although most slaves would prefer freedom, the slave of a king realizes the prestige of his position, and would rather not be freed.[243]

A Jewish slave must serve his master for six years. If at the end of this six-year period he wishes to remain in his master's service, he must be subjected to having a hole pierced in his ear. The Gemara explains the significance of this ritual: "On Har Sinai his ear heard the words, 'For Bnei Yisrael are servants to Me,'[244] signifying that we were to be Hashem's own servants, and not the servants of other servants, yet he willingly enslaved himself to another person. Therefore, let his ear be pierced."[245]

Why is this ritual performed only at the end of six years, when he wishes to extend his term of servitude? Why was his ear not pierced when he initially sold himself? At the time he sold himself, he was obviously forced to do so by the pressures of poverty. However, when he extended his term, he received no money in compensation. He freely and willingly accepted the yoke of subjugation, since he "loved his master,"[246] as the *pasuk* states. It is this kind of enslavement that infringes on our debt of servitude to Hashem: a service of love.

By lovingly crowning Hashem as our king, we merited a corresponding measure of kingship for ourselves. For this reason the angels descended to crown each Jew with two crowns, one for *na'aseh*, and one for *nishma*.

The greatest accolade to which a human being can aspire is to be known as a loyal servant of the King. This was the title that Hashem bequeathed to Moshe Rabbeinu, when he said, "My servant Moshe is trusted in all My house."[247] In recognition of Moshe's loyal service of Hashem, he was granted a crown of splendor, as we say in Shacharis for Shabbos: יִשְׂמַח מֹשֶׁה בְּמַתְּנַת חֶלְקוֹ כִּי עֶבֶד נֶאֱמָן

---

243. *Tosefos, Gittin* 11b s.v. *Gittei nashim.*
244. *Vayikra* 25:55.
245. *Kiddushin* 20a.
246. *Shemos* 21:5.
247. *Bamidbar* 12:7.

קְרָאתָ לּוֹ כְּלִיל תִּפְאֶרֶת בְּרֹאשׁוֹ נָתַתָּ לּוֹ, *Moshe rejoiced in the portion he was granted, since he was called a faithful servant by You. You placed a crown of splendor upon his head.*

There is no greater joy in all the world than the peace of mind that comes with knowing that one faithfully serves his Creator.

The Gemara often discusses the heretical sects founded by Tzadok and Baitus, who had once been students of the Sage Antigonus of Socho. When they heard their Rebbi teach that we must be like servants who serve their master with no thought of reward,[248] they misinterpreted this to mean that there is in fact no reward for the righteous. "Must a laborer toil from morning to night, only to be denied his wages?" they asked. Disheartened by this thought, they abandoned Torah observance, and founded their own cults, which rejected the teachings of the Sages.[249]

Tzadok and Baitus failed to understand the intrinsic difference between a slave and a laborer. Had we been mere laborers, perhaps they would have been correct to insist that we should labor for reward. In truth, however, we are much more than mere laborers. Having declared *na'aseh v'nishma*, we shackled ourselves with chains of devotion, to do every bidding of our beloved Master — with no thought of any reward, other than the very privilege to serve Him.

In the Gemara we find yet another example of this intrinsic debate between the heretical followers of Tzadok and the faithful Sages:

Once there was a Tzadoki who observed Rava concentrating on a Torah teaching. Rava was so engrossed in his studies, that he did not notice that he was sitting on his fingers, causing them to bleed.

"You are an impetuous nation, who put your mouths before your ears (placing *'na'aseh'* before *'nishma'*)," said the Tzadoki. "You are still just as impetuous as ever. You should have first asked to hear Hashem's commandments. If you felt that you were able to observe them, you could have accepted. If not, you could have refused."

---

248. *Pirkei Avos* 1:3.
249. *Avos D'Rebbe Nosson* Ch. 1. See also *Rambam*, commentary on *Pirkei Avos* 1:3.

"We trust Hashem implicitly," explained Rava. "Therefore, the *pasuk* says of us, 'The sincerity of the straightforward will guide them.' You, however, always search for complaints. Of you the *pasuk* states, 'The crookedness of the traitors will rob them.'"[250]

The Tzadoki in this story followed the ideology of his predecessor, Tzadok, and could not possibly understand the "impetuous" love of Klal Yisrael for Hashem. Rava, like his predecessor Antigonus, remained a faithful servant of Hashem. He placed "*na'aseh*" before "*nishma*," with no thought of personal benefit.

I once heard from the Lev Simcha of Ger, in the name of his father, the Imrei Emes, an interesting incident that occurred in the Beis Midrash of his grandfather, the Sefas Emes, during Succos. The Sefas Emes said to his chassidim, that when saying the words *Ana Hashem* — "Please, Hashem," in *Hallel*, it is an auspicious time for all one's prayers to be answered. A debate then erupted among the chassidim over how to interpret the Sefas Emes's words. Some thought he referred to the *pasuk*, "Please, Hashem, save us." Others thought he referred to, "Please, Hashem, grant success."

The next morning during Hallel, the controversy between them was evident. When they reached the *pasuk*, אָנָּא ה' הוֹשִׁיעָה נָּא — "*Please, Hashem, save us*," some of them would cry out with great fervor. When they reached the *pasuk*, אָנָּא ה' הַצְלִיחָה נָא — "*Please, Hashem, grant success*," the others would cry out with equal emotion.

The Imrei Emes said that he did not join either group, since they were both in error. The Sefas Emes referred to neither of these *pesukim*. He referred to the *pasuk*, אָנָּה ה' כִּי אֲנִי עַבְדֶּךְ — "*Please, Hashem, for I am Your servant*."

I have often said that the relevance of this teaching is especially appropriate to the holiday of Succos, "the season of our joy." The Rambam writes:

Although there is a mitzvah to rejoice on all the holidays, the festival of Succos was marked by special rejoicing in the Beis HaMikdash, as the *pasuk* states, "You shall rejoice before Hashem your God, for seven days."[251]

250. *Shabbos* 88a.
251. *Rambam, Hilchos Lulav* 8:12.

Elsewhere, the Rambam writes that the recital of *Hallel* is a special expression of joy. For this reason we do not recite *Hallel* on Rosh Hashanah and Yom Kippur, days that are made somber by the fear of judgment.

As such, the recital of *Hallel*, the expression of joy, on Succos, the holiday of joy, is the most auspicious time for a Jew to call out to Hashem from the innermost depths of his heart, and proclaim, "Please, Hashem, for I am your servant." This is our greatest joy: that we have the privilege to serve Hashem. It is no wonder that such a prayer has great power to shake the Heavens.

May Hashem grant us the privilege to subjugate ourselves to Him, with pride and joy, and to serve Him faithfully, with all our hearts and souls.

פרשת משפטים

Parashas Mishpatim

Seeing the Sounds

I N THIS WEEK'S *PARASHAH*, THE TORAH CONTINUES ITS
description of perhaps the most significant event in the history
of the world, Kabbalas HaTorah. Regarding this epic turning
point in the development of Klal Yisrael, the Torah cautions us,
"Guard yourselves, lest you forget the events you saw with your
own eyes."[252] The Ramban lists this warning as one of the six hundred and thirteen mitzvos.[253]

Why does the *pasuk* stress that we witnessed Kabbalas HaTorah
with our own eyes? It would seem that the mitzvos we heard with
our ears were even more significant than the awesome sight of Har
Sinai burning like a fiery furnace, and hovering in the air over our
heads.

The Torah tells us that when Bnei Yisrael received the Torah
on Har Sinai, they "saw Hashem's voice."[254] Our Sages explain that
they could see the sounds and hear the sights.[255]

The depth of this teaching can be understood in light of Rav

---

252. *Devarim* 4:9.
253. *Sefer HaMitzvos.*
254. *Shemos* 20:15.
255. *Mechilta, Yisro.*

Chaim of Volozhin's observation, that of all our senses, there is none as descriptive as sight. The other senses can sometimes deceive, but once a person has seen something with his own eyes, he has no doubt at all of its veracity.[256] Therefore, for the majority of mankind, sight is the most significant of the five senses. "Seeing is believing," as people are wont to say.

However, Bnei Yisrael value the tradition we have received from the words of our forefathers, even more than our own sense of sight. For example, we cannot see Hashem, as the *pasuk* states, "Man cannot see Me and live,"[257] yet we are so certain of His existence that the Rambam writes, "Everything that exists in Heaven and earth, and all that is between them, have no existence other than what they draw from the ultimate truth of His own existence."[258]

What is man if not the breath of life that Hashem has blown into his lungs? This breath of life, the immortal soul, cannot be seen. Nor can we see the angels that constantly circle the world, doing Hashem's bidding. Yet we have no doubt at all of their existence, having received a tradition in an unbroken chain from generation to generation. For this reason, the Ramban[259] and Sefer HaChinuch[260] write that our faith is founded not on what we perceive with our own eyes, but on the tradition we have received from our forefathers.

When Bnei Yisrael stood at Har Sinai, we were elevated to such an exalted level that we could "see the sounds." This means to say, that we could recognize the veracity of the words we heard, as if we had seen them with our own eyes. At the same time, we could "hear the sights," meaning that this visible, physical world became so distant from our thoughts, that it was as if we had only heard about it, and had never seen it with our own eyes.[261]

With this we can explain an interesting episode related in the Gemara:

---

256. *Nefesh HaChaim* III, note on Ch. 11. See also *Bnei Yissaschar: Sivan.*
257. *Shemos* 33:20.
258. *Yesodei HaTorah* 1:1.
259. *Devarim* 4:9.
260. Introduction.
261. See *Meshech Chachmah, Chukas; Meor Einayim, Beshalach.*

R' Yochanan taught that in the future, Hashem will take gems thirty cubits tall and thirty cubits wide, carve from them openings ten cubits wide and twenty tall, and place them by the gates of Yerushalayim.

One of his students mocked this teaching. "Today no gem is even as big as a bird's egg, and in the future such giant gems will be found?" he asked. Later, the student was traveling by boat when he saw in the Heavens a vision of angels carving the giant gems that R' Yochanan had described.

"Who are these for?" he asked.

"In the future, Hashem will place these gems by the gates of Yerushalayim," the angels told him.

The student then returned to R' Yochanan and said, "Teach, Rebbi, teach. I have seen exactly what you described."

"*Reika*! (empty one)," R' Yochanan scolded him. "Had you not seen it, you would not have believed. You mock the words of the Sages." R' Yochanan then set his eyes upon him, and turned him into a pile of bones.[262]

Why did R' Yochanan scold the student only after he returned to verify R' Yochanan's words with his own testimony? Why did he not turn the student into a pile of bones when the student first challenged his teachings?

When the student returned to R' Yochanan, amazed by the sight he had seen, he demonstrated that he valued the vision of his own eyes over the tradition he heard from his rebbi, who based his teachings on *pesukim* from the Torah. This is what angered R' Yochanan. The student had obviously attained a lofty spiritual level, having been able to converse with angels. Accordingly, he should have been able to "see the voice" of R' Yochanan, accepting his Torah teachings as if he had seen them with his own eyes.

The punishment of being transformed into a pile of bones was *middah k'neged middah* (in equal and appropriate measure) to his sin. In outward appearance, the human body is no more than a bag of bones, held together by meat and sinews. It is given life by the invisible soul within it. Since the student valued only what was visible to his eyes, he was transformed into a lifeless pile of bones

---

262. *Bava Basra* 75a.

— all that is visible of man initially. Thus, R' Yochanan called him *reika,* empty one, as if to say, "Are you empty of the holy soul, which you cannot see? Just as you believe in your own soul, you should believe my words."

In a similar vein, the Gemara states elsewhere:

Rav Sheishes was blind. When everyone went to greet the king, he went along with them. A Sadducee then taunted him, saying, "Why does the broken bucket go to the river?" (Just as it cannot draw water from the river, so too you cannot see the king.)

"Come and I will show you that I can see the king better than you can," answered Rav Sheishes.

When the first contingent of the king's men passed before the spectators, there was a great roar of applause. "The king has come," the Sadducee told Rav Sheishes.

"He has not yet come," answered Rav Sheishes.

When the second contingent passed, there was again a great uproar. "Now the king has come," the Sadducee said.

"He has not yet come," answered Rav Sheishes again.

When the third contingent passed, there was silence. "Now the king has come," said Rav Sheishes.

"How did you know?" asked the Sadducee.

Rav Sheishes explained, "The kingdom of mortal men parallels the kingdom of Heaven, of which it is said, 'Go out and stand on the mountain before Hashem.' And behold, Hashem passed by him. Before Hashem, there was a great and mighty wind, which uprooted mountains and crumbled stones — but Hashem was not in the storm wind. After the storm wind there was a great noise — but Hashem was not in the noise. After the noise there was a fire — but Hashem was not in the fire. After the fire there came a still thin sound ..."[263]

When the king came, Rav Sheishes recited a *berachah* ("Blessed are You, Hashem ... Who shared His honor with flesh and blood").

The Sadducee then asked him, "Why do you recite a *berachah* over something you cannot see?" What was the fate of the Sadducee? Some say that his peers gouged out his eyes. Others say that Rav Sheishes set his eyes on him and turned him into a pile of bones.[264]

---

263. *I Melachim* 19:12.
264. *Berachos* 58a.

This Gemara also teaches us that the truth should not be determined by what our eyes behold, but by what our ears receive. Rav Sheishes, who could not see at all, was more aware than the Sadducee not only of what occurs in Heaven above, but even of the mundane occurrences of this lower world. When the Sadducee obstinately refused to concede that he perceived less than Rav Sheishes, and went so far as to mock Rav Sheises for reciting a *berachah* over what he could not see, he was punished *middah k'neged middah*, and his eyes were gouged out. Alternatively, he was transformed into a pile of bones like R' Yochanan's student.

The prophet describe the awaited Redemption, with the *pasuk*, "And all flesh as one will **see**, that the mouth of Hashem has spoken."[265] As it was when we first received the Torah, the truth of Hashem's word will be so obvious, that not only will we be able to hear it with our ears, but we will see it with our very eyes. For this we pray in the *Kedushah* for Shabbos Mussaf: וְיַשְׁמִיעֵנוּ בְּרַחֲמָיו שֵׁנִית לְעֵינֵי כָּל חָי לֵאמֹר הֵן גָּאַלְתִּי אֶתְכֶם אַחֲרִית כְּרֵאשִׁית לִהְיוֹת לָכֶם לֵאלֹקִים — "And in His mercy, He will let us hear again, before the eyes of all living things, 'Behold, I have redeemed you, at last as at first, to be for your God.' "

---

265. *Yeshayahu* 40:5.

פרשת תרומה
Parashas Terumah

The Eternal Mikdash

O UR SAGES TELL US THAT THERE IS A CELESTIAL BEIS HaMikdash in Heaven, directly above the physical Beis HaMikdash here on earth.[266] When the Beis HaMikdash on earth was destroyed, the Beis HaMikdash in Heaven was destroyed along with it. Over the course of the generations, the Heavenly Beis HaMikdash is slowly being rebuilt, brick by brick, by the Torah and mitzvos of Bnei Yisrael. When it is at last complete, it will finally be revealed, and descend as a fiery edifice.[267] Rebbe Naftali of Ropshitz writes as follows:

וּבְנֵה אוֹתָהּ בְּקָרוֹב בְּיָמֵינוּ בִּנְיַן עוֹלָם — *"Rebuild it (Yerushalayim) soon and in our days, as a permanent structure."*[268] In Hebrew, the prefix of the letter "ב" can mean either "in" or "with." Therefore, we can interpret this prayer to mean "Rebuild it *with* our days." Hashem rebuilds the Beis HaMikdash out of the days of Bnei Yisrael. With each day that a Jew serves Hashem, he furthers the construction of Yerushalayim and the Beis HaMikdash. Some build an entire row of

---

266. See *Rashi, Shemos* 15:17.
267. *Rashi, Succah* 41a.
268. From *Shemoneh Esrei.*

bricks with their mitzvos, while others place just one brick. As a Jew serves Hashem day by day, he contributes towards the completion of the Beis HaMikdash, may it be soon in our days.[269]

Just as the mitzvos of the *tzaddikim* contribute to the construction of the Beis HaMikdash in Heaven, the misdeeds of the wicked hinder its construction. My Rebbe and mentor, the Klausenberger Rav *zt"l*, said that his great-grandfather, the Divrei Chaim of Tsanz, once sat at his *tish*, with his chassidim assembled around him, and revealed to them that he could see the Beis HaMikdash standing in Heaven. It had already been completed and was ready to descend, and all that was still lacking was the *paroches*. At that point, an elderly chassid, whose heart pined over the length of the *Galus*, cried out, "Why does the Rebbe not make a *paroches* himself, through his Torah and mitzvos?"

The Divrei Chaim's face flushed, and he said, "Have I not already made one? Time and time again, I have woven *parochos* for the Beis HaMikdash, but each time a wicked person transgresses a terrible sin, and tears my *paroches* apart."

How is the Beis HaMikdash in Heaven built? How can we take part in this vital endeavor, to hasten its construction, and bring the world to its ultimate perfection?

Each vessel of the Beis HaMikdash corresponds to a certain task in the service of Hashem. Although the physical Beis HaMikdash and its vessels have been destroyed, the spiritual task that each vessel represented can still be achieved. When we apply ourselves to that task, we create the spiritual essence of that vessel Above.

The three most crucial vessels, around which every service of the Beis HaMikdash revolved, were the Menorah, Shulchan (Table), and *Mizbei'ach* (Altar). Each one signified a different aspect of our service of Hashem.

What was the task of the Menorah? The Gemara states that if a person desires wisdom, he should face slightly southward as he davens, just as the Menorah was located on the southern wall of the Beis HaMikdash.[270] Similarly, the Bnei Yissaschar writes that reciting the Torah portion describing the Menorah is a potent *segulah*

---

269. *Zera Kodesh, Ki Seitzei.*
270. *Bava Basra* 25b.

for understanding the Torah.[271] Furthermore, our Sages tell us that the reward for diligently lighting the Chanukah Menorah is to be blessed with Torah scholars for sons.[272] All this seems to indicate that the Menorah's task was to spread the light of Torah. The Menorah shed spiritual light in the world, just as it shed physical light in the Beis HaMikdash.[273]

The *Mizbei'ach* corresponds to prayer. The daily prayer service was enacted in place of the *Korban Tamid* offerings that were brought on the *Mizbei'ach* in the morning and afternoon, and the remainder of its meat that was burned on the *Mizbei'ach* at night.[274] Accordingly, the Prophet enjoined us, וּנְשַׁלְמָה פָרִים שְׂפָתֵינוּ — *"let [the words of] our lips serve in place of the cow offerings."*[275] The world stands on the merit of Torah, *Avodah* (service), and Acts of Kindness.[276] Rabbeinu Yonah explains that *Avodah* refers to offering of sacrifices while the Beis HaMikdash stood, or prayer now that the Beis HaMikdash has been destroyed. Prayer is considered "the *Avodah* of the heart." [277]

If the Menorah and *Mizbei'ach* corresponded to the first two pillars of the world, Torah and *Avodah*, it stands to reason that the Shulchan corresponds to the third pillar: Acts of Kindness. In the Jewish home, this takes the form of food served on the table to hungry guests. Yet, in a broader sense, it refers to all forms of kindness and giving.

II

Similarly, the garments worn by the Kohanim served to atone for sins such as *lashon hara* and arrogance.[278] By rectifying these traits within ourselves, we help weave these garments in

---

271. *Igra D'Firka* 172.
272. *Shabbos* 23.
273. *Netziv, HaEmek Dvar: Tetzaveh.*
274. *Berachos* 26b.
275. *Hoshea* 14:3.
276. *Pirkei Avos* 1:2.
277. *Taanis* 2a.
278. *Arachin* 16a.

Heaven. By strengthening these three pillars of Torah, Prayer, and Kindness, we help form the spiritual essence of the vessels in the Beis HaMikdash Above, thus fulfilling the *pasuk*, "Make for Me a Mikdash, and I will dwell among you."[279]

What aspect of the Beis HaMikdash is still lacking in Heaven? What remains for our generation to complete? The Divrei Chaim testified that in his own time, the *paroches* was still lacking. Yet, he also explained that while certain elements of the Beis HaMikdash are created through our mitzvos, other elements are destroyed by our sins. Therefore, it is quite possible that the primary obligation of our generation is not necessarily the *paroches*, but some other aspect of the Beis HaMikdash.

Rabbi Yitzchak of Komarna wrote that in the end of days, when the Aron Kodesh in Heaven is completed, the Redemption will at last arrive.[280] This points toward the paramount importance of Torah study in our generation. In full agreement, the Ohr HaChaim's explains that our Final Redemption has been delayed for so long because it must be orchestrated by Moshe Rabbeinu, but Moshe "has no desire to redeem a nation that is lax in Torah study," as the Zohar states.[281]

Moshe is called the "*Raaya Mehemna*," the Faithful Shepherd of Israel, who led our forefathers through the Desert, carrying them in his merit, as a mother carries her infant. He put his life on the line to challenge Hashem for our survival, demanding that his name be erased from the Torah, if Hashem would destroy us. How then can we understand the Ohr HaChaim's assertion, that Moshe has no desire to redeem us?

It seems that Moshe does desire to redeem us, but he is simply unable to do so, as long as we are lax in our Torah study. Moshe's power lies in the Torah. If we fail to strengthen his hand by diligently applying ourselves to its study, he cannot help us.

If only we had eyes to see, or ears to hear, we would see Moshe Rabbeinu pleading with us, "My beloved children, help me to help you! Dedicate yourselves to the love and study of Torah. Complete

---

279. *Shemos* 25:8.
280. *Heichal Berachah, Vayeira.*
281. *Ohr HaChaim, Parashas Tetzaveh.*

the Aron Kodesh in Heaven, the final piece of the Beis HaMikdash, so that I can herald your Redemption at last."

III

While the Beis HaMikdash stood, it was the primary resting place of the *Shechinah* in this world. However, even after the Beis HaMikdash was destroyed, the *Shechinah* has never left us. The Gemara interprets the verse, "I shall be for them a miniature sanctuary,"[282] as a reference to the shuls and yeshivos that were founded in Babylon. Furthermore, the *Shechinah* also rests in each Jewish home that is dedicated to the service of Hashem, and is therefore also considered a *"mikdash mi'at"* — a miniature sanctuary. Rashi tells us that before the Mishkan was built, the *Shechinah* rested in the homes of the *tzaddikim*.[283] The same is true in our own generation.

To a certain extent, a Jewish home is even holier than a shul, as the Kedushas Levi writes. In shuls, we perform Rabbinic commandments, such as communal prayer, while in the home we perform Torah commandments such as mezuzah and *hachnassas orchim* (welcoming guests).

Perhaps this is the meaning of the *pasuk* וַיִּטֹשׁ מִשְׁכַּן שִׁלוֹ אֹהֶל שִׁכֵּן בָּאָדָם — *"And he abandoned the Mishkan in Shilo, the tent wherein He dwells with man."*[284] Although the Beis HaMikdash has been destroyed, and the *Shechinah* no longer dwells in Shilo or Yerushalayim as it once did, it still dwells among us in our homes, shuls, and yeshivos, and in the heart of every Jew who dedicates himself to Hashem's service, by supporting the pillars of Torah, Prayer, and Kindness.

---

282. *Yechezkel* 11:16.
283. *Shabbos* 55b.
284. *Tehillim* 78:60.

They Shall Make for Me a Mikdash

וְעָשׂוּ לִי מִקְדָּשׁ וְשָׁכַנְתִּי בְּתוֹכָם.

They shall make for Me a Mikdash and I shall dwell among them.[285]

THE RISHONIM DEBATE WHETHER THE THIRD AND final Beis HaMikdash will be built by human hands, like the first two, or will descend from Heaven as a structure of fire made by Hashem's own hands, as implied by the verse, מִקְדָּשׁ ה׳ כּוֹנְנוּ יָדֶיךָ — *"The Mikdash, Hashem, that Your hands have established."*[286]

The Rambam[287] states clearly that Mashiach will build the third Beis HaMikdash, assisted by the rest of Klal Yisrael. The Sefer HaChinuch[288] states the same. Rashi[289] and Tosafos,[290] however, argue that the third Beis HaMikdash will descend in a state of completion from Heaven in all its perfect splendor.

The Zohar[291] supports this opinion:

Since the (third) Beis HaMikdash will be built by HaKadosh Baruch Hu, it will endure forever. Of this it is written, *"The glory of this latter Temple will be greater than [that of] the first."*[292] Whereas the first Beis HaMikdash was built by human hands, the final Beis HaMikdash will be built by HaKadosh Baruch Hu Himself. Therefore it is written, *"If Hashem will not build the house, the builders labor in vain."*[293]

---

285. *Shemos* 25:8.
286. Ibid. 15:17.
287. *Hilchos Melachim* 11:1.
288. Mitzvah 95.
289. *Rosh Hashanah* 30a.
290. *Shevuos* 15b.
291. *Bereishis* 28a.
292. *Chaggai* 2:9.
293. *Tehillim* 127:1.

The Maharam Shik[294] writes that in fact the Beis HaMikdash might be built in either way, depending on the manner of our Redemption. Our Sages explain a seeming contradiction in the verse that states of the Redemption, בְּעִתָּהּ אֲחִישֶׁנָּה — "In its proper time, I will hasten it."[295] Will the Redemption arrive in due time, or will it be hastened to arrive before its time? The Gemara explains that if we so merit, then the Redemption will be hastened to arrive before its time. If not, then we will have to wait until the destined time for the Redemption.

Similarly, through our Torah and mitzvos, we can build the Beis HaMikdash by our own hands. However, if we fail to do so, then we will have to wait for Hashem to build the Beis HaMikdash Himself, and send it down from Heaven as a fiery structure.

In either case, it is certain that no political power will be the instrument through which the third Beis HaMikdash will be built. The Midrash[296] states that in the time of R' Yehoshua ben Chananya, the wicked empire (Rome) gave orders to rebuild the Beis HaMikdash. Offices were then set up from Akko to Antiochia to provide gold and silver for all the laborers who were needed.

However, the plan ultimately failed since the third Beis HaMikdash cannot possibly be built by any world power, but only by the Torah and mitzvos of Klal Yisrael or, if necessary, by Hashem Himself.

כִּי אַתָּה ה' בָּאֵשׁ הִצַּתָּהּ וּבָאֵשׁ אַתָּה עָתִיד לִבְנוֹתָהּ — "For You, Hashem, have caused it to be consumed by fire; and with fire You will rebuild it" (from the Nacheim prayer, recited in the Shemoneh Esrei of Tishah B'Av).

May it be soon and in our days.

---

294. Teshuvos Y.D. 203.
295. Yeshayahu 60:22.
296. Shemos Rabbah 64.

פרשת תצוה
Parashas Tetzaveh

The Garments of Priesthood

וְעָשִׂיתָ בִגְדֵי קֹדֶשׁ לְאַהֲרֹן אָחִיךָ לְכָבוֹד וּלְתִפְאָרֶת ... וְלִבְנֵי אַהֲרֹן תַּעֲשֶׂה כֻתֳּנֹת וְעָשִׂיתָ לָהֶם אַבְנֵטִים וּמִגְבָּעוֹת תַּעֲשֶׂה לָהֶם לְכָבוֹד וּלְתִפְאָרֶת.

You shall make vestments of sanctity for Aharon, your brother, for glory and splendor ... For the sons of Aharon make Tunics and make them Sashes; and you shall make them Headdresses for glory and splendor.[297]

THE WORDS *KAVOD* (GLORY) AND *TIFERES* (SPLENDOR) seem synonymous. However, the Chasam Sofer explains that they in fact represent two opposite traits, which merge to create a delicate balance. Whereas *kavod* signifies the honor and distinction of the priesthood, *tiferes* signifies the humility of the Kohanim, who recognized their own relative smallness, as they stood in Hashem's infinite Presence. For this reason Yaakov, who said, "I have been made small by all Your kindness,"[298] personified the attribute of *tiferes* — the splendor of humility.[299]

---

297. *Shemos* 28:2,40.
298. *Bereishis* 32:11.
299. *Zohar, Shir HaShirim* 25a.

As we previously discussed in the essay *"The Eternal Mikdash"* *(Parashas Terumah)*, although the Beis HaMikdash and its vessels have been destroyed, the spiritual service that these vessels exemplified still exists, and are performed by their counterparts in our own Torah study, mitzvah observance, and character improvement.

The same is true of the *bigdei Kehunah*, which are no longer worn, but the function they served still exists. Today, there are other "priestly garments" — namely, tzitzis and tefillin, which we wear in the service of Hashem. Through them, the balance between *kavod* and *tiferes* is preserved.

Tefillin represent the honor and glory of priesthood. For this reason, a mourner is exempt from wearing tefillin on the first day of his mourning, when he "rolls in the dust of misery."[300] Tzitzis, on the other hand, represent humble servitude. The Gemara refers to them as "a badge of servitude."[301] Together, they represent the *kavod* and *tiferes* of Klal Yisrael, who are a "kingdom of priests, and a holy nation."[302]

The Most Beloved Korban

Our Sages tell us that the *ketores* is the most beloved of all the *korbanos*. So much so, that even after the Mishkan and its vessels were completed; the sacrifices were slaughtered and offered on the *Mizbei'ach*; the Shulchan was set, and the Menorah was kindled; the *Shechinah* still did not descend to rest upon the Mishkan, until after the *ketores* was offered.[303]

The Zohar states that nothing has such power to drive back the force of death in the world as the *ketores*, which "binds judgment to mercy, with a fragrance that is pleasant to the *af*."[304] The Ramban explains this based on a play on words, in which the Hebrew word *"af"* can mean either "nose" or "anger." As such, there is a double meaning here, that just as the *ketores* is pleasant to smell, it also

---

300. See *Kesubos* 6b, *Moed Katan* 21a, *Shulchan Aruch O.C.* 38:5.
301. *Menachos* 43b.
302. *Shemos* 19:6.
303. *Midrash Tanchuma, Tetzaveh* 15.
304. *Zohar* III, 224a.

serves to assuage Hashem's anger over our sins.[305]

The Arizal[306] notes that יב״ק, the first letters of the *pasuk*, יָשִׂימוּ קְטוֹרָה בְּאַפֶּךָ, "They shall place *ketores* before You,"[307] is equal in gematria to the Names י-ה-ו-ה and אֱלֹקִים together, thus representing the unification of Hashem's Name. י-ה-ו-ה is Hashem's Name of Mercy, while אֱלֹקִים is His Name of strict judgment.[308] *Ketores*, which in Aramaic means "tie," binds these two Names together.

Behind our most difficult trials hides Hashem's greatest kindness. Hashem has no interest in making us suffer, yet sometimes He must cloak His goodness behind a guise of difficulty, for reasons known only to Him. Ultimately, the meaning for our suffering will be revealed, and we will understand how "everything the Merciful One does is for the best."[309] In the meantime, however, we must trust in Him in perfect faith, that His *gevurah* (strictness) is nothing but a representation of His *chesed* (kindness).

The Vilna Gaon explained the significance of the *pasuk*, "With *gevurah*, His right hand rescues."[310] Generally, Hashem's right hand represents His loving kindness, while His left hand represents His strictness. As our Sages tell us, "The right hand draws close, while the left hand pushes away."[311] Nevertheless, the *pasuk* here stresses His *gevurah* can also be a representation of His right hand's kindness.

For this reason, מְכַלְכֵּל חַיִּים בְּחֶסֶד — "*He dispenses life, with kindness,*" is said in the second *berachah* of *Shemoneh Esrei*, which begins אַתָּה גִבּוֹר לְעוֹלָם ה׳ — "*You are eternally mighty, Hashem.*" Hashem masks His kindness behind a curtain of seeming severity. *Ketores* has the power to reveal the hidden kindness, thus uniting Hashem's attributes of *chesed* and *gevurah*. The Zohar states:

"And Moshe said to Aharon, 'Take the pan, fill it with fire from the *Mizbei'ach*, and place upon it *ketores*. Take it quickly to the congregation to atone for them, for anger has gone forth from Hashem.

---

305. Ramban, commentary to the Torah: *Shemos* 30:1.
306. *Likutei Torah, V'Zos HaBerachah.*
307. *Devarim* 33:10.
308. *Shemos Rabbah* 3:6.
309. *Berachos* 60b.
310. *Tehillim* 20:7.
311. *Sotah* 47a.

The plague has begun.' Aharon did as Moshe said. He ran to the congregation, and behold, the plague had begun among the people. He placed the *ketores* (on the fire) and atoned for the nation, standing between the dead and the living, and the plague was halted."[312]

The forces of evil and the accusers cannot withstand the *ketores*. It is the secret of everything, and the connector of everything. At Minchah time, when judgment hovers over the world, David concentrated on this prayer, as it is written, "Let my prayer be as *ketores* before You."[313] This prayer ascends and drives away the fury of harsh judgment that reigns at that time. The *ketores* pushes it away, rescinding all anger and accusation.[314]

———•———

The Gemara states as follows: מִיָּד כָּל אֶחָד וְאֶחָד לוֹ אוֹהֵב וּמָסַר לוֹ דָּבָר ... אַף מַלְאַךְ הַמָּוֶת מָסַר לוֹ דָּבָר שֶׁנֶּאֱמַר וַיִּתֵּן אֶת הַקְּטֹרֶת וַיְכַפֵּר עַל הָעָם — וְאוֹמֵר וַיַּעֲמֹד בֵּין הַמֵּתִים וּבֵין הַחַיִּים וְגוֹ' אִי לַאו דְּאָמַר לֵיהּ מִי הֲוָה יָדַע ("After Moshe ascended to Heaven, and defeated the angels in a debate over who should receive the Torah) the angels all befriended him and gave him gifts ... the Angel of Death also gave him a gift, as we learn from the pasuk, "[Aharon] placed the ketores, and atoned for the nation... standing between the dead and the living."[315] Had the Angel of Death not revealed this secret, how could Moshe have known (that ketores can halt a deadly plague)?[316]

How does this *pasuk* prove that the Angel of Death itself revealed the secret of *ketores*? Perhaps Moshe realized it through his prophetic powers? Or perhaps one of the other angels or even Hashem Himself told him?

The Arizal[317] explains that since the eleven ingredients of the *ketores* are the very source from which the Angel of Death draws its power to exist, no other being could have revealed them without its consent. Hashem never delivers a creation's source of vitality into the hands of another, without that creation's consent.

---

312. *Bamidbar* 17:11-13.
313. *Tehillim* 141:2.
314. *Zohar* I, 230a.
315. *Bamidbar* 17:12.
316. *Shabbos* 89a.
317. *Likutei Torah, Tetzaveh.*

On Yom Kippur, the holiest day of the year, on which Bnei Yisrael are forgiven for their sins, the Kohen Gadol enters the *Kodesh Kodashim* to offer the *ketores*. The Gemara states:

R' Yishmael ben Elisha said: I once entered deep within [the *Kodesh Kodashim*] to offer *ketores*, and I saw *Akasri-keil, Kah,* Hashem of Hosts, sitting on a high and exalted throne. He said to me, "Yishmael, My son, bless Me."

I said to Him, "May it be Your will that Your mercy overrule Your anger; May Your mercy extend over all Your attributes; May You deal with Your children with the Attribute of Mercy, and waive for their sake the strict demands of justice." And he nodded His head in approval.[318]

The Ben Ish Chai explains that the expression לִפְנַי וְלִפְנִים refers not only to the inner recesses of the Beis HaMikdash, in the *Kodesh Kodashim*, but also the inner recesses of the Heavens. R' Yishmael ascended to the uppermost reaches of creation, to the Highest planes of existence, where he was able to converse with Hashem, and arouse His Heavenly mercy. All this was through the power of the *ketores*, which binds one world to the next, and binds mercy to judgment.

———•———

Although the Beis HaMikdash has been destroyed, and we can no longer offer the *korbanos* on a physical level, nevertheless, our study of the Torah portions of the *korbanos* enacts the same effect on a spiritual level. This is true also of the *ketores* offering. The Igra D'Parka writes that if a person concentrates while reading the portion of the *korbanos* after *Ashrei*, he weakens the forces of evil, and saps their power. Even if a decree of death has been passed upon him or upon a member of his family, the decree can be revoked through the recital of *ketores*.[319]

Rav Chaim Pilachi advises a potent *segulah* of reading the Torah portion of *ketores*, written on parchment in *Ksav Ashuris* script.[320] The Ben Ish Chai further advises counting the eleven ingredients of

---

318. *Berachos* 7a.
319. *Igra D'Firka* 36.
320. *Kaf HaChaim* 17:18.

the *ketores*, while reading them aloud. One is thereby merited as if he had actually offered them in the Beis HaMikdash. [321]

The Zohar states:

Come and see. Anyone who is pursued by harsh judgments must make use of the *ketores*, and return in *teshuvah* before his Creator. The *ketores* helps to fend off the harsh judgments, if he sets himself to recall the *ketores* twice each day, morning and night, as the *pasuk* states, "*ketores* of spices each morning," and "burn it in the afternoon."[322]

Ketores is the constant support of the world, as the *pasuk* states, "A constant *ketores* before Hashem, throughout your generations."[323] This is the support of the world below, and the support of the world Above. Wherever the *ketores* is not recalled each day, judgments from Above hover, death abounds, and foreign nations rule over us, as it is written, "A constant *ketores* before Hashem." This is what constantly stands before Hashem, more than all the other forms of service. The service of *ketores* is beloved and cherished by HaKadosh Baruch Hu, more than all other forms of services and desires in the world. Although prayer is greater than all else, the *ketores* is even more cherished and beloved before HaKadosh Baruch Hu.

Come and see the difference between prayer and *ketores*. Prayer was instituted in place of the *korbanos* that Bnei Yisrael offered. Of all their *korbanos*, there was none as significant as *ketores*. Furthermore, prayer serves to rectify what its needed, whereas *ketores* has even greater effect to rectify, unite, and illuminate more than anything else. How so? It drives away filth, purifies the Mishkan, and thereby everything is illuminated, rectified, and united as one. Therefore, *ketores* should be recited before prayer each day, as a beloved korban that HaKadosh Baruch Hu desires.[324]

---

321. *Ben Ish Chai,* First Year, *Mikeitz* 8.
322. *Shemos* 30:7-8.
323. Ibid.
324. *Zohar* II, 219a.

פרשת כי תשא
Parashas Ki Sisa

The Covenant of the Torah

וַיֹּאמֶר ה׳ אֶל מֹשֶׁה כְּתָב לְךָ אֶת הַדְּבָרִים הָאֵלֶּה כִּי עַל פִּי הַדְּבָרִים הָאֵלֶּה כָּרַתִּי אִתְּךָ בְּרִית וְאֶת יִשְׂרָאֵל.

HASHEM said to Moshe, "Write these words for yourself, for according to these words have I sealed a covenant with you and Yisrael."[325]

OUR SAGES INTERPRET THE EXPRESSION עַל פִּי, WHICH literally means, "by the mouth," as an allusion to the *Torah She'beal Peh*, the Oral Tradition of Torah study. From here they learn that Hashem forged a covenant with Bnei Yisrael only in the merit of the *Torah She'be'al Peh*.[326] This covenant is nothing other than our intimate relationship with Hashem, as expressed by the presence of His *Shechinah*, Which once dwelled in the Beis HaMikdash, but now dwells in our shuls, yeshivos, and all places where Torah is studied. The Zohar states:

From the day the Beis HaMikdash was destroyed, and the offerings were discontinued, HaKadosh Baruch Hu has nothing but

---

325. *Shemos* 34:27.
326. *Gittin* 60b.

words of Torah, and the novel Torah concepts that are constantly developed.[327]

The Zohar serves as an interesting parallel to the Gemara, which states:

From the day the Beis HaMikdash was destroyed, Hashem has nothing except for the four cubits of halachah alone.[328]

The expression "halachah" used in the Gemara refers to the tradition of accepted rulings, handed down from one generation to the next. The Zohar adds that Hashem is equally fond of the novel Torah concepts that are developed in each generation. Both forms of Torah study cause Hashem's presence to be manifested.

The Midrash states:

There are purchases in which the seller sells himself along with the merchandise. HaKadosh Baruch Hu said to Bnei Yisrael, "I have sold you My Torah, and I have sold Myself along with it." ... This can be compared to the case of a king who had an only daughter. When another king married her and wished to take her back with him to his land, her father said, "My daughter is my only child. I cannot bear to part from her, but I cannot tell you not to take her, since she is your wife. So please do for me this kindness, that wherever you go, make for me a small chamber, that I may dwell with you, since I cannot part from my daughter."

So too, HaKadosh Baruch Hu said to Bnei Yisrael, "I have given you My Torah. I cannot part from it, nor can I prevent you from taking it. Rather, wherever you may go, make for Me a chamber, that I may dwell together with you, as the *pasuk* states, 'Make for Me a Mikdash, and I will dwell among you.'"[329, 330]

This Midrash provides the key for understanding how Hashem's Presence is felt among us. The *Shechinah* rests wherever Torah is studied. The instruction to build a Mishkan, and later a Beis HaMikdash, was an outcome of Hashem's unwillingness to part from the Torah that He granted us. For this reason, we learn in *Pirkei Avos*[331] that if even one person sits alone and studies Torah,

---

327. *Zohar, Parashas Balak.*
328. *Berachos* 8a.
329. *Shemos* 25:8.
330. *Shemos Rabbah* 33.
331. 3:6.

the *Shechinah* rests upon him, since the *Shechinah* and the Torah are inseparable. The Zohar states:

How beloved is the Torah to HaKadosh Baruch Hu. In any place where words of Torah are heard, HaKadosh Baruch Hu and all His hosts come to listen, and HaKadosh Baruch Hu comes to dwell there.[332]

With this we can well understand why the Ramban understood the Mishkan as a means of continuing the revelation of Sinai.

However, the parable of the king and his only daughter does not seem to fit the case of Hashem's granting the Torah to Bnei Yisrael. When a person sells a material possession, he must part from it, or accompany the buyer wherever he goes. However, when a person teaches wisdom to another, the teacher's wisdom is in no way diminished. Why then does Hashem have to accompany Bnei Yisrael, in order to remain with the Torah?

When Hashem granted us the Torah, he gave not only a specified body of wisdom, but mastery over the Torah, such that our Sages tell us that "the Torah is not in the Heavens," as we learn in the following Gemara:

(R' Eliezer and the Sages debated an issue regarding ritual impurity) … on that day, R' Eliezer presented all the arguments in the world, but the Sages refuted them all. Finally he said, "If the halachah is in accordance with me, the carob tree will prove it." The carob tree was then uprooted and moved one hundred cubits, or four hundred cubits according to some versions.

"No proof can be brought from a carob tree," the Sages objected.

"If the halachah is in accordance with me, the water canal will prove it," said R' Eliezer, and the water began to flow backward in the canal.

"No proof can be brought from a water canal," the Sages said.

"If the halachah is in accordance with me, the walls of the study house will prove it," said R' Eliezer, and the walls began to cave in, until R' Yehoshua scolded them, saying, "Torah scholars may have their debates, but it is no business of yours!" To honor R' Yehoshua's command, they stopped falling, but to honor R' Eliezer they did not return to their original upright position — and

---

332. *Zohar* III, 118a.

until this day [*when the Gemara was recorded*], they still stand at an angle.

"If the halachah is in accordance with me, the very Heavens will prove it," said R' Eliezer, and a voice emanated from the Heavens proclaiming, "Why do you argue with R' Eliezer? The halachah is always in accordance with him."

R' Yehoshua then stood on his feet and declared, "It is not in the Heavens!"[333] What does this mean? R' Yermiyah said that since the Torah was given on Har Sinai, we no longer heed Heavenly voices that contradict what was taught at Sinai, that halachah follows the majority opinion.

R' Nosson later met Eliyahu HaNavi, and asked him how HaKadosh Baruch Hu responded to this debate. Eliyahu told him that Hashem smiled and said, "My sons have defeated me."[334]

In every generation, new situations arise, and the Torah scholars in that generation have the responsibility to apply the Torah's timeless laws and principles according to their understanding, based on their vast knowledge. Thus, the Torah is in their hands.

Elsewhere, the Gemara states:

The Heavenly Academy debated the laws of *tzaraas*. If a white mark on the skin precedes a white hair, it is a definite sign of impure *tzaraas*. But if a white hair precedes a white mark on the skin, then according to HaKadosh Baruch Hu it is pure, but the entire Heavenly Academy argued that it is impure.

"Who shall decide for us this matter?" they asked. "Let Rabbah bar Nachmani decide it," they said, since he claimed to be the foremost authority on the tractates of *Negaim*[335] and *Oholos*.[336] An envoy was sent to summon him, but the Angel of Death could not take his soul, since his mouth never ceased speaking words of Torah. A wind then came and blew through the trees, making a strange sound. Rabbah thought it was a troop of mounted soldiers. "Let me die, and not be delivered into the hands of the government," he said. He expired, and ascended to Heaven, with the words "It is pure," on his lips. A Heavenly voice then proclaimed,

---

333. *Devarim* 30:12.
334. *Bava Metzia* 59b.
335. Which deals with the laws of *tzaraas*.
336. Which deals with how impurity is transferred under a roof.

"Fortunate are you, Rabbah bar Nachmani, that your body is pure, and your soul expired in purity."[337]

In this fascinating episode, we see that Hashem Himself debates points of halachah with the Heavenly Yeshivah, and required the services of Rabbah bar Nachmani, a mortal Torah scholar, to decide in His favor, that if a white hair precedes a white mark on the skin, it is not a sign of *tzaraas*. Although Rabbah bar Nachmani concurred with Hashem, the Rambam rules to the contrary, in accordance with the Heavenly Academy.[338] The *Kesef Mishnah* explains that since Rabbah bar Nachmani did not offer his opinion until the moment of his death, his opinion has no force in halachah, since "the Torah is not in Heaven."

Mortal man was given a startling degree of authority to apply the Torah. Furthermore, the entire world was created through the Torah, as the Zohar states, "[Hashem] gazed into the Torah and thereby created the world."[339] As such, the events of this physical world depend on how the halachah is determined, based on the rulings of Torah scholars in each generation. For example, Beis Din has authority to add an extra month to the year, to ensure that the cycle of lunar months correctly matches the solar seasons. Aspects of physical maturity that depend on a person's age will be adjusted accordingly, such that a person's body might retrogress a month at the moment of Beis Din's decision.[340]

The Torah itself, and the physical world that is shaped around it, are thus in the hands of the Torah scholars. Regarding this level of authority over the Torah, the Midrash applies the parable of the king who could not bear to part from his daughter. As it were, Hashem divested Himself of rulership over the Torah, and granted it to Bnei Yisrael.

Accordingly, we can understand the significance of the covenant forged between Hashem and Bnei Yisrael, in the merit of the *Torah She'be'al Peh*. It is a covenant of unity between Hashem and the holy Torah, in which Hashem can never forsake His beloved Torah, nor can He forsake those who are responsible for the Torah,

---

337. *Bava Metzia* 86a. See *Derashos HaRan,* 5.
338. *Hilchos Tzaraas* 2:9.
339. *Zohar* II, 161b.
340. *Talmud Yerushalmi, Nedarim;* cited in *Shach Y.D.* 189 s.k. 13.

the Torah scholars of each generation, who use their God-given powers of intellect to bring to light and determine novel rulings and applications of the Torah, which are binding in Heaven and on earth.

The Power of the Half Shekel

וְלֹא יִהְיֶה בָהֶם נֶגֶף בִּפְקֹד אֹתָם.

So there will not be a plague among them when counting them.

REISH LAKISH SAID: IT WAS CLEARLY KNOWN IN ADVANCE *before He Who spoke, and the world came into being [i.e. God] that Haman was destined to weigh out shekalim (i.e. silver coins) for the purpose of destroying the Jews. Therefore, He caused the Jews to precede their shekalim to [Haman's] shekalim. And thus we learned in a Mishnah: on the first of Adar, they [the Sanhedrin] proclaim regarding the payment of the shekalim.*[341]

The decree of Haman and Achashveirosh *"to destroy, to slay, and to exterminate all the Jews, from young to old, children and women"* was so harsh that God preempted it with the cure, and from the wound itself affixed the bandage to heal it; namely, shekalim for shekalim. We do not find such preemptive measures with any other decree.

This cure, the half shekel, had the power to turn a curse into a blessing, the Attribute of Judgment into the Attribute of Mercy. As we know, counting the Jewish people is a danger to them, but when they are counted using the half shekels blessing is ever present. Not only are they not harmed when they are counted, *"... so there will not be a plague among them when counting them,"*[342] but they are blessed through them. As the Zohar explains[343]

---

341. *Megillah* 13b.
342. *Shemos* 30:13.
343. *Ki Sisa*, Part II, 187b.

*Come and see. The blessing from Above does not dwell upon any-
thing counted. If so, how were Bnei Yisrael counted? An atonement for
their souls [i.e. the half shekel] was collected from each of them, and
these were not counted until they were all collected. First Bnei Yisrael
were blessed, then the coins were counted, and then Bnei Yisrael were
blessed again, so that Bnei Yisrael were blessed at the beginning and at
the end thereby preventing a plague among them.*

Thus we see that through the half shekels Bnei Yisrael are blessed
and the danger is not only preempted but entirely nullified.

Chassidic commentators have noted that the middle letter of the
word מַחֲצִית is the "צ" which stands for צְדָקָה, *charity*. The two adjacent
letters are "ח" and "י" which together spell חַי, *alive*. The outermost
letters are "מ" and "ת" which together spell מֵת, *dead*. This is to hint to
us that this mitzvah has the power to add life and keep death at bay.

We find this *segulah* in general with the mitzvah of *tzedakah*, as
we see in the Gemara[344]

*It was taught in a Baraisa: They related the following story about
Binyamin the righteous, who was appointed administrator over the
communal charity fund. Once, during years of famine, a woman came
before {Binyamin] and requested assistance. She said to him: "My master, sustain me!" [Binyamin] said to [the woman]: "I swear by the Holy
Temple that there is nothing in the charity fund for me to distribute
to you." [The woman] said to [Binyamin]: "My master, if you do not
sustain me, a woman and her seven sons will perish!" Moved by the
woman's plea, [Binyamin] rose and provided her with sustenance from
his own funds. After a time [Binyamin] took ill and was close to dying.
The ministering angels thereupon said to the Holy One, Blessed is He:
"Master of the Universe! You have said that one who preserves one
Jewish soul is regarded as if he preserved an entire world, and Binyamin
the righteous, who preserved a woman and her seven sons during a
famine, should die after these few years on earth?!" Immediately upon
hearing this argument [the Heavenly Court] tore up [Binyamin's]
decree, and in the merit of his charity he was spared. It was taught in a
Baraisa: [The Heavenly Court] added twenty-two years to his lifetime.[345]*

---

344. *Bava Basra* 11a.
345. It is known in the name of the Gaon of Vilna that twenty-two years
were added to his life because the Gemara (*Bava Basra* 9b) states that one

This mitzvah has a wondrous potency to stir the heavenly Attribute of Mercy and increase life, as the wisest of all men, Shlomo HaMelech, said, [346]וּצְדָקָה תַּצִּיל מִמָּוֶת — *"and charity rescues from death."* This is even more potent in the mitzvah of מַחֲצִית הַשֶּׁקֶל which also has the power to annul decrees against the Jewish people. The righteous who steps in and gives charity—he is the one who keeps death at bay and brings life.

———◆———

Chassidic commentators say that a *tzaddik* has the power to nullify harsh decrees and turn the Attribute of Judgment into Mercy through certain letter permutations. For example, in סֵפֶר[347] הַתּוֹלְדוֹת it states that נֶגַע, *affliction*, can be switched around to spell עֹנֶג, *pleasure*; צָרָה, *calamity*, to רְצָה, *appeasement*; צָרַעַת, *leprosy*, to עֲצֶרֶת, *a holy assembly*. Thus through the mitzvah of *tzedakah* the death sentence is distanced, the letters "מת" further away from the "צ", the צדקה, and life is added, the letters "חי" being adjacent to it.

There is a basis for this found in the words of the תּוֹסְפוֹת[348] who write that Bilam wanted to curse the Jews at the specific time of day when God's anger is present. Bilam said כַּלֵּם, *destroy them*, but God changed it from כַּלֵּם to מֶלֶךְ, *king*, as the verse states, וּתְרוּעַת מֶלֶךְ בּוֹ — *"and the friendship of the King is in him."*[349] We see that decrees and curses can morph into blessing through permutation of the letters.[350]

———

who gives alms to the poor is blessed six times, and one who comforts him with words is blessed elevenfold. Thus Binyamin the Righteous who acted this way with eight people merited eighty-eight blessings, and the Gemara states (*Sotah* 22b) that a good merit is sustainable for three months. If each of the eighty-eight blessings he received lasted three months, then eighty-eight multiplied by three equals 264 months, which is exactly twenty-two years.

346. *Mishlei* 10:2,11:4.

347. *Sefer HaToldos Parashas Noach.* See also *Degel Machane Ephraim* on *Parashas Emor.*

348. *Avodah Zarah* 4b.

349. *Bamidbar* 23:21.

350. For further insight see the *Zohar* III, 179a, regarding Kohanim having the ability to turn חֵרֶם, *excommunication* or *destruction*, into רַחֵם, *mercy.*

When we maintain the half shekel custom of our fathers, this too stirs the Heavenly Mercy and suppresses the Angel of Death, adding bounty, life and mercy to all of Am Yisrael. As we say in the פַּרְשַׁת שְׁקָלִים for יוֹצֵר,

אוֹר פָּנֶיךָ עָלֵינוּ אָדוֹן נְסָה, וְשֶׁקֶל אֶשָּׂא בְּבֵית נָכוֹן וְנִשָּׂא, וּבְצֶדֶק הֶגֶה עֶרֶךְ כִּי תִשָּׂא, גּוֹנְנֵנוּ בְּמָגֵן א-ל רָם וְנִשָּׂא — *"O Master, raise the light of Your face upon us, and let me raise a shekel in the firm and exalted Temple. In the merit of the Torah reading in Ki Sisa, protect us as with a shield, O exalted and uplifted God."*

The Covenant of the Oral Tradition

כְּתָב לְךָ אֶת הַדְּבָרִים הָאֵלֶּה כִּי עַל פִּי הַדְּבָרִים הָאֵלֶּה כָּרַתִּי אִתְּךָ בְּרִית וְאֶת יִשְׂרָאֵל.[351]

Write these words for yourself, for according to these words have I sealed a covenant with you and Israel.

THE HOLY ONE DID NOT ENTER INTO A COVENANT WITH the Jewish people but for the Oral Torah as it says: *"for according to these words have I sealed a covenant with you and Israel."* [352]

What exactly is this covenant, and why was it sealed specifically through the Oral Torah? The essence of this covenant is the resting of the *Shechinah*, the Divine Presence, among Bnei Yisrael. To understand what this covenant signifies we must examine first what the resting of the *Shechinah* means, and what is so significant about this Divine revelation.

The Zohar states,[353] *from the day that the Beis HaMikdash was destroyed and the sacrifices were annulled, all that remains for God are the words of the Torah and Chidushei Torah of the mouth.*

---

351. *Shemos* 34:27.
352. *Gittin* 6b.
353. Vol. III, 202a.

These words of the Zohar are astounding. From the Gemara[354] we learn that "since the day that the Temple was destroyed, the Holy One, Blessed is He, has nothing in His world but the four cubits of Halachah," teachings that have been passed down from generation to generation. Yet the Zohar illuminates for us that the novelty of the Torah, the innovation and newness found in it by those who learn it, is what sustains God's Divine presence in the world. They are the reason God finds pleasure in His world. This warrants further explanation. Let us begin by explaining the words of our Sages concerning the building of the Mikdash and its destruction, and through this we will be able to understand the necessary prerequisites to God's *Shechinah* dwelling among Bnei Yisrael. The Gemara states,[355] *Rav Yehudah said in the name of Rav: What is the meaning of that which is written:"Who is the wise man who will understand this, etc."? This matter [i.e. why the land was lost] was asked of the Sages and of the prophets, yet they could not explain it, until the Holy One, Blessed is He, Himself explained it, for it is written:"and Hashem said: Because of their forsaking My Torah etc." ... that they did not recite the blessing on the Torah first.*

The Ran quotes Rabbeinu Yonah[356] who explains how Rav knew that the land was destroyed due to their lack of reciting the blessing on the Torah first

If the reason [the land was destroyed] was because they weren't learning at all (as is implied from the pasuk), why weren't the Sages and prophets able to explain this? It's a simple, known reason. Rather, certainly they were busy with Torah study—and therefore the Sages and prophets were stumped as to why the land was destroyed. Only God Himself was able to explain this, for he knows the depths of people's souls and he knew that they were not making the blessings on Torah study, meaning that it was not so important in their eyes to warrant a blessing on its study, because they were not studying it for the sake of heaven.

But the question still stands: Is it possible that the Sages of Am Yisrael and the prophets, who were experts in all the internal

---

354. *Berachos* 8a.
355. *Nedarim* 81a.
356. *Megillas Sesarim* by Rabbeinu Yonah.

workings of the Jewish nation's soul and its secrets did not realize that Bnei Yisrael no longer valued the Torah and no longer studied it for the sake of heaven? The question is magnified by the Bach's version of the Gemara which adds that the question was posed to the ministering angels as well. How could it be that angels who know all the thoughts in people's hearts[357] did not notice that Bnei Yisrael weren't occupied with Torah for its own sake? Leaving these questions aside, it's even more difficult to explain why the Beis HaMikdash was destroyed because of their lack of Torah study for its own sake, when our Sages clearly teach us[358] that Torah study even not for its own sake is still a great mitzvah and a person should learn even though it is not for its own sake, for through learning it not for its own sake, he will eventually come to learn it for its own sake. Furthermore, during the time of the destruction, Bnei Yisrael were guilty of far greater sins—adultery, idol worship, and murder, and the Gemara elsewhere[359] states that it is because of these three sins that the Beis HaMikdash was destroyed. So how can we reconcile these discrepancies?

Perhaps we can reconcile this discrepancy with the words of the Medrash relating the mitzvah of building a Temple. Clearly the reason for its destruction is rooted in the rationale behind its being built — i.e. when the reason for which it was built is no longer present, it is inevitable that it will be destroyed. The Medrash states,[360] *Is there such a thing as merchandise whose seller is sold with it? Said Hashem [to the Jewish people]: I have sold you My Torah, and I have been sold with it, as it states, "let them take for Me a portion." This is likened to a king who had an only daughter. One of the kings came, took the daughter, and wanted to go back to his own land to marry her. Said the king to him: "My daughter is an only child. To part with her—that I cannot bear. To tell you not to go—that I cannot do, for she is your wife. So do this one favor for me: every place you go, make a small chamber for me so I can live with you, for I cannot leave my daughter." So said the Holy One, Blessed is He, to Bnei Yisrael: I gave*

---

357. See *Tosafos* on *Shabbos* 12a. For further insight see the *Noam Elimelech* on *Parashas Behaaloscha*.
358. *Pesachim* 50b.
359. *Yoma* 9b.
360. *Midrash Tanchuma, Terumah* 3.

you the Torah. I cannot bear to part with it and I cannot tell you not to take it. Rather, in every place you go, make one house for me so that I may dwell in it, as the pasuk states: "and they shall make for Me a sanctuary."

The Medrash opens the door for us to understand the concept of Divine Presence among Bnei Yisrael. God said "to part with her [the Torah] — that I cannot bear." Any place where His Torah is studied, there He dwells. This is the reason He commanded them *and they shall make for Me a sanctuary — because God cannot bear to part with the Torah He gave them.* This is the meaning of the continuation of the *pasuk so that I may dwell among them.*

This also sheds light on the words of R' Chalafta ben Dosa of Kfar Chanania:[361] *How do we know this even of one (who sits and engages in Torah study — that the Divine Presence rests with him)? For it is said:"In every place where I cause My Name to be mentioned, I will come to you and bless you."*

Every place where Torah is studied as it should be, even by one person, God says, " to part with her — that I cannot bear."

Come and see what the Zohar states,[362] *How beloved is the Torah before God, for in every place where the Torah is heard the Holy One, Blessed is He, and all His entourage listen to every word, and the Holy One, Blessed is He, comes to dwell with him, as it says;"In every place etc."*[363]

But at first glance this parable to a king and his daughter does not apply to what it is meant to represent. When a person marries off a daughter, it is understood that she leaves her father's household to go to her husband's. No person can be in two places at once. So too with any gift that is given by one person to another, it is transferred from the giver's domain to the recipient's. So we can understand what the king said: "My daughter is an only child, to part with her — that I cannot bear."But someone who confers wisdom on another, his own knowledge is in no way diminished. The teacher does not have to part with that which he is teaching;

---

361. *Pirkei Avos* 3:7.
362. *Zohar* III, 118a.
363. See also the Ramban in his commentary at the beginning of *Parashas Terumah*, where he discusses that the dwelling of the *Shechinah* in the Mikdash is a continuation of God's presence at Har Sinai at *Matan Torah*.

they can both retain and gain from that knowledge. Why, then, did God tell Bnei Yisrael: "I cannot bear to part with it [the Torah]," and command them to make a dwelling place for Him?

In truth, when God gave the Torah to Am Yisrael, it wasn't merely knowledge and wisdom which he imparted to them; rather he gave them the power to "control" the Torah, and to use the Torah to dominate the whole creation. From the moment the Torah was given, one does not even rely on a *Bas Kol,* a Heavenly echo, to decide in halachah because לֹא בַּשָּׁמַיִם הִיא שֶׁכְּבָר נִתְּנָה תּוֹרָה מֵהַר סִינַי — *"it [the Torah] is not in heaven, for the Torah was already given [to man] at Har Sinai."* The Gemara[364] relates how R' Eliezer and his colleagues had a disagreement concerning the ritual status of a specific type of oven. R' Eliezer's opinion was rejected even though he shook the foundations of the world: a tree uprooted itself, the water canal flowed backward, the walls of the Beis Medrash leaned and were about to fall, and even a *Bas Kol* proclaimed he was right, saying, "What argument do you have with R' Eliezer whom the halachah follows in all places!" Nevertheless, these things were inadmissible as evidence of R' Eliezer's being right; his opinion was not accepted. When R' Yehoshua stood up and stated לֹא בַּשָּׁמַיִם הִיא — *"[Torah] is not in Heaven,"* he set a halachic principle applicable not only in that case but for all future times, namely, that God gave the Torah to Am Yisrael and gave its scholars the authority to determine halachah.

Furthermore, we find in the Gemara,[365] *At that moment, they were disputing the following Mishnah in the Heavenly Academy: If the bahares (i.e.a snow-white spot, one of the skin discolorations symptomatic of tzaraas) preceded the white hair, [the baheres] is tamei. But if the white hair preceded the baheres, it is tahor. If there exists a doubt as to which came first, the Holy One, Blessed is He, says the leprous mark is tahor, and the entire Heavenly Academy say it is tamei. As a result of this dispute they said, "Who will decide this issue? Rabbah bar Nachmani will decide." They chose him to decide the issue, for Rabbah bar Nachmani had once said, "I am unique in my knowledge of Negaim; I am unique in my knowledge of Oholos."*

---

364. *Bava Metzia* 59b.
365. Ibid. 86a.

They sent an agent after him to fetch him. However, the Angel of Death could not approach him since his mouth did not cease from its recitation of Torah. At that point a wind blew, and made loud noises among the reeds. [Rabbah bar Nachmani] thought it was a brigade of horsemen who were coming to arrest him. He said, "May the soul of that person (myself) pass on so that he will not be given into the hands of the government." As he was dying, he said, "Tahor, tahor." A Heavenly echo issued forth and said, "Fortunate are you, Rabbah bar Nachmani, for your body is tahor and your soul departed with the utterance of the word tahor!"[366]

God and the Heavenly Academy argued as to whether a doubt in *tumas negaim* is *tamei* or *tahor*. Rabbah bar Nachmani, who had the credentials to decide this matter, ruled *tahor* in accordance with Hashem. Despite this, the Rambam[367] rules *tamei*. The Kesef Mishnah explains the Rambam's reason:

Since he [Rabbah bar Nachmani] said this at the time of the departing of his soul, this is included in the ruling that "[Torah] is not in heaven," and should therefore not be relied upon against the common ruling that we rule like Tanna Kamma (who ruled tamei).

See how far reaching is the power of the Torah, that God in His mercy vested in Am Yisrael the ability to overpower, so to speak, God's own opinion.

Not only did God give Am Yisrael the authority over the Torah, He also gave them the power to manipulate nature via the Torah. As is brought in the Yerushalmi[368]

The hymen of a three-year-old girl who cohabited does not regenerate. But if the Beis Din vote to make the year a leap year (thereby causing her third birthday to have not yet arrived), it will regenerate. This is what the pasuk[369] "to the God Who fulfills for me" is referring to.

God gave His world over to those who learn Torah and toil in it in purity, to build and to destroy, to uproot and to plant.

This is a wondrous power that Bnei Yisrael have: to use their God-given brain to augment and expound on the Torah. Bnei

---

366. See *Derashos HaRan, Derush* 5, on this point.
367. *Hilchos Tumas Metzora* 2:9.
368. *Perek HaNodeir Min HaMevushal*. Also brought in *Shach, Yoreh De'ah* 189:13.
369. *Tehillim* 57:3.

Yisrael control halachah through their knowledge. This is why God said to them: "I gave you the Torah, but I cannot bear to part with it…in every place you go, make one house for me so that I may dwell in it." This is what God bequeathed to the Jews: this ability to handle the Torah, interpret it, and enhance it. Perhaps now we can explain the words of our Sages:[370] *God did not enter into a covenant with the Jewish people but for the Oral Torah, as the pasuk states, "… for according to these words have I sealed a covenant with you and Israel."* What is unique about the Oral Torah more than the Scripture? Why is the covenant premised on the Oral Torah specifically? Based on what we have learned above, it is clear. The covenant with the Jewish people and God resting His *Shechinah* among the Jews is dependent on the Oral Torah, because it is within the realm of Oral Torah that Bnei Yisrael hold sway over the Torah, and have the ability to delve deeper into it and develop their part in it, which is why God said: "to part with it — that I cannot bear."

כְּתָב לְךָ אֶת הַדְּבָרִים הָאֵלֶּה כִּי עַל פִּי הַדְּבָרִים הָאֵלֶּה כָּרַתִּי אִתְּךָ
בְּרִית וְאֶת יִשְׂרָאֵל.[371]

"Write these words for yourself, for according to these words have I sealed a covenant with you and Israel."

Why was Moshe commanded to write these words down—specifically after the sin of the Golden Calf—in the second לֻחוֹת, the *Tablets*, rather than in the first?

The Ramban explains that Moshe was commanded to write these words as a *new* covenant that God made with the Jewish people. With God's forgiveness for the sin of the Golden Calf came a new covenant, as the Ramban writes:[372] *God, Blessed be He, had to make with them a covenant on the forgiveness that He extended to them [for their sin with the Golden Calf] and so [Moshe] wrote the forgiveness, and the conditions [on the new covenant].*

---

370. *Gittin* 60b.
371. *Shemos* 34:27.
372. Ibid.

We see from these words that God stipulated new conditions with his forgiving Bnei Yisrael for this sin, and in forgiving them He renewed His covenant with them.

The main principle of this covenant is the clear knowledge that the Oral Torah was also given to Moshe at Har Sinai, and no one has the right to take the Torah and do with it as he or she pleases. Those who made the Golden Calf were not idol worshipers, rather they merely intended to make a calf, an icon, similar to the Cheruvim above the Ark. When Bnei Yisrael fulfilled God's will the Cheruvim faced each other, and when they did not fulfill God's will the Cheruvim faced away from each other.[373] So what was so wrong with what they did? Says the Beis HaLevi, "The Cheruvim would also have been considered idol worship had they not been commanded to make them."

God wanted us to learn this lesson forever, that we can only rely on the words of our Sages and do as they command us, and the Oral Torah bears as much credence as the Written Torah. And just as the Written Torah cannot be studied by heart, so too the Oral Torah (literally "Torah of the heart") cannot be written. Thus, God did not enter into a covenant with the Jewish people but for the Oral Torah as the *pasuk* says, *"… for according to these words have I sealed a covenant with you and Israel."*

---

373. *Bava Basra* 99a.

פרשת ויקהל
Parashas Vayakhel

The Cheruvim

וַיַּעַשׂ שְׁנֵי כְרֻבִים זָהָב מִקְשָׁה עָשָׂה אֹתָם מִשְּׁנֵי קְצוֹת הַכַּפֹּרֶת. כְּרוּב אֶחָד מִקָּצָה מִזֶּה וּכְרוּב אֶחָד מִקָּצָה מִזֶּה מִן הַכַּפֹּרֶת עָשָׂה אֶת הַכְּרֻבִים מִשְּׁנֵי קְצוֹתָיו. וַיִּהְיוּ הַכְּרֻבִים פֹּרְשֵׂי כְנָפַיִם לְמַעְלָה סֹכְכִים בְּכַנְפֵיהֶם עַל הַכַּפֹּרֶת וּפְנֵיהֶם אִישׁ אֶל אָחִיו אֶל הַכַּפֹּרֶת הָיוּ פְּנֵי הַכְּרֻבִים.

"He made two Cheruvim of gold — hammered out did he make them — from the two ends of the Cover: one Cheruv from the end at one side and one Cheruv from the end at the other; from the Cover did he make the Cheruvim, from its two ends. The Cheruvim were with wings spread upward, sheltering the Cover with their wings, with the faces toward each other; toward the Cover were the faces of the Cheruvim."[374]

THE KLI YAKAR EXPLAINS THE SIGNIFICANCE OF THE Cheruvim as follows:

The Cheruvim over the Aron resembled the angels of the same name, whose faces are like those of children. They

---

374. *Shemos* 37:7-9.

represent the Torah scholar. To be worthy of teaching Torah, he must be angelic[375] and free from sin like a newborn baby.

The Torah scholar must be pure in all his relationships, both with Hashem and with his fellow man. To represent our obligations toward Hashem, the Cheruvim stretched their wings upward. To represent our obligations toward our fellow man, the Cheruvim faced each other, displaying the love that binds the Torah's adherents together in peace and brotherhood. They faced toward the lid of the Aron, to show that their entire motivation was solely for the sake of the Torah (unlike those who enjoy teaching to display their own erudition, for their own honor, and not for the honor of the Torah)....

"And I will meet you there."[376] HaKadosh Baruch Hu has no dwelling place in the world, other than the four cubits of halachah[377] — where Torah is studied amid peace and brotherhood, and the students have no interest in defeating one another in debate. From there (between the Cheruvim) Hashem's voice would resonate throughout the Mishkan.[378] The Aron was the most exalted of all the sacred vessels. Through it, Divine bounty would flow to them all. Our Sages tell us that the Aron would carry those who carried it, as a lesson to those who provide for Torah scholars. It seems as if they support the Torah scholars, while in fact the Torah scholars are supporting them.[379]

The location of the Cheruvim in the Mishkan highlights their great significance. They stood atop the Aron Kodesh, in the *Kodesh Kodashim*, the holiest place in the world, where even angels are forbidden to enter, and only the Kohen Gadol may enter on the holiest day of the year.[380]

They resembled the angels of Heaven, with faces of newborn babies.[381] This is to teach us that in our quest for Torah, we must be pure of sin like newborn babies, and realize that our destiny, the

---

375. *Chagigah* 15b.
376. *Shemos* 25:22.
377. *Berachos* 8a.
378. See *Rashi, Bamidbar* 7:89.
379. *Kli Yakar, Shemos* 25:17,22.
380. See Talmud *Yerushalmi, Yoma* 7b; *Succah* 21b.
381. *Succah* 5b, *Bava Basra* 99a.

spiritual height to which we aspire, is greater than that of the angels themselves. After Adam was exiled from Gan Eden, Cheruvim were positioned as sentries to guard the path to the Tree of Life. So too, golden Cheruvim were positioned above the Aron Kodesh, to guard the Torah, the veritable Tree of Life. By internalizing the message they teach us, we prove ourselves worthy of the greatest gift, and are allowed entrance into the chambers of Torah wisdom.

What was the message of the Cheruvim? First, they raised their wings to Heaven, teaching us to subjugate our hearts to Hashem, in sincere recognition that our fate is in entirely in His hands, as the Gemara states:

"And it was, when Moshe raised his hands, Israel was victorious."[382] Was it Moshe's hands that brought success or failure? Rather, this teaches us that as long as Bnei Yisrael lifted their eyes upward, and subjugated their hearts to their Father in Heaven, they were victorious. But if they failed to do so, they were defeated. Similarly, another *pasuk* states, "And you shall make a snake and place it on a flagpole. Anyone who was bitten shall see it and live."[383] Did the snake really kill or grant life? Rather, when Bnei Yisrael would raise their eyes upward and subjugate their hearts to their Father in Heaven, they were healed. But if they failed to do so, they would die from their bite wound.[384]

Secondly, the Cheruvim faced each other, stressing the crucial prerequisite of being kind and considerate toward our peers. If we are not scrupulously observant of the mitzvos *bein adam l'chaveiro* (between man and his fellow), we cannot possibly hope to draw close to Hashem through the mitzvos *bein adam la'Makom* (between man and his Maker).

The Ramban[385] writes of the Ten Commandments, that the first five represent the mitzvos *bein adam la'Makom*, such as believing in Hashem, and not worshiping idols; while the second five represent the mitzvos *bein adam la'chaveiro*, such as not stealing and not lying in court. Rashi[386] notes that the Hebrew word for Tablets, *Luchos*, is

---

382. *Shemos* 17:11.
383. *Bamidbar* 21:8.
384. *Rosh Hashanah* 29a.
385. *Shemos* 20:12-14.
386. *Devarim* 9:10.

written in such a way that it could be read *Luchas*, in the singular form (לוּחַת). This teaches us that although they were divided in two, they should be viewed as one single, inseparable unit. If a person strives to perfect himself in one area, while ignoring the other, his achievements will not be met with Divine favor.

Rav Yisrael Salanter writes that when Moshe Rabbeinu saw the Golden Calf, he wanted to destroy the first Tablet, on which the mitzvos *bein adam la'Makom* were carved. Although Bnei Yisrael had worshiped idols, and proved themselves unworthy of these mitzvos, he thought that they could still receive the second Tablet, of mitzvos *bein adam la'chaveiro*. Hashem then told him that this was impossible, since the entire Torah, the mitzvos *bein adam la'chaveiro* and *bein adam la'Makom* together, form one single unit, which cannot be divided.

The position of the Cheruvim symbolized these two crucial prerequisites to Torah greatness. They raised their wings to Heaven, symbolizing our need to strengthen ourselves in mitzvos *bein adam la'Makom*, and faced each other in love and unity, symbolizing our need to strengthen ourselves in mitzvos *bein adam la'chaveiro*.

Perhaps the same symbolism can be found in Birkas Kohanim. When blessing the congregation, the Kohanim raise their hands, reminding us to raise our eyes to Heaven, to subjugate our hearts to Hashem; and they face us with love and compassion, reminding us to strengthen the bonds of brotherhood that unite us.

פרשת פקודי
Parashas Pekudei

The Mishkan Mirrors Creation

אֵלֶּה פְקוּדֵי הַמִּשְׁכָּן מִשְׁכַּן הָעֵדֻת אֲשֶׁר פֻּקַּד עַל פִּי מֹשֶׁה עֲבֹדַת
הַלְוִיִּם בְּיַד אִיתָמָר בֶּן אַהֲרֹן הַכֹּהֵן. וּבְצַלְאֵל בֶּן אוּרִי בֶן חוּר לְמַטֵּה
יְהוּדָה עָשָׂה אֵת כָּל אֲשֶׁר צִוָּה ה' אֶת מֹשֶׁה. וְאִתּוֹ אָהֳלִיאָב בֶּן
אֲחִיסָמָךְ לְמַטֵּה דָן חָרָשׁ וְחֹשֵׁב וְרֹקֵם בַּתְּכֵלֶת וּבָאַרְגָּמָן וּבְתוֹלַעַת
הַשָּׁנִי וּבַשֵּׁשׁ.[387]

*These are the reckonings of the Tabernacle, the Tabernacle
of Testimony, which were reckoned at Moshe's bidding. The
labor of the Leviim was under the authority of Issamar, son of
Aharon the Kohen. Betzalel, son of Uri son of Chur, of the tribe
of Yehudah, did everything that Hashem commanded Moshe.
With him was Oholiav, son of Achisamach, of the tribe of
Dan, a carver, weaver, and embroiderer, with turquoise,
purple, and scarlet wool, and with linen.*

SAYS THE MIDRASH:[388] *"THESE ARE THE RECKONINGS OF
the Tabernacle…"* Said R' Yaakov son of R' Assi: why does the
verse state: *"Hashem, I love the House where You dwell, and*

---

387. *Shemos* 38:21-23.
388. *Tanchuma Pekudei* 2.

the place where Your glory resides"[389]? *Because it [the House] is equal to the creation of the world. How so? [Regarding] the first day [of creation] it says: "In the beginning of God's creating the heavens and the earth,"*[390] *and it states: "stretching out the heavens like a* **curtain***,"*[391] *and [regarding] the Mishkan it says: "you shall make* **curtains** *of goat hair."*[392] *[Regarding] the second day [of creation] it says: "let there be a firmament"*[393] *for the purpose of* **separating** *between the waters beneath the firmament and the waters above the firmament, and in the Mishkan it says: "the Partition shall* **separate** *for you between the Holy and Holy of Holies."*[394] *[Regarding the third day [of creation] it mentions* **water***, as it says: "let the* **waters***…be gathered"*[395] *and in the Mishkan it says: "You shall make a copper laver and its base of copper … and put* **water** *there."*[396] *On the fourth day [of creation He] created* **luminaries** *as it says: "let there be* **luminaries** *in the firmament of the heavens,"*[397] *and in the Mishkan it says: "You shall make a* **Menorah** *of pure gold."*[398] *On the fifth day [of creation He] created the fowl as it says: "let the waters teem with teeming living creatures, and* **fowl** *that fly"*[399] *and in the Mishkan offerings were brought from sheep and* **fowl** *[and in the Mishkan it says:] "the Cheruvim shall be with* **wings** *spread upward"*[400] *On the sixth day [of creation]* **man** *was created as it says: "So God created* **Man** *in his image"*[401] *in the glory of his Creator, and in the Mishkan it says:* **"men"** *referring to the High Priest who was anointed to work and serve in front of God. On the seventh day [of creation it says:] "Thus the heaven and the earth were* **finished***," and in the Mishkan it says: "All the work*

---

389. *Tehillim* 26:8.
390. *Bereishis* 1:1.
391. *Tehillim*104:2.
392. *Shemos* 26:7.
393. *Bereishis* 1:6.
394. *Shemos* 26:33.
395. *Bereishis* 1:9.
396. *Shemos* 30:18.
397. *Bereishis* 1:14.
398. *Shemos* 25:31.
399. *Bereishis* 1:20.
400. *Shemos* 25:20.
401. *Bereishis* 1:27.

*[of the Tabernacle] was **completed**."*[402] *In the creation of the world it says: "God **blessed**," and in the Mishkan it says: "And Moshe **blessed** them." In the creation of the world it says: "God **completed**," and in the Mishkan it says: "it was on the day that Moshe **finished**." In the creation of the world it says: "and He **sanctified** it." And in the Mishkan it says "and he anointed it and **sanctified** it."*[403] *Why is the Mishkan equal to [the creation of] heaven and earth? To teach us that just as heaven and earth are witnessed for Bnei Yisrael as it says: "I call heaven and earth today to bear witness against you,"*[404] *so too the Mishkan bears testimony for Bnei Yisrael as it says: "These are the reckonings of the Tabernacle, the Tabernacle of Testimony."*[405] *Therefore is says "O Hashem, I love the House where You dwell, and the place where Your Glory resides."*[406]

From the words of this Midrash we see that the details of the Mishkan correspond to the details of the creation of the world. The Mishkan is the world in miniature, a microcosmic representation of the world. Thus, we can infer that just like the world is eternal so too is the Mishkan. Indeed, the Mishkan that Bnei Yisrael made in the Wilderness was made for temporary use and yet it is eternal; no strangers ever took control of it and it never fell into the hands of our enemies. The Mishkan and its vessels are a testimony to Bnei Yisrael now, as it was back then.

The Seforno writes:[407] ***The Tabernacle of Testimony***: *Our pasuk tells us the virtues of this Mishkan because of which it was worthy of being eternal and never falling into the hands of their enemies. First,* מִשְׁכַּן הָעֵדוּת, *it is the "Tabernacle of Testimony"; the Two Tablets of Testimony are housed in it. Second,* אֲשֶׁר פֻּקַּד עַל פִּי מֹשֶׁה — *"which were reckoned at Moshe's bidding." Third,* בְּיַד אִיתָמָר— *"the labor of Leviim was under the authority of Issamar," for all the shifts of the Mishkan were under the auspices of Issamar. Fourth,* וּבְצַלְאֵל בֶּן אוּרִי בֶן חוּר לְמַטֵּה יְהוּדָה עָשָׂה — *"Betzalel son of Uri son of Chur of the tribe of Yehudah did [it]." The heads of the artisans in charge of making*

---

402. *Shemos* 39:32.
403. *Bamidbar* 7:1.
404. *Devarim* 30:19.
405. *Shemos* 38:21.
406. *Tehillim* 26:8.
407. *Shemos* 38:21.

the Mishkan and its vessels were the distinguished and the righteous of the generation, and so the Divine Presence dwelled in that which their hands created, preventing it from falling into the hands of the enemies. But the Temple that Shlomo built, where the workers who built it were from Tyre, was different. Even though the Divine Presence dwelled in it, parts of it were damaged and it was necessary to repair the deterioration of the Temple; and in the end everything fell into the hands of their enemies. The second Temple, where none of the above virtues were present, fared worse: the Divine Presence wasn't even there and it fell into the hands of their enemies. It was not a Tabernacle of Testimony because the Tablets were not housed in it. It['s bulding] was commended by Koresh and the Leviim weren't there, as Ezra himself says: [408] וָאָבִינָה בָעָם וּבַכֹּהֲנִים וּמִבְּנֵי לֵוִי לֹא מָצָאתִי שָׁם — "I then scrutinized the people and the Kohanim, but I could find no Leviim there." Those who built it were from Sidon and Tyre, as is mentioned in the Book of Ezra.

The Mishkan that Moshe made was constructed by the chosen of the generation and therefore no foreign legion ever took hold of it, for foreigners were not able to lay a hand on that which was consecrated. But the Mishkan that Shlomo built had craftsmen who had been sent by Hiram king of Tyre. Even though the construction of the Mishkan was done in holiness, these gentile craftsmen had no way of knowing the secret of God's resting His Presence in His House of Cedars. Thus the number of days during which God would dwell in the House were limited, and once those days were up, the foundations of the House — as though the foundations themselves decided to do so—became unstable. God's Divine Presence is dependent on the *heart*, on our love for Him, our pining for Him, by truthfully asking Him to dwell among us.

Says Rashi:[409] וַיְבָרֶךְ אֹתָם מֹשֶׁה — "and Moshe blessed them. He said to them, "May it be God's will that the Shechinah rest in the works of your hands. May the pleasantness of my Lord, our God, be upon us, and [make] the work of our hands, etc." This is one of the eleven consecutive songs that begins "A prayer by Moshe" and continues until the psalm that begins, "A song of David: Kindness and justice…"

---

408. *Ezra* 8:15.
409. *Shemos* 39:43.

The Midrash states, [410] *In the future all the nations of the world will gather all the silver and gold in the world and build a House for God. And God will mock them and will not desire any house but the House that Bnei Yisrael built for him, as the pasuk states:* אִם יִתֶּן אִישׁ [411]אֶת כָּל הוֹן בֵּיתוֹ בָּאַהֲבָה בּוֹז יָבוּזוּ לוֹ — *"were any man to offer all the treasure of his home to entice you away from your love they would scorn him to extreme."*

This Midrash warrants explanation: Why would God not want the house offered by the nations of the world—after all it will be more glorious than its predecessors?

We find the answer in the words written by Ramban:[412] *The esoteric significance of the Mishkan is that the Glory that rested upon Mount Sinai at the time of the giving of the Torah should rest upon [the Tabernacle], but unlike at Sinai, in a concealed manner. And note that just as it is written there, regarding Mount Sinai, "the **glory** of Hashem upon Mount Sinai"[413] and it is further written "Behold, Hashem our God has shown us His glory and His greatness,"[414] so too here regarding the Tabernacle, it is written, "and the **glory** of Hashem filled the Tabernacle."[415] Furthermore, regarding the Tabernacle it says twice, "and the **glory** of Hashem filled the Tabernacle," parallel to the two expressions "His **glory** and His **greatness**"[416] mentioned at Mount Sinai. Thus the glory that originally appeared to [the people] at Mount Sinai remained constantly with Bnei Yisrael in the Tabernacle and whenever Moshe entered [the Tabernacle], he would receive the same level of Divine communication that was spoken to him at Mount Sinai. And just as [Scripture] said regarding the Giving of the Torah: "from heaven He caused you to hear His voice in order to teach you, and on earth He showed you His great fire,"[417] so too regarding the Tabernacle it is written, "he heard the voice speaking to him from atop the Cover ... from between the two Cheruvim; and He spoke to*

---

410. *Tanna D'Vei Eliyahu* 28.
411. *Shir HaShirim* 8:7.
412. *Shemos* 25:1.
413. Ibid. 24:16.
414. *Devarim* 5:21.
415. *Shemos* 40:34.
416. *Devarim* 5:21.
417. Ibid 4:36.

him."[418] *The words "and He spoke to him" are repeated at the end of that verse in order to convey what [the Sages*[419]*] said through a tradition, that the Voice would come from heaven to above the Ark- cover and speak to [Moshe] from there. For every communication with Moshe originated in heaven during the day and was heard by Moshe as though it was emanating from between the two Cheruvim. This too was in a manner similar to the Giving of the Torah, of which it is written, "and you heard His words from the midst of the fire."*[420] *This is why [the Cheruvim] were both made of gold. Scripture likewise states, "at the entrance of the Tent of Meeting, before Hashem; where I shall set My meeting with you to speak to you there..., and it shall be sanctified with My glory."*[421] *For that was to be the meeting place for communication and it would "be sanctified by My glory." One who examines carefully the verses written at the Giving of the Torah, and understands what I wrote above, will understand the esoteric significance of the Mishkan and the Beis HaMikdash.*

Hence, not everyone wishing to partake in the construction of the Mishkan could do so. The masses could not join in the making of the Mishkan lest they damage it. Only Moshe and Betzalel were able to do so. As the Baal HaTurim writes,[422] **Betzalel made the Ark:** *In [the making of] all [the vessels] it does not mention Betzalel's name except for [the making of] the Ark, to teach that Betzalel knew the secret of the Ark and the Merkavah,*[423] *for the Ark parallels God's Throne.*

On the other hand, we find that the Ramban writes:[424] *And so [the Sages] said in Midrash Rabbah: "Why with regard to all the other vessels of the Tabernacle is it written 'you [singular] shall make' while regarding the Ark it is written 'they shall make an Ark'? Rabbi Yehudah Bar Shallum said: The Holy One, Blessed is He, said, 'Let everyone come and be involved in the making of the Ark, so that they*

---

418. *Bamidbar* 7:89.
419. *Devarim Rabbah* 14:22.
420. *Devarim* 4:36.
421. *Shemos* 29:42-43.
422. Ibid. 37:1.
423. God's Chariot.
424. *Shemos* 25:10.

may merit having a connection to the Torah.' " [425] *The connection that the Midrash mentions regarding the Ark is either that each person should donate one gold article for use in making the Ark, or that he render some small assistance to Betzalel, or that they participate mentally and direct their thoughts to the matter.*

The Ark of Testimony is more exalted than the other vessels of the Mishkan—*"Let everyone come and be involved in the making of the Ark."* But how do they become involved? *"That each person should donate one gold article for use in making the Ark, or that he render some small assistance to Betzalel, or that they participate mentally and direct their thoughts to the matter."*

Betzalel opened the doorway to holiness, to the secrets of the *Merkavah*[426] and when they made the Ark they tapped into Betzalel's thoughts and intentions. Hence, וְעָשׂוּ אָרוֹן— *"they shall make an Ark,"* is in plural. This is to teach us that the primary aspect of the construction of the Mishkan and its vessels were its hidden intentions and a purity of heart, and only through this will the *Shechinah* dwell in the Mishkan. This is what David HaMelech referred to when he wished to build the Beis HaMikdash. וְיָדַעְתִּי אֱלֹקַי כִּי אַתָּה בֹּחֵן לֵבָב וּמֵישָׁרִים תִּרְצֶה אֲנִי בְּיֹשֶׁר לְבָבִי הִתְנַדַּבְתִּי כָל אֵלֶּה וְעַתָּה עַמְּךָ הַנִּמְצְאוּ פֹה רָאִיתִי בְשִׂמְחָה לְהִתְנַדֶּב לָךְ[427] — *"I know, my God, that You examine the heart and desire in integrity. I have offered all these donations in the uprightness of my heart, and now I see Your people, who are present here, to offer donations to You with gladness."*

Building the Mikdash is comparable to creating a microcosmic world. This is what our Sages refer to when they say, regarding Betzalel's wisdom,[428] *Said Rav Yehudah in the name of Rav: Betzalel knew how to join the letters with which heaven and earth were created. For it is written here, regarding Betzalel, "He filled him with Godly spirit, with wisdom, with understanding and with knowledge"*[429] *and it is written there, regarding the Creation: "Hashem founded the earth with wisdom; He established the heavens with understanding,"*[430] *and*

---

425. *Shemos Rabbah* 34:2.
426. God's Chariot.
427. *Divrei HaYamim* 29:17.
428. *Berachos* 55a.
429. *Shemos* 31:3.
430. *Mishlei* 3:19.

it is written in the next verse: "Through His knowledge the depths were cleaved."

To direct one's thoughts means to join letters as God did when He created the world to be ready for Him to reveal himself. Building the House is hidden and sublime, dependent on the feelings in the heart, the purity of mind, the secret of Godly thought. Thus the Zohar states,[431] *The lower world [this world] was not complete in its existence till Avraham came and the world existed [because of him], but [it] was not complete . . . Yitzchak came and held the world in his left hand and the world was sustained further. When Yaakov came he held the middle [of the world] and it was established* וְאִתְכָּלִיל *on both sides. The world now existed and would not collapse. Despite all this, the world was not complete until Bnei Yisrael accepted the Torah at Har Sinai and the Mishkan was erected. Only then did the worlds [upper and lower] exist and become complete.*

With the creation of the Mishkan, Creation was completed. God established a world in which the *Shechinah* can dwell. The Godly desire was fulfilled the day that Moshe erected the Mishkan.

We can now understand the words of our Sages:[432] *R' Shmuel bar Nachmani said in the name of R' Yonasan: Betzalel [which can be read B'tzel El, namely, "in the shadow of God"] was so named on account of his wisdom, which was demonstrated in the following incident: When the Holy One, Blessed is He, said to Moshe, "Go and tell Betzalel to make me a Tabernacle, Ark, and vessels," Moshe went and reversed the order and said to Betzalel, "Make an Ark, vessels, and a Tabernacle." Betzalel said to him: "Moshe, our teacher! The practice of the world is that first a person builds a house and then he brings vessels into it. But you say, 'Make for me an Ark, vessels, and then a Tabernacle.' Into what shall I put the vessels that I make? Perhaps the Holy One, Blessed is He, said to you as follows: 'Make a Tabernacle, and then an Ark and vessels'"? Moshe said to him: "Perhaps you were in the shadow of God [B'tzel El] and that is how you knew this."*

The question is clear: Why was Moshe so amazed by Betzalel's answer? It is only logical that one first builds a house and then

---

431. *Zohar* III, 117a.
432. *Berachos* 55a.

makes the articles that go inside it. But what impressed Moshe was that Betzalel said, מִנְהָגוֹ שֶׁל עוֹלָם — "*the practice of the world.*" Betzalel did not learn this from the builders and carpenters alone, rather from the creation of the world. Moshe Rabbeinu understood the depths of Betzalel's thought process, that building the Mishkan is like creating the world. What Betzalel meant was that this was God's practice when He created the world: first he created the world and only then created the animals and the people. This is also how the Mishkan must be. This is truly the knowledge of someone who was בְּצֵל אֵ-ל, *in the shadow of God*, someone who knows that the Mishkan parallels the creation of the world. Since Betzalel knew this secret, he was fitting and deserving of working on the Mishkan, because he knew how to join the letters with which Mishkan and earth were created.

It is imperative that we know that the Mishkan did not fall into the hands of our enemies. Its power did not cease; it is still in our hands. The toiling in Torah represented by the Ark; the light of our faith that glows from the Menorah; our tables that resemble the Show bread; the Altar ramp that was constructed in place of steps; which alludes to the caution a person must exercise concerning the honor of his friend lest he embarrass him; the robe with bells on the fringe that sounded when the Kohen entered the Mikdash, which parallels sins committed with the voice; the Breastplate that parallels judgment; and the Tzitz that atones for brazenness. The Mishkan of Moshe no strangers ever took hold of. It endures still. As the Midrash states,[433] *Speak to the Children of Israel and let them take for Me a portion.*[434] *Everything about which God said, לִי — "for Me," endures in this world and in the next. How so? The verse states "The land shall not be sold in perpetuity for the entire land is for Me,"[435] in this world and in the next. "For Me is every firstborn"[436] in this world and in the next. "And the Leviim are for Me"[437] in this world and in the next. Bnei Yisrael, as it says: "And you shall be*

---

433. *Tanchuma Terumah* 3.
434. *Shemos* 25:2.
435. *Vayikra* 25:23.
436. *Bamidbar* 3:13.
437. Ibid. 8:14.

for Me a kingdom of ministers and a holy nation."[438] *In this world and in the next. "And let them take for Me"*[439] *in this world and the next.*

These are the reckonings of the Tabernacle, the Tabernacle of Testimony. What is the testimony? That as long as Bnei Yisrael are occupied with Torah study and the offerings, it serves as a testimony that they will not descend to *Gehinnom.*[440] As we said above, this is what we mean by the Mishkan still being here—as long as Bnei Yisrael are busy with Torah, doing what they are supposed to, the Mishkan endures.

For Glory and for Splendor

I T IS GENERALLY PRESUMED THAT THE TERMS כָּבוֹד, *GLORY,* and תִּפְאֶרֶת, *splendor*, are synonymous. Yet, as the *Chasam Sofer* explains[441] these two terms are not only not synonymous but are in fact antonymous. כָּבוֹד denotes greatness and elevation, while תִּפְאֶרֶת is rooted in humility, as we see with Yaakov whose predominant characteristic is תִּפְאֶרֶת and utmost humility; he is the one who stated: [442] קָטֹנְתִּי מִכֹּל הַחֲסָדִים . . . אֲשֶׁר עָשִׂיתָ אֶת עַבְדֶּךְ— *"I have been diminished by all the kindnesses ... that You have done Your servant."*

We have explained numerous times that even though the *Beis HaMikdash* is no longer extant and the mitzvos of the *Mikdash* ceased with its destruction and cannot be performed nowadays, nevertheless the internal principles they represent are still relevant today, for the Torah is eternal.[443]

---

438. *Shemos* 19:6.
439. Ibid. 25:2.
440. *Shemos Rabbah* 51:7.
441. *Toras Moshe, Parashas Tetzaveh.*
442. *Bereishis* 32:11.
443. See comments on "וְעָשׂוּ לִי מִקְדָּשׁ," *Parashas Terumah* with regard to the essence of each of the vessels in the Mikdash and what each one teaches us.

The same is true of the בִּגְדֵי כְהוּנָה, *the garments of the Kohanim*, that were made לְכָבוֹד וּלְתִפְאֶרֶת, *for glory and for splendor*. For although the garments of the Kohanim are non-existent today, the בִּגְדֵי כְהוּנָה of Bnei Yisrael, who are also described as מַמְלֶכֶת כֹּהֲנִים וְגוֹי קָדוֹשׁ, *a kingdom of priests and a holy nation*, are still in existence. This is manifest in the two mitzvos that we observe through donning namely, tefillin and tzitzis. The tefillin are for כָּבוֹד, as the *pasuk* states, פְּאֵרְךָ חֲבוֹשׁ עָלֶיךָ[444]— *"don your headgear upon yourself."* This is why an אָבֵל, *someone in mourning*, is exempt from donning tefillin on the first day, because he is rolling in dust and not in glory.[445] Tzitzis, on the other hand, are called [446]חוֹתָם שֶׁל טִיט, *a clay seal*. *Tosafos* there[447] explain that tzitzis resemble the mark they would use to mark a slave. Tzitzis are the mark on Bnei Yisrael; they testify that Bnei Yisrael are the servants of God. Thus, we see that tzitzis represent servitude and humility while the tefillin represent majestic glory. The two together are לְכָבוֹד וּלְתִפְאֶרֶת, the special priestly garments of a kingdom of priests and a holy nation.

———•———

The mitzvah of tzitzis is not an obligatory mitzvah in itself, rather is only incumbent upon someone who has a four-cornered garment; In the absence of this garment, he is exempt. At first glance, this seems strange for tzitzis is equal to all the other mitzvos in the Torah.[448] Why, then, is it not a mitzvah incumbent upon us? It seems that the reason it is not compulsory is because tzitzis, as mentioned above, is the symbol of our subservience, a sign of servitude. Therefore, we have to accept it upon ourselves with love — it is not something that can be forced upon us — for the whole purpose of Bnei Yisrael's servitude to God is that it is self-appointed, undertaken with joy and love.[449]

---

444. *Yechezkel* 24:17.
445. See *Moed Kattan* 21a, *Kesubos* 6b, and *Shulchan Aruch, Orach Chaim*, 38:5.
446 *Menachos* 43b.
447. S.v. *chosem*.
448. *Nedarim* 25a.
449. See comments on *Parashas Yisro, Na'aseh* precedes *Nishma*.

The Tabernacle of Testimony

THE DETAILS OF THE MISHKAN, THE COMMANDMENT TO build it and its construction, are written about quite extensively—in the *parshiyos* of *Terumah* and *Tetzaveh* before חֵטְא הָעֵגֶל, *the sin of the Golden Calf,* and again after in the *parshiyos* of *Vayakhel* and *Pikudei*. Why is this reiteration necessary?

We can answer this with the following parable: A father has a well-mannered, diligent son who brings him much *nachas*. The father buys his son a precious gift, but before he has a chance to give it to him he hears from the son's teacher, much to his chagrin, that the boy is not behaving properly and that he is no longer as studious as he was previously. The father says to the teacher, "How unfortunate this is—I had been intending to give him this precious gift!" The teacher told the father not to worry, that the gift can be used to help the boy improve and set him back on the right track. The gift can be given to the boy on the condition that he mends his ways.

So too was it between God and the Jewish people. God wanted to dwell among the Jews even before they committed the sin of the Golden Calf.[450] But after they sinned, the commandment to construct the Mishkan, and God dwelling among them, served as proof that He had forgiven them.[451] Hence it is called הָעֵדוּת מִשְׁכָּן, — "*a Mishkan of testimony,*" for it testifies that God forgave them. Furthermore, God made a condition with them that if they did not follow His ways, the Mikdash would be destroyed because of their sins.

Although the Mishkan indicates that God forgave them for חֵטְא הָעֵגֶל, the forgiveness was not complete. God said, וּבְיוֹם פָּקְדִי וּפָקַדְתִּי עֲלֵהֶם חַטָּאתָם[452] — "*on the day that I make My account, I shall bring their sin to account against them.*" As Rashi explains,[453] there is

---

450. See the *Ramban* on *Parashas Tetzaveh* 29:46 where he explains that the service in the Temple was a צוֹרֶךְ גָּבוֹהַּ, a fulfillment of Divine desire, not just a fulfillment of a human need.
451. As stated in *Rashi* at the beginning of *Parashas Pekudei*.
452. *Shemos* 32:34.
453. *Rashi*, ibid.

no calamity that befalls the Jewish people that does not contain something in it to atone for the sin of the Golden Calf.

Additionally, the *pasuk* states, אֵלֶּה פְקוּדֵי הַמִּשְׁכָּן מִשְׁכַּן הָעֵדֻת — *"these are the reckonings of the Tabernacle, the Tabernacle of Testimony."* Rashi explains that the word Mishkan is mentioned twice to allude to the two Mishkanos שֶׁנִּתְמַשְׁכְּנוּ עַל עֲוֹנֹתֵיהֶם שֶׁל יִשְׂרָאֵל — *"that were taken as collateral because of Bnei Yisrael's sins."* There is a play on the word מִשְׁכָּן, *Tabernacle,* to be read as מַשְׁכּן, *collateral.* But were the two Temples really taken as *collateral*? They were destroyed! Rather, it seems to reason that God took the two Temples as a מַשְׁכּוֹן, *collateral,* for the debt incurred by Bnei Yisrael's sins. We see God's mercy in this, namely that He did not force Bnei Yisrael to pay for their sins immediately but rather took collateral — the two Temples — and poured His wrath on an inanimate object rather than on His beloved children. He keeps that collateral till we pay back the debt of our sins, and when we merit paying up that debt, God will once again return that מַשְׁכּוֹן, may He do so speedily in our days.